BASEBALL HISTORY 3

Baseball and American Society

Series ISBN 0-88736-566-3

1. Blackball Stars
   John B. Holway
   ISBN 0-88736-094-7 CIP 1988

2. Baseball History, Premier Edition
   Edited by Peter Levine
   ISBN 0-88736-288-5 1988

3. My 9 Innings: An Autobiography of 50 Years in Baseball
   Lee MacPhail
   ISBN 0-88736-387-3 CIP 1989

4. Black Diamonds: Life in the Negro Leagues from the Men Who Lived It
   John B. Holway
   ISBN 0-88736-334-2 CIP 1989

5. Baseball History 2
   Edited by Peter Levine
   ISBN 0-88736-342-3 1989

6. Josh and Satch: A Dual Biography of Josh Gibson and Satchel Paige
   John B. Holway
   ISBN 0-88736-333-4 CIP forthcoming, 1991

7. Encyclopedia of Major League Baseball Team Histories
   Edited by Peter C. Bjarkman
   Volume 1: American League
   ISBN 0-88736-373-3 CIP forthcoming, 1990

8. Encyclopedia of Major League Baseball Team Histories
   Edited by Peter C. Bjarkman
   Volume 2: National League
   ISBN 0-88736-374-1 CIP forthcoming, 1990

9. Baseball History 3
   Edited by Peter Levine
   ISBN 0-88736-577-9 1990

10. The Immortal Diamond: Baseball in American Literature
    Peter C. Bjarkman
    ISBN 0-88736-481-0 (hardcover CIP forthcoming, 1991
    ISBN 0-88736-482-9 (softcover) CIP forthcoming, 1991

11. Total Latin American Baseball
    Peter C. Bjarkman
    ISBN 0-88736-546-9 CIP forthcoming, 1991

12. Baseball Players and Their Times: A History of the Major Leagues, 1920–1940
    Eugene Murdock
    ISBN 0-88736-235-4 CIP forthcoming, 1991

13. The Tropic of Baseball: Baseball in the Dominican Republic
    Rob Ruck
    ISBN 0-88736-707-0 CIP forthcoming, 1991

14. The Cinema of Baseball: Images of America, 1929–1989
    Gary E. Dickerson
    ISBN 0-88736-710-0 CIP forthcoming, 1991

15. Baseball History 4
    Edited by Peter Levine
    ISBN 0-88736-578-7 forthcoming, 1991

16. Baseball and American Society: A Textbook of Baseball History
    Peter C. Bjarkman
    ISBN 0-88736-483-7 (softcover) CIP forthcoming, 1991

BASEBALL HISTORY 3

An Annual of Original Baseball Research

Edited by
Peter Levine

Meckler

BASEBALL HISTORY

An Annual of Original Baseball Research

Publisher
Alan M. Meckler

Cover art: John Hull, "Midwest League, All Star Game: Clinton," 1988, acrylic on canvas, from the collection of Tal Smith, Houston, Texas. Reproduced by permission of Tal Smith. Artwork courtesy of Grace Borgenicht Gallery, New York, New York.

ISSN 1047-3521
ISBN 0-88736-577-9

Meckler Publishing, 11 Ferry Lane West, Westport, CT 06880.
Meckler Ltd., Grosvenor Gardens House, Grosvenor Gardens,
London SW1W 0BS, U.K.

Printed on acid free paper.
Printed in the United States of America.

Contents

EDITOR'S NOTE

This year's edition of *Baseball History* unites the talents of established writers and poets with the efforts of some talented newcomers to provide a rich tapestry about the game both in the United States and abroad. On the international scene, Gary Gildner, best known for his poetry and fiction, offers a beautiful account of his experiences coaching a Polish baseball team only a year before Eastern Europe's astonishing political transformation. Evocative of the game's appeal and importance in a different part of the world is historian Rob Ruck's rich interview with Juan Marichal and his experiences in the Dominican Republic. Rounding out our global reach, is a story of a young Jewish-American who played baseball in Berlin at the 1936 Olympic Games, well-told by Louis Jacobson, a young man just beginning what promises to be a fine career as a writer.

Closer to home, historian Bruce Kuklick, who is completing a social history of Shibe Park, offers an interesting look at the last days of the Philadelphia Athletics, while sociologist Michael Kimmel suggests some interesting connections between baseball's popularity and the redefinition of American masculinity at the close of the 19th century. Jim Sumner, whose talent for retelling interesting stories about unusual circumstances has previously graced these pages, offers us one about Tom Zachary. Jack Kavanagh, just beginning this third career, provides a compelling reminiscence of his days as an usher at Ebbets Field on the eve of World War II. Once again, W. P. Kinsella rounds out this year's issue with the title story of his next collection of baseball stories, and Fred Roberts orchestrates reviews of last year's crop of baseball books. I hope you enjoy our efforts.

Peter Levine

The Warsaw Sparks

GARY GILDNER

AUTHOR'S NOTE: *In 1987 I went to Poland on a Fulbright to teach at the University of Warsaw. One January day a Warsaw sportswriter came knocking on my classroom door. He had a big problem. The baseball team he'd organized the year before could not win; would I—who, he had heard, was a pitcher—come help? I told Dariusz it was a little late for me to attempt a comeback—I was 49—but I'd be glad to give his team some tips. The offer led to an adventure that, after it was over, I thought I might turn into a novel; but the facts and the education I had been given that season wouldn't let me. What follows is the first chapter of a memoir,* The Warsaw Sparks, *which the University of Iowa Press brought out last spring.*

We were ten Juniors, sixteen Seniors, the organizer, his assistant, and me, the coach. We were one American, two Cubans, and twenty-six Poles and on a rainy, gloomy Saturday in late May, high on two victories in a row and our first road trip, we set out by bus from Warsaw for the coal mining town of Rybnik to play baseball the next day—a Juniors game at ten A.M. and the big one, against a tough, experienced team, at noon. It was 350 kilometers to Rybnik, a scheduled seven-hour trip, counting the stop for supper on the way. Dariusz, the organizer, said we should be in our hotel, in bed, by ten-thirty. "Then sleep," he said. "Then Sunday, half-past seven, sharp, stand up! Then clean, eat, bus to game, play, win. No problem." At ten-thirty on Saturday night, however, we were waiting in a dark parking lot somewhere in dark Rybnik—road-weary, sleepy, and hungry—while Dariusz went to ask the manager of a night club if he would feed us. It was our last chance for supper after eight hours on the road, and it was still raining.

The restaurant that Dariusz planned for us had been inexplicably closed. The next one we stopped at, which he went into alone, to scout, was "no good," he announced to the team. To me he said, "Very big prices, very nothing amounts. Also," he added. "horse meat only." Then we took some wrong turns. In Częstochowa, about three-quarters of the way to Rybnik, we asked a pedestrian how to get to Katowice. In soot-colored Katowice, in the heart of the coal country, we asked three pedestrians for help. "No proper signs!" Dariusz would wail. Finally we got straightened out and it was decided to push on to Rybnik—which we should reach by nine, an hour before the restaurants in Poland closed—and eat there. We arrived at nine-thirty. It took us fifteen minutes to find a parking place for the large touring coach and then to find, on foot, the one restaurant open to us. When we achieved the restaurant, the manager told us, *"Nie ma."* You hear this expression a lot in Poland. Literally it means, "There is not." Depending on the situation, the time of day, and especially on the speaker's mood, it can also mean, "There never was," "There never will be," "He or she is not here," "I don't know what you're talking about, don't bother me." Here it seemed to mean no food, period. We walked back to the bus in the rain. Players began to count up the sandwiches and apples some of them had left from snacks they'd brought. In the rear of the bus, meanwhile, Jacek Koncki, a Seniors outfielder, was hurting: his right eye was weeping and refused to open. To his teammates who noticed it, he said it was nothing.

Dariusz returned to the bus and said the night club would feed us. A few players gave a little cheer; others said, "Let's see first." Mainly we were silent, tired, chilled. We followed Dariusz through narrow cobblestone streets in the rain. I wanted to win that game the next day—the Seniors game, the one that mattered—and began to imagine colds coming on, lethargy on the bases, dropped balls. I could see, as I had in games, a perfect throw from the shortstop popping out of Froggy's mitt. Froggy was our first baseman. He was nineteen. During practice, fooling around, he could "pick up" a ball off the ground with this feet and, in the same motion, "flip" it to someone nearby. A nifty little trick that was easy for him after years of playing soccer. But in *this* game, under pressure and having to use his hands, Froggy would sometimes freeze. Though he could hold his glove up to receive the thrown ball, he could not always react fast enough to close it. Despite a couple of errors per game by Froggy, however, plus half a dozen others, the Sparks' season record so far was 2–1. The previous season, their first, they lost all fourteen games they played—one game by the score of 42–5, other games, more typically, by 25–0 and 20–0 scores. I wanted to turn these guys into a real baseball team. Walking over the slick cobblestones, I made a mental note to wear the same yellow practice jersey I'd worn in the last two games, instead of the new peach-colored shirts we'd just been issued; then I had to laugh at myself. Walking along, I also flashed through a montage of street scenes from maybe half the foreign films I'd ever seen—its principal features all seemed to be right there in Rybnik: hunched-over, shadowy figures with their collars turned up, rain, a lonely lamp post giving gauzy light, nothing good around the corner. As we approached the night club, I heard Alejandro, the Seniors' sixteen-year-old center fielder from Cuba, mutter, "*Nie ma,* mon. *Nie ma.*"

The night club looked, from the outside, like a small town IGA back home that had gone out of business, its plate-glass front painted an industrial green. We filed in like refugees. We piled our coats and hats on a counter, behind which a big-bosomed Polish woman with an Afro smiled as if she'd been waiting all day for us. And now here we were! She put on Mariusz Szpirowski's baseball cap that said "Chicago Bears" on the crown, and directed us—*"Proszę, proszę!"* ("Please, please!")—up a small flight of stairs into the main room. It was fairly large. A couple of dozen tables for four and six occupied the near half, a dance floor and band the far half. People were dancing. I couldn't tell how big the band was, though way back in the farthest reach, under very subdued purple light, there seemed to be at least a guitar and an organ. If the Rybnik night club had a name, I didn't catch it—or see anything written in neon; but someone on the planning committee, I thought, must have checked out some American Legion Halls and some Holiday Inns in places like North Dakota, and listened to a lot of three-piece combos play "Misty" into the wee hours.

The Sparks brightened visibly. This was a considerable leap from the restaurant that Dariusz had planned for them. There, the food would have been pretty ordinary—much like cafeteria fare—with sweetened tea to drink. And absolutely no atmosphere. Here, waiters in tuxedos brought jumbo bottles of Coke to our tables. Older players like Jake, the catcher, and July, the left-handed pitcher—both of whom were graduate students—had glasses of wine, as well. And Dariusz ordered double portions for everyone: a very good fillet of ocean perch, mashed potatoes, coleslaw. For atmosphere, we had the fox-trotting dancers to watch and tunes like "Blue Velvet" and "The Isle of Capri"—in mainly jumpy renditions—to listen to. When the band took a break and the dancers returned to their tables, we could check out the girls close up. There was one near me in a sleeveless white blouse and powder blue skirt who was blonde and rosy and could almost have been in the wedding party of a Brueghel picture but for her expression and manner, which seemed typical of many girls in the room—and typical of several young women I knew in Warsaw. She sat and smoked and alternately sipped from a glass of wine and a glass of Coke, and either seemed bored with the boy she was with or reluctant to make conversation because, well, it was his place to speak first. You might have thought she could take all this or leave it, it didn't matter one way or the other. You might have thought she had seen a lot of Greta Garbo and Marlene Dietrich movies. The boy, stocky as a middle linebacker, wore a longish crewcut and a white shirt open at the neck, and he sat, smoked, alternately sipped wine and Coke, and presented, roughly, the same expressions the girl did. When they made eye contact, it was brief—like a dash, or maybe a sentence fragment. They wore no wedding rings, but I guessed they would probably marry each other, and their nights out, when they could afford them, would be much like this one.

The table where I sat, with Dariusz, his assistant Henry, and the bus driver, was served first—we were simply closest to the kitchen—and when I finished eating I went to see how the Sparks were getting along. It was after midnight. We still had to find our hotel. Everyone was seriously into his food—everyone except Jacek Koncki. He sat with his face in his hands; he hadn't touched his plate. "What's wrong with Pizza Hut?" I asked. (I had given him that nickname because he was one of three Jaceks on the Seniors team but the only one who always wore a Pizza Hut T-shirt to practice. And he came to all the practices, a record most of his teammates could not match.)

"He got something in his eye," Pete, a pitcher, told me. Pete was one of five Seniors who spoke English, and I asked him now to translate for us.

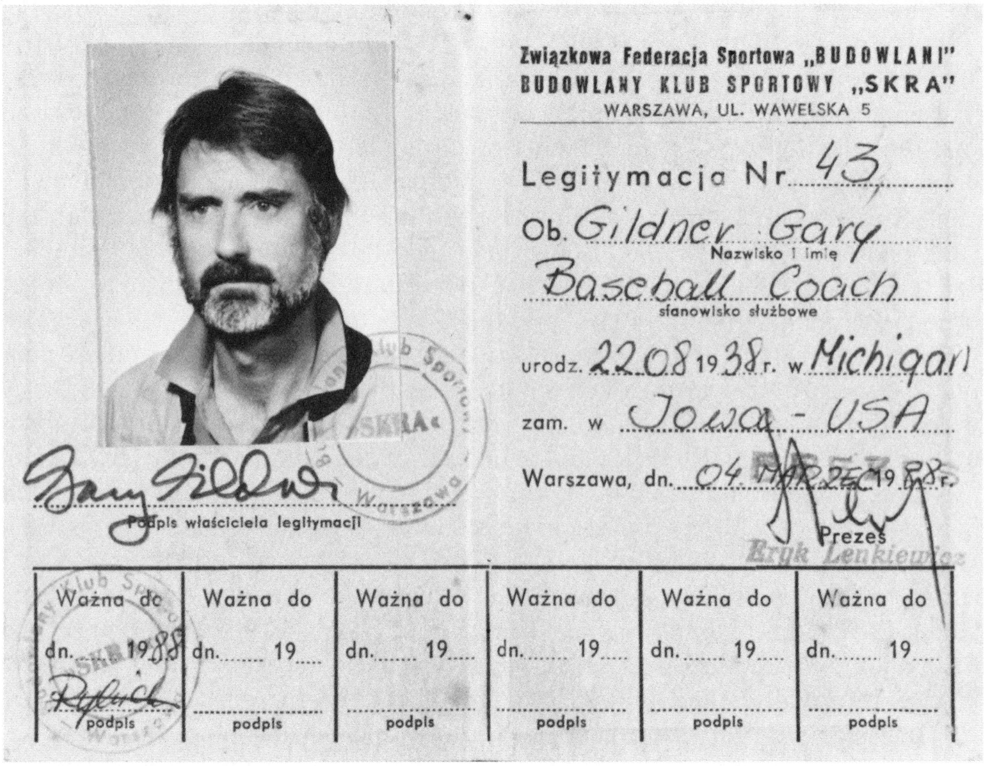

Związkowa Federacja Sportowa „BUDOWLANI"
BUDOWLANY KLUB SPORTOWY „SKRA"
WARSZAWA, UL. WAWELSKA 5

Legitymacja Nr 43
Ob. Gildner Gary
Nazwisko i imię
Baseball Coach
stanowisko służbowe
urodz. 22.08 1938 r. w Michigan
zam. w Iowa - USA
Warszawa, dn. 04 MARZEC 1988 r.
Prezes

Podpis właściciela legitymacji

Ważna do	Ważna do	Ważna do	Ważna do	Ważna do	Ważna do
dn. 1988	dn. 19	dn. 19	dn. 19	dn. 19	dn. 19
podpis	podpis	podpis	podpis	podpis	podpis

My Baseball legitymacja—*or I.D.*

"What's wrong, Pizza Hut?"

He shook his head.

"Let me see your eye," I said.

He took away his hands and let me look. In the night club's poor light I could only see that his right eye was closed to a wet slit and somewhat swollen. He put the heel of his palm up to rub it.

"Don't touch it," I said. To Pete I said, "He hasn't eaten a thing."

"I know. He was sick in the toilet," Pete said.

Jacek suddenly got up from the table and lay down on three chairs against the wall. He moaned something.

"He says he is dizzy," Pete said.

Dariusz joined us and he and Pete spoke in Polish. Then Dariusz said, "We must take Pizza Hut to hospital." We got directions to the hospital from the coat-check woman in the Afro—she still had on Mariusz' Chicago Bears hat, wished us luck, *"Powodzenie!"*—and then we all walked back to the bus. Henry helped Jacek along. It was still raining. On the way I asked Pete what had happened to Jacek's eye. He said he didn't know. "Maybe when we stopped to pee—in that forest—a tree branch hurt him. Maybe on the bus someone did this"—he opened his raincoat, pulled out his suspender strap, and snapped it against his chest. "Maybe," Pete said, "there was an accident. I don't know."

In the touring coach we made a couple of agonizingly slow, jockeying-back-and-forth turns, and soon we were heading out of Rybnik. Apparently one of our turns was wrong. Dariusz, nervous, stood by the door looking for a pedestrian to help us. The driver said something and Jake, behind me, gave a sad laugh.

"What now, Jake?" I said.

"This is some kind of comedy," he said.

"Explain it," I said.

"The driver says we are running out of gas."

It was one A.M. and very quiet on the bus. The driver made a difficult turnaround on a narrow, tree-lined road, almost slipping his front wheels into a ditch. I watched the windshield wiper on his side miss about six inches of glass—the six inches, by my reckoning, that lay in the most direct line between his eyes and the road. Jake said, "Only in Poland is this possible." I thought he meant the driver's wiper blade wearing out in the middle, and I said, "Oh no, in America that's where they go first, too. It's practically a law."

"What is?" Jake said.

"Wiper blade wear-out."

"Wiper blade wear-out?"

"Windshield wiper. That," I pointed. "That place not getting scraped."

"I'm not following you, Coach."

"It's not important. How's Jacek?"

"He's in the back, lying down. He's not rubbing his eye. But what is practically a law? I mean, if you don't mind telling me."

Like a good many young Poles who spoke English, Jake taught it, privately, for extra income. With me, he enjoyed practicing. Sometimes—to paraphrase Robert Frost, who said poetry is the stuff that gets lost in translation—Jake and I would get lost in translation. As the bus eased back into the center of Rybnik, I said to him, "You lived in the States. You know we make a kind of joke about things going wrong, or suddenly not working, exactly when we want them *not* to go wrong, don't you?"

"I was only a boy when I lived there," he said.

"Well, I might be telling some guy, for instance, that I ran out of gas while rushing my pregnant wife to the hospital, and he'd say, 'It never fails.' "

"Like us now with Jacek," Jake said.

"More or less," I said.

"In America, though, people don't really run out of gas," he said. "Or if they do, it's very easy to buy more. Not like here."

"Jake, you're giving me a hard time on this."

"But I really don't get it about wiper blades," he said.

"Same thing. You want them to work when it's raining—and just when it starts to rain, they fail."

"But they *are* working," he said.

From his point of view, he was right, of course. In Poland if the windshield wiper is moving back and forth and the rubber blade is scraping off water—never mind how much—everything is working. The real thing, like the poetry lost in a translation, is not missed. Or to put the matter plainly: in a country where many things do not work at all, what's a little blur in the middle?

The driver stopped and Dariusz called to a woman who was waiting at a taxi stand. He spoke very fast to her and she got on the bus. She would show us the way to the hospital. We got there quickly and dropped off Henry and Pizza Hut and the woman. Dariusz would return later, after checking us into the hotel.

We found the Hotel Pracowniczy (Workers' Hotel) without incident. Inside, however (it was now one-thirty, or six hours to wake-up) the clerk told Dariusz she had room for maybe half of us. He looked stunned, betrayed. He raised his voice at her, saying he had reservations. She was a small sparrowlike woman in her thirties wearing a plain brown house-dress and holding a cigarette burning down to the filter. We were all gathered around her in the lobby with our backpacks, duffel bags, bats, batting helmets, and two sets of catcher's gear; several players also carried jumbo Cokes they'd bought as we left the night club. In a room off the lobby, a blue TV screen was showing an army in retreat: soldiers with their heads turbaned in bandages, or hobbling on makeshift crutches, made their dazed way behind groaning trucks. I could hear heavy gears working and somber violins, and in the lobby I could smell a rag-smoke odor coming from the woman's burning filter. Dariusz raised his voice again.

She gazed at some keys in her hand as if the world had been unfair and flowerless for as long as she could remember, and here was one more day of it. She sighed. Finally, her shoulders sagging, she led us down a hallway as if to a place she knew nothing about. For a few crazy moments I felt that I was back home—in one of the old railroad hotels you can still find in America if you stay off the freeways and instead follow the two-lanes to towns like Osceola, Iowa, and Valentine, South Dakota, and pull up on Main Street. They are the hotels where engineers and brakemen and conductors used to stay—and some of them still do. A clerk waits behind the desk, or in the small lobby across the way, watching a fuzzy TV and chewing on a match; near him, a pretty girl with crimson lips and honey skin smiles out morning and night, month after month, from a herbicide calendar. The rooms smell of pine cleaner and used tobacco, of old shoes and linoleum and maybe a little of rye whiskey; and if the rough blanket on the bed smells of these things too, the sheets are fine. The peg on the door will hold your shirt and pants, the window opens, you can catch a whiff of new-cut hay, maybe see a piece of moon, and if you're tired enough and just want to sleep, your chances are pretty good.

The Hotel Pracowniczy had all of this except the moon, the rye whiskey, and new-cut hay, and the rooms the woman showed us were larger, big enough for five single beds and a central table and chairs. I could imagine a Polish family on vacation in there, gathered around a meal of kielbasa and bread, white cheese, and radishes, to save on a restaurant bill: the husband, wife, their two kids, and either his mother or hers—the *babcia,* the grandmother, the most visible and perhaps the most powerful family member of all in Poland, if not the most powerful force, pound for pound, in the whole country. I had seen *babcias* on trams and autobuses, tough as drill sergeants, chewing out drunks; I had seen them take on store clerks practiced in the rude whine and the sulk, and I had seen the clerks change their tunes; I had seen these estimable women sweep down on possible disaster large and small—a bloody head on a playground, a run in a pretty girl's stocking—and take charge, repair. The *babcia*'s principal duty in life was to mind her grandchildren while the parents worked. Here was her real territory, where she gave to the young, so that it layered their bones, an understanding of discipline, order, patience, prayer, diet, custom, costume, manners, and fate, which they would receive nowhere and from no one else. In the five months that I had been coaching the Sparks, I sometimes saw myself as one of these old women in a rage for form.

How the sighing, flowerless hotel clerk was suddenly able to produce rooms for us was never explained to me, and I was too tired to ask. Passports and Polish I.D. cards were quickly collected. It was two o'clock Sunday morning. Dariusz led me and the bus driver up a flight of stairs to a two-bedroom suite that was several cuts above the quarters the players were given. In fact, it seemed in a different hotel. We had our own bath, a kitchen, a parlor with a color TV set (the driver turned it on at once), and each bedroom contained two beds covered with brilliantly white, ironed sheets and down comforters whose surprising softness I hadn't felt in a long time. I wondered if the clerk had these rooms ready for big Communist party dogs, perhaps even General Jaruzelski himself—the head of state—if they came barking in the night.

"Very nice," I said to Dariusz.

"Only one in complete hotel," he said.

"This *is* a workers' hotel, Dariusz?"

"Yes, yes, of course."

"Why is there a difference between here and downstairs?"

"Always a difference," he said, "even in Poland." Then—no time for dialectics—he said Henry and the driver would share one room, he and I the other. "Now, you sleep," he said. "Tomorrow, baseball." He left for the hospital and, dog-tired, I crawled under a worker's comforter. I thought—or maybe dreamt—back to my Grandpa Szostak's farm house in northern Michigan, where my own *babcia,* her frost-blooming breath smelling of apples, tucked me under a quilt full of the duck's most intimate feathers, in a room closer to the stars than any I have slept in since.

When I woke I didn't know where I was right away. Scotland? Montana? I had awakened in gray-lit, coal- and linoleum-smelling rooms in both of those places. Then I saw a jumbo Coke on the floor and remembered the night club, our game against the miners. In the other bed I saw July. What had happened to Dariusz? My watch said seven o'clock. Through the window the sky was the color of whale skin, but the rain had stopped. I got up, showered fast in cold water (there was no hot), and put on my uniform—the yellow stretch hose, powder blue knickers, my yellow practice jersey. Dariusz had got a Boston Red Sox uniform through the American Embassy and had taken it to a Polish tailor, instructing him to copy it thirty times—substituting "SKRA" for "BOSTON" on the shirts. The knickers turned out best. They were big and baggy—like the knickers you see in photos of Babe Ruth and Ty Cobb—but instead of loops for a belt there was elastic around the waist. In case the elastic didn't keep the knickers up, there was a strip of nylon hem tape for a drawstring. As for the peach-colored shirts, the tailor skipped buttons and fashioned one-piece, one-size (large) pullovers. He also made large neck openings. On the more muscular Sparks this was no real problem, but on the slimmer, smaller players the shirts barely covered their collarbones and hung like pajama tops borrowed from a burly uncle. Our shoes were soccer shoes and our hats were anything we could find with a bill. Dariusz was very proud of our uniforms. "Polyester," he told me. "One hundred percent!"

The word "SKRA" across our shirt fronts signified our sponsor. The season I am writing about—1988—there were eight baseball teams in the Polish Baseball and Softball Association (Polskiego Związku Baseballu i Softballu—or PZBall) and each team was sponsored by, and named for, a local sports club. Officially, we were Robotniczny Klub Sportowy Skra Warsaw. *Robotniczny* means "workers." *Skra* means "spark." In English our team was "Spark—Workers' Sports Club of Warsaw."

"What kind of workers?" I once asked Dariusz, trying to make a connection between *robotniczny* and *skra.* Most of the other teams in Poland were sponsored by clubs whose names seemed to be associated with occupations. The team we were playing that Sunday, for example, was Klub Sportowy Górnik Boguszowice. *Górnik* means "miners" and Boguszowice is a section of Rybnik. Thus we were playing the coal miners of Boguszowice. Were they playing the electricians of Warsaw?

"Gary, you listen," Dariusz said. "Three levels in Communistic state: workers, farmers, thinkers. *Robotniczny* is workers—with hands."

"In our case, workers who put up electric wires?" I asked.

"I don't understand," he said.

"I am trying to find out if *Skra,* our name, means electricians. You know, light bulbs, zip-zip for trams," I said.

"*Skra* means *Skra,*" he said. "A name, nothing more."

"Like the Tigers of Detroit? The Cubs of Chicago?"

"Yes, yes, I know. And the Mets of New York, my favorite. The very fine Dwight Gooden." At that point, Dariusz wanted to discuss the speed of Gooden's fastball, not linguistics.

* * *

After dressing I woke up July, then knocked on the other bedroom door. Jake came out. "Where are Dariusz and Henry?" I asked him. He said he didn't know. "The hotel clerk last night had no beds for me and July, so Dariusz brought us up here. He said we needed our strength today. Maybe he and Henry slept on the bus." While I waited for Jake and July to dress, Dariusz came in looking rumpled and puffy-eyed.

He shook my hand. "This bed was OK?" he said.

"Fine," I said. "Where did you and Henry sleep?"

He waved the question away. "Listen," he said, "we must talk. Quietly, you understand? You, me, Jake, July." Whenever Dariusz wanted to give me important information, he asked one of the players who spoke English to translate for him. Here—in Jake and July—he had two translators.

"I tell about Pizza Hut," he said. Then he delivered a burst of Polish to Jake. Jake said, "Dariusz wants you to understand the hospital in Rybnik is very good, the best maybe in Poland. The doctor who examined Pizza Hut is also very good—a specialist. Because of all the mining down here, the way of life, the government gives the workers good care."

"The best," said Dariusz.

"What about Pizza Hut?" I said.

"I know, I know," Dariusz said, and delivered another burst of Polish. Jake said, "Pizza Hut must not be moved for ten days, maybe two weeks. He must lie easy. It's a question of his central eye—the middle part—I don't know how it's called in English."

July said, "I don't know either. Where the light comes."

"His retina?" I said.

"Yes, that part," Jake said. "It might break loose."

Dariusz said something in Polish, looking sad.

Jake said, "Dariusz thinks we should not worry the others before the game. He says we should only tell them Pizza Hut is under observation and resting. Later we can tell them."

"Ask Dariusz how serious it is," I said.

"Yes, yes, I know," Dariusz said. "Maybe fifty percent OK, no problem. Maybe fifty percent operate." He spoke to Jake in Polish, and Jake said, "Dariusz wants you to understand Pizza Hut will have the best doctor in Poland."

"I understand," I said. Then we went down to wake up all the other Sparks for breakfast.

* * *

In the hotel dining room, which we had to ourselves, none of us was moving very fast. We moved as if our bones hadn't collected into their best arrangements yet. In their peach and powder blue outfits, the younger players looked even younger, the short, shorter. Many of the Sparks were still half asleep. At the far end of the dining room, we lined up at a low window with a counter; on the other side stood two women in white nylon smocks. You could not see their faces unless you bent down and leaned through the window—but you could see, very clearly, their amply filled bras and deep cleavages because the smocks were not much thicker than mist. It was like being served by two pairs of breasts.

One woman stood before a steaming tub full of sweetened black tea. She ladled the tea into mugs without handles and set them on the counter. The other woman gave us, in turn, a plate containing several slices of smoked ham, a bun, a square of butter, a wedge of tomato on a leaf of Bibb lettuce, and a big dill pickle. A bowl of strawberry jam, thick and juicy as stew, sat on the counter, along with extra buns and loaves of dark rye bread.

The dining room was long and narrow; tables filled it from end to end in four strict rows. Three rows were of tables for two, the last row, of tables for four. When you left the food line, you had a choice, as it were, of four other lines. In Poland the line and symbols of it are everywhere, present as the crucified Christ in all the Catholic churches, spiritless as a stone in a pile of stones. You line up for virtually everything: groceries, magazines, movies, baby clothes, toilet paper (when there *is* toilet paper), also to have your key copied, your watch fixed, or to have a look at a rare Chopin in the philatelist's shop. And close by, as a kind of antidote, there will hang a calendar or a poster featuring a woman's creamy breasts. Just waiting for you, day after day . . . as the herbicide girl waits on the American prairie. In the dining room of the Workers' Hotel that morning, sitting in our strict rows, we had the women in their nylon smocks.

Dariusz and I sat with the Cubans, Tony and Alejandro. At thirty and sixteen, they were the oldest and youngest players on the Seniors team. (Without Tony our average age was twenty.) Tony was our third baseman. He was also a Third Secretary in the Cuban Embassy and because of that, and because I was an American, the Warsaw press found in us good—and sometimes creative—copy. The illustrated sports magazine *Sportowiec,* for example, ran a story headlined *"Dyplomacja na bazie"* ("Diplomacy on the bases"). It was true, as the reporter said, that Tony, who had played the game half his life before coming to Poland two years ago, was our best performer. It was also true that the reporter and I had had this exchange:

"Why, when you are not being paid for it, are you coaching the Warsaw team?"

"Because I love baseball."

"Really?"

"Absolutely."

But it was not true that I was a former Detroit Tiger and in America earned $300 an hour coaching pitchers and hitters; that "news" probably came from Dariusz' enthusiasm. Dariusz too loved baseball. He was also a sports journalist. Since professional ethics prevented him from writing about us (though God knew he wanted to, in boldface and by the meter), he encouraged his colleagues to promote his passion. He told me that baseball was "the most intelligent game in history. You know this is so!" He felt that it should—and would!—replace soccer as the national sport. "Soccer is no grace, no *thinking.* I must write about this stupid game but you understand me, Gary, my heart has no feeling there." Dariusz was thirty-two. He had a flat-footed walk that reminded me of Charlie Chaplin in a hurry, but his round face was a small boy's delighted to his cheeks at being invited to tag along with the big guys. He was a member of the board of PZBall and a man who searched Warsaw for stars.

The first time I met Dariusz, he came knocking one January day on my classroom door at Warsaw University, where I was teaching a course in American literature. I was, in fact, deep into a discussion of who Ted Williams was, and what he represented to the main character of Russell Banks' novel, *Continental Drift.* I had brought to class my Detroit Tigers cap as a visual aid, and was wearing it when I answered the knock. Dariusz apologized profusely for interrupting, but he had heard at the American Embassy that I was a baseball player—and could we talk? Quickly? He had with him, to translate, a young man named Grzegorz, who was wearing, in addition to his winter coat, an old Rawlings mitt that had seen much use (and could have used, I noted, a good dose of neat's-foot oil). Caught by their visual aid, I invited them in. They said no, no, they only wanted to know if I would help the Warsaw baseball team. I said, "How? When?" They said we could discuss this tomorrow. The following afternoon they came to my apartment. Standing in the doorway, Grzegorz said, "Dariusz apologizes, but can you go with us?"

"Right now?" I said.

"Yes, if that is not inconvenient," said Grzegorz. "We are having practice tonight."

Minutes later we were pushed together on a rush-hour autobus, making our way across town to Gwardia gymnasium, where I would meet the Skra players at their first practice of the season. It was the middle of January, the day already dark. I could see sleet falling in the headlights of cars going past. Suddenly Dariusz began searching around in his shoulder bag, and came out with a Topps bubble gum card of Dwight Gooden. Showing it to me, he said, "Much quickness. Very great, I think, yes? We *need* this." Grzegorz said, "What Dariusz is hoping you will do for the team is make us presentable. Last year was a disaster." I'd do what I could, I said. "What position do you play?" Grzegorz asked. I had to smile. I explained to him that I'd played high school and American Legion ball and had once been scouted by the Tigers after pitching a Legion no-hitter. But that was the high point of a short career. I developed arm trouble my last year in high school and became strictly a fan who played catch now and then. The Detroit cap in my duffel bag, I told Grzegorz, only meant that I was still crazy about the game and rooted for the Tigers.

The autobus pulled up at the Gwardia stop. As we walked in the snow to the gym, Grzegorz spoke Polish to Dariusz, and Dariusz, beaming, said to me, "You will pitch once more!" I said to Grzegorz, "Tell Dariusz I'll be very happy, and honored, to supply some coaching. But I'm forty-nine years old and I don't think I should attempt a comeback."

Grzegorz said, "A comeback?"

I said, "I'm too old to pitch."

Dariusz said, "A revelation! I am seeing much happiness. It's OK! It's OK!"

Now in Rybnik, eating breakfast with Tony and Alejandro, Dariusz looked worried. He counted the players twice. He asked Tony how he'd slept. Tony, in a sweater and warm-up jacket, said, *"Dobrze"* ("Fine"). He was a quiet, reserved, good-looking man with a mustache. Besides being our best and oldest player, he was also, at five-feet-two, our shortest . . . and the one who seemed most affected by the weather. We were most likely to see Tony at practice if the sun was shining. If it was the least bit chilly when he showed up, he wore, unless he was fielding, white cotton gloves. Dariusz then asked Alejandro how he felt, and Alejandro, already fidgeting to get going, said *"Dobrze! Dobrze!"* Long-limbed, wiry, curly-haired Alejandro was the Sparks' talker, having played enough baseball in Cuba to know the tradition and value of chatter. When I heard him in the outfield crooning his Spanish-Polish interludes of encouragement and praise, his sputters of razz, I wished I had him in the infield, or behind the plate, to fire up his quieter teammates at close range. Out where he was, much of his song was lost on the wind. He too wanted to be closer to the action, if not everywhere at once. Often he'd suggest to me, after Froggy muffed a play at first base or a ball went through Norbert's legs at shortstop or Jake threw wild down to second, that he, Alejandro, could play first base, shortstop, catcher. "Pitch too maybe! OK?" At the beginning of practice when we warmed up our arms, he'd want me to observe his specialty, his submarine ball, which he delivered from an almost hairpin position, releasing the ball near his shoe tops. Never mind that a herky-jerky, all arms-and-legs motion (that is, a desire to fox the batter; that is, *style*) was his principal aim—which was also the case with his next specialty, the knuckler, and his next, the sinker. Never mind, he'd indicate, smiling grandly: he, Alejandro, Cuban tinker and confidence man, could pitch, *sí,* and catch (*"Fuego, amigo! Fuego!"* he'd yell from a catcher's crouch, thumping his mitt), and play anywhere else that I needed him. So far, that was center field, where he could catch any ball that was catchable, and then achieve—with speed and accuracy—home plate with his throw.

Tony and Alejandro were allowed to play on the team because PZBall had a rule that each club could take on three foreigners. The only other foreigner playing Polish baseball, as far as I knew, was a Cuban named Juan Echevarría. He was founder, coach, and first baseman of Robotniczny Klub Sportowy Stal Kutno. *Stal* means "steel" and Kutno is a town of 50,000 that makes steel; it's located 127 kilometers west of Warsaw. Echevarría, a contract worker in Poland

The Sparks in Warsaw's SKRA Stadium, before our season's opener against Jastrzębie. Kneeling (l-r): George, Norbert (partially hidden), Pete, Chuck Powers of the Los Angeles Times, *Capt. Paweł, Alejandro, Greg Stabeusz, and Andrzej Majchrowski (whose medical school studies soon forced him to quit the team). Standing (l-r): Pizza Hut, Blackie, Jake the catcher, Mark, July (behind Mark in sunglasses), Adam, Tony, Marek, Chris Płatek (Paweł's younger brother), Jackson Diehl of* The Washington Post, *Mariusz, me, Froggy Darryle Johnson of the U.S. Embassy, Henry, Tomasz Konarzewski (who left the team after a few games), and Komo. We're wearing our practice clothes; our new uniforms were not ready yet. Dariusz is not here because he was up in the press box.*

who married a Kutno woman and decided to stay there, formed Stal Kutno in 1984. When anyone asked him about the history of Polish baseball, Dariusz would give plenty of verbal ink to Echevarría, mainly because Juan was the one who introduced him to the game. In the larger picture, Polish baseball's genealogy, Dariusz told me, went back to the old Polish game of *palant,* which went back to 1474. *Palant* had a bat (about half the size of a baseball bat), a leather ball (softer than a baseball, about twenty percent smaller), and a single base (a wooden post in the ground, placed a certain distance from where the batter stood). The batter played against a gathering of fielders. Like a tennis player serving, the batter hit the ball, then had to run to the post and back. He was "out" if a fielder either caught the ball in the air or, having fielded a grounder, hit the batter with the ball before he could get back to the starting point. According to Dariusz, *palant* was last played in Poland in 1967. "Death," he told me, "came natural in Silesia." Silesia is the coal-mining region in southern Poland where Rybnik is located. Rybnik is the town where the Polish Palant Union buried itself and then rose up as a softball team—thanks to the Czechs who taught it the rules. Klub Sportowy Silesia Rybnik became Poland's first softball team, Górnik Boguszowice became its second, and they played each other until 1982, at which time the Czechs taught them baseball. The Polish workers liked this game *bardzo, bardzo* ("very, very much"). Three more Silesian teams were quickly formed: another one in Rybnik (Kolejarz), one in Jastrzębie, and one in Rój-Zory. All five of these baseball teams were within twenty kilometers of each other. Then an outsider came in—Cyprzanów. Cyprzanów is a village of about 400 located ninety kilometers west, and a beautiful little turn south, of Rybnik. It is almost in Czechoslovakia, among rolling hills so storybook-like it seems right and proper that Cyprzanów is not even shown on the *Samochodowa Mapa Polski* (the official Polish road map). There is a church on a hill, and a red brick road winds through the village. The road leads to a creek. You cross over a bridge and come to a sheep meadow. That's where Ludowy Zespól Sportowy Cyprzanów (Folk Sports Union of Cyprzanów) plays baseball, among strict white chalk lines and clusters of sheep droppings that no one pays much attention to. Juan Echevarría's Kutno team was formed the same year as Cyprzanów's, and the next year, 1985, PZBall—with seven teams—began league play.

"Gary, you listen. I talk now about first shadows of Warsaw team." This was Dariusz' favorite part of the story, the part where he fell in love. The day he told it to me Pete was translating, but having a hard time getting *his* part in because Dariusz, using both Polish and English and snapping his fingers for words he wanted quickly, was excited all over again. The gist of the story was that in October 1985, Dariusz' paper sent him to Kutno to cover a game and interview Juan. Dariusz came home with his head full of much quickness and thinking and his heart full of passion, and he immediately began beating the capital city's bushes for baseball players. He found them mainly across the Vistula River, in the east part of Warsaw called Praga, where, if you go there, people in west Warsaw will say, you must keep your hands on your wallet and your eyes open and not stay after dark. Thieves, pimps, prostitutes, and Hungarian gypsies live in Praga, they say. Praga, they say, is working class—by which they mean that

Praga has none of the cultural lights that their side of the Vistula has, like the Great Theatre, the palaces, Old Town, the university, the five-star hotels, Łazienki Park, the church where Chopin's heart is buried. Praga is also where the Russian army was camped in the summer of 1944, watching—doing nothing to help, most Poles will tell you—when the Polish home army attempted its "Uprising" against the occupying Germans and was crushed. Praga was where, in the fall of 1986, you could buy black market Russian caviar, the best, for twenty dollars a kilo, and where Dariusz found the first shadows of his baseball team.

He found Adam Ziółkowski (called "Blackie" by his teammates because of his black hair and black mustache and perhaps because of his black temper too), who declared himself the first baseman—he liked the idea that a runner could go nowhere without getting past *him*. Dariusz found Mariusz Szpirowski, a muscular high school student whose rugged good looks made him seem older, to play second base; and he found jumpy little Norbert Gajduk, also a student, to play shortstop. Norbert's right arm, of which he was justly proud, was a real baseball arm; his throws to first base or home plate were on-a-line stingers, absolute honeys to witness, and part of a problem that would come up later. Dariusz found pitcher-infielder Piotr (Pete) Załęcki who, when tempers flared, stepped in as peacemaker. Pete too was in high school that year, and wondering where his life was going. Dariusz found outfielder Paweł Płatek, who ground lenses for glasses and who, like Alejandro, could catch anything. Where Dariusz, walking, made me think of Chaplin, curly-haired Paweł, smiling, made me think of Harpo Marx. Unlike all the other Sparks, Paweł was totally unflappable, which was why they voted him team captain. Dariusz found outfielder Grzegorz (Greg) Stabeusz, who was his translator the first time we met. Greg was a university student majoring in business; he'd spent his junior high years in New York City, hence his English and the Rawlings glove. Dariusz found catcher Cezary Komorowicz (called "Komo"), who, whenever he had to reach high or to the side to catch a baseball, would perform a somersault. He could also speak Japanese. Komo preferred to meditate to loosen up, rather than stretch or run laps. He wore wire-rimmed spectacles and looked like a humorless revolutionist, but when he went to catch or throw a baseball he seemed to want to imitate a moth above a candle flame. He was twenty-three and married when Dariusz found him, and he did not last long as a Spark. Dariusz found three more players that fall of 1986: a pitcher named Mark Gierasimowicz, 16, a big, hard-throwing kid with a pompadour of hair so blond it was almost white; a pitcher named Jacek Małecki, 19, who was dark and bony and threw very hard too, and who became our first loss; and slow, steady Pizza Hut, 17, who often appeared to be ready for a nap because of his houndlike brown eyes. All of these ten original Sparks were among the Seniors getting up now from their breakfast in Rybnik—except Greg, who was home studying for an exam; Komo, who had become an umpire and was working the game in Kutno (the strange is not so strange in Poland); Jacek Małecki, who cut some tendons in the wrist of his pitching arm by falling in a pile of junk glass; and Pizza Hut. Dariusz counted the players again as they left the dining room.

"Ten Juniors, only *fifteen* Seniors," he said to me.

"*Spokojnie,* Dariusz," I said. *Spokojnie* means "calm down" and is a word we all used often.

"OK, OK," he said. He lit one of his foul-smelling Polish cigarettes. "But you listen, Gary, I think about Jacek, about Norbert, about Paweł, and now Pizza Hut." He was counting on his fingers our injuries so far—indicating a streak of very bad luck. Jacek Małecki's injury occurred a month before the season began; most likely he was lost for the year. The day before our opener, Norbert twisted his ankle running down some steps and was gimpy for two games. Then Paweł twisted his ankle kicking a soccer ball around with some little kids; he missed our last game and was doubtful for today's. Now gone was Pizza Hut, a dependable reserve outfielder, whose injury troubled Dariusz the most. "I don't know how we must behave!" he said. We walked out to the bus, and he counted everyone again.

Górnik Boguszowice played its home games just outside Rybnik, about a fifteen-minute ride from our hotel. Leaving the mainly soot-colored town—the twin towers of a brick church looking more black than red, more like towers where grief's story, not joy's, rose from the worshipers' lips—leaving this town where coal and its acid odors and an ancient faith in "black gold" held the Poles in a grip there seemed to be no getting out of—not for a long time—I was surprised to see, suddenly, so much green rolling ahead. It was the morning-after-an-all-night-rain green, a green that made you feel everything was not lost, at least not for today. It was a green that said, "You are forgiven. Breathe." We passed meadows bearing bright dandelions, little orchards whose slick-limbed cherry trees grew among tall grasses. We passed a milk cow chewing her cud in belly-high timothy beside the narrow road, and farther out, man-size scarecrows made from rags and straw were guarding a field of something young, something with brave shoots. We passed houses of brick and houses of cement block (in many upper windows, pillows and blankets were piled to take the air), and we passed people walking to church on the road's shoulders in their Sunday best: willowy blonde girls under white hats, broad-hipped women in dresses printed with flowers, old men all buttoned up in dark suitcoats, *babcias* arm in arm with each other, with a younger woman, or alone with a cane. The whale skin–colored sky was behind us and going away, going down behind distant smoke stacks. Up ahead, the sky was blue and white and the sun, just where we wanted it, was breaking through.

At a fork in the road offering two equally attractive tree-shaded lanes, Dariusz hesitated, then told the driver which one to take. After a kilometer or so, it seemed to be the wrong one. We weren't finding the crossroads that Dariusz remembered from his visit out here last year. He stood at the door looking for a pedestrian, becoming visibly more nervous. I tried to calm him down with a joke. I said to Jake, "Tell Dariusz it's very simple: next time we go anywhere we should bring along an American Indian." Jake translated this, but Dariusz remained frozen to his mission. Finally he spotted a boy on a bike. The boy straightened us out. When we got to Klub Sportowy Górnik Boguszowice and were leaving the bus, Dariusz said to me, "Gary, I promise you something—next time to Rybnik, no improvisation! No night club. I make reservation for *all* meals and complete hotel. Please, no American Indian."

He was so apologetic I felt ashamed. "I get lost a lot myself, Dariusz," I said. "But I tell you, no more improvisation!"

"Right. Let's play baseball."

* * *

Most baseball diamonds in Poland were laid out on soccer fields, which usually resulted in a deep left field, an even deeper straight-away center field, and a short right field. Since almost all the players threw and batted right-handed and tended to hit the ball to left and center, that layout worked fairly well. (The occasional ball hit to deep right, and into the stands that were often there, was a ground-rule double.) What did not work well, however—and thank God it was dying out as the Poles came to understand baseball better—was their fussy practice of laying down canvas carpet on the pitcher's mound, at home plate, and along the base paths, to save the grass. When the field at Skra was being prepared for our first game that season, I told the Klub manager we were going to play baseball, not conduct a wedding, and I took the carpet away. The Górnik diamond did not have carpet; in fact, the base paths were dirt (or dirt and cinders—these guys were tough indeed) and the pitcher threw from a true mound. Right field was short—about 175 feet, ending in a thick stand of oak trees—but otherwise here was a real ball field. It was also very soggy from all the rain. Third base, in the worst shape, was a small pond. Tony found a shovel and, wearing his white cotton gloves, dug a hole about twelve feet away from the base—in foul territory—and then scooped out a canal leading from the pond to the hole. It was a wonderful piece of engineering: the water flowed.

The Junior Sparks did not flow. Neither did the Górnik Juniors, for that matter. They played a five-inning game (the limit for Juniors unless one team was ahead by ten runs after three innings; then a "knock down" was declared and the team behind spared further humiliation). They played a game in which two groups of adolescents slipped and rolled over in the wet grass a goodly number of times, made an occasional catch, an occasional put-out at first base, hit the ball maybe six times, walked a lot because they were small or afraid to swing the bat, struck out a lot because they were eager to swing at anything (especially when the pitch came in hat-high), and, in short, demonstrated that they had spent the important part of their youth bouncing soccer balls off their foreheads and feet instead of throwing and catching and hitting baseballs. The Junior Sparks were all seventeen and eighteen years old (eighteen was the cut-off for Juniors; there were no age restrictions for Seniors) and, except for one player, had never held a baseball until six months ago. (The exception was our center fielder, Paweł Tymiński, who had lived briefly in New York City.) I didn't know about the Górnik Juniors' experience, but they did not seem to possess any more skill or savvy than we did. That surprised me, in view of the fact that Boguszowice had been playing the game five years longer than Warsaw. It also surprised me that our Juniors were physically much bigger than theirs—I had expected to see size and muscle on *all* the players in Silesia. Our catcher, Mariusz ("Whale") Tumulski, a good eater who made his mother and grandmother happy over the years, was not an outrageously big kid for a Pole (six feet,

190 pounds), but he looked almost freakish next to these local boys. In any case, it was a sloppy game that Górnik won by a score of 14–12. The young Sparks were not overly disappointed. They knew they were learning a difficult sport and found consolation in the handful of decent plays they'd made. They also knew that the next game was the one that counted.

* * *

PZBall rules declared that a Seniors pitcher could pitch only seven innings. (The limit was three for a Junior.) When I asked Dariusz why, he said, "Is necessary." He explained that prior to the rule, a team would pitch—exclusively—the player who could perform that function the best. Thus few, if any, new pitchers were being developed. There was another way to look at the situation: an outstanding pitcher in the Polish league—like an outstanding pitcher in Little League in America—could win a game practically all by himself. All he had to do was throw hard and throw strikes. If he had a good curveball too, the only help he needed on the field, for most games, was a catcher. Silesia Rybnik had such a pitcher—Jan Cnota. Storybook Cyprzanów, of the sheep meadow, had a pitcher almost in Cnota's class named Janusz Rzytki. In the first year of PZBall, 1985, Silesia Rybnik won the championship, Cyprzanów finished runner-up. Silesia Rybnik successfully defended its title in 1986 and 1987. I didn't doubt that the abilities of Cnota and Rzytki did a lot to encourage the seven-inning rule—especially since games were scheduled only on Sunday, which gave a pitcher all week to rest up. We would meet these two strong arms in our sixth and seventh games, both on their turf. And in our fifth game we'd go against Juan Echevarría's steelworkers, who had faced Cnota in their season's opener and lost only 7–5, a real baseball score—a score that did not indicate a minefield full of errors and walks. Meantime—today—we had Boguszowice's coal miners, who were fighting mad, we heard, because they'd lost their first three games (to Cyprzanów, Kolejarz, and Kutno) and wanted our fancy big city hides. I hoped that the sight of July, wearing aviator shades and plugged into his Walkman when he stepped off the bus, made them see stars.

July's full name was Arkadiusz Lipiec (Arcady July), and though he was hardly a summer rustic of the Peloponnesus gazing contentedly upon fleecy sheep, he *was* the guy reclining on one elbow in the sunshine, not thinking about too much at the moment, oh maybe a little bit about his girlfriend Agnieszka, and maybe a little bit about his girlfriend Renata, and how he might discover, maybe, which one was his real love. July was twenty-four. He drove a fast royal blue Ford Sierra (bought by his engineer father in West Germany, with dollars earned in Libya), and he combed his thinning blond hair forward, like Caesar, but in almost every other way July was laid back. He was also a rare item in Polish baseball, a left-hander, and because of that and his snaky motion, he spooked the hell out of most batters. Never mind that a right-hand hitter ought to fare better against a southpaw, it was the fact that July threw from over *there,* and fast, that gave the jumpy hitters visions of their kissers crushed. That was what the Sparks who faced July in batting practice told me (reminding me of the myth I believed years before, in Midget League, that all lefties were wild and could kill you), and for that reason and because he could throw strikes, but mainly because he was laid back, July was my starting pitcher. I hoped to get at least two innings out of him, then bring in our ace, high-kicking Mark Gierasimowicz, to pitch the next seven. If July—who did not have his baseball legs yet—could go three innings, all the better; then I'd still have Mark in case the game went an extra inning. In reserve, I had two more pitchers: Pete and a young bull named Adam Jaworski who, before he turned to baseball, threw the javelin for the national track team. Pete had good control but not a lot of speed. Adam had speed; frightening speed. His problem—which most of the Sparks shared—was that until he played an inning or two and could get calmed down, his beating, thumping heart was raging to escape his chest. In each of our first three games—all at home and all started by Mark—we walked at least two batters, committed at least two errors, and spotted the opposition at least three runs before we even came up to hit. Today we were up first. I hoped we could get rid of our jitters right away at the plate. But if not, I hoped that laid-back July, when we took the field, would help us be cool for a change out there. We wouldn't have Paweł's cool too, unfortunately; during our warm-up he still couldn't run full speed on that ankle.

The chief umpire was the president of PZBall, Jan Liszka. He called for the two captains (Mariusz was our acting captain in place of Paweł) and explained some rules: if one team was ahead by ten runs after five innings, the game was over; if a ball was hit into the oak trees in right field, it was a double; if a ball was hit beyond the yellow flags in left or center—and no one caught it—it was a home run; if either team had a complaint during the game, the umpire would discuss it only with the captain; if a player on the field swore, he would be ejected.

After the umpire finished his instructions, I quickly gathered the Sparks in a huddle to review our signs.

I held up my palm.

"No swing!" they said. "Take."

I pulled at my chin.

"Steal!"

I pulled at my earlobe.

"Bunt!"

I made as if to tie my shoelace—our sign for the squeeze play.

"Must bunt!"

I brushed my arms.

"Erase! Change sign!"

Then I told them the batting order. It went like this:

Jerzy (George) Biń, rf
Norbert Gajduk, ss
Tony Valcarcel, 3b
Mariusz Szpirowski, 2b
Alejandro Tellez, cf
Marek Sobkowicz, lf
Adam (Blackie) Ziółkowski, dh

—hitting for Jacek (Jake) Kalinowski, c
Tomasz (Froggy) Małkowski, 1b
Arkadiusz (July) Lipiec, p

Although the Sparks knew ahead of time pretty much what the lineup would be, they didn't want to know the batting order any sooner than necessary; having that knowledge to carry around would only add juice to their beating hearts. We touched hands at center-huddle, then broke away with a yell—"OK!" The Sparks lined up along first base, Górnik lined up along third (they were big fellows, unlike their Juniors), and the two opposing players closest to home plate slapped hands in greeting, followed by the next two moving up to the plate, and so on. The umpire then yelled, *"Pałka!"* ("Bat!") and we were ready to go. I trotted down to the coach's box at first base.

The Górnik pitcher, a guy with a five o'clock shadow heavy as Richard Nixon's, walked George on four pitches. He walked Norbert on five pitches, and then he lost Tony on a 3 and 2 count. We had the bases full. Mariusz, our clean-up batter, could hit the ball a kilometer, but was himself hit—in the ribs. Like many Poles who are hit by pitches, Mariusz' initial reaction was rage. He threw down the bat. But seconds later he flashed a sweet smile at the pitcher—"It's nothing, forget it"—and raced happily to first base, scoring George. Alejandro struck out, swinging from his heels for Cuba (at high pitches!). Marek, playing left field in place of Paweł, walked, forcing in Norbert. Like Pizza Hut, Marek came to practice faithfully and, like Dariusz, was passionate about this game. When he arrived at first base, he said, "Coach, I am nervous. Let me steal to calm down." I said, "Marek, the bases are loaded." He looked mortified. "I'm sorry, Coach."

Blackie came up. Blackie was on probation. In our season's opener, playing first base, he made a nice catch of a high throw from Norbert at shortstop and the batter was out. Blackie was so pleased that he thrust a triumphant fist into the air and performed a little parade in front of the happy local crowd that took him and his euphoria into short right field. Meanwhile, a runner on second base, taking advantage of Blackie's celebration, ran to third and, seeing that Blackie was still full of himself, continued on toward home. Blackie woke up just as the runner crossed the plate, and *then* he threw the ball to Jake—who all this time had been shouting for it, but Blackie heard nothing except the cheers from the stands for his wonderful catch at first. Between innings I spoke to him about this error. He hung his head and said he would make amends. When he came up to bat, he hit a triple. He stood on third base with his fist held high. From the coach's box across the diamond at first, I returned his salute. Then I signaled for him to take a lead. He could take a big one because not only was the pitcher ignoring him and winding up but the third baseman was playing a good dozen feet from the bag. Blackie could easily have taken six steps toward home. Instead, he continued to stand on the base, like a Polish prince who had just recaptured his rightful land, telling me (I could see the word issuing from his mouth, could almost hear above my own shouting its self-assured, completely-in-control tone), "Moment, moment." Blackie was at that moment a Polish prince indeed—not a factory worker, not a twenty-two-year-old guy who still lived at home with his parents and grandmother in a two-room apartment because that was the way it was in Poland unless you had dollars, or joined the hated Milicja (the State Police) and right away got a nice apartment and a nice salary, or had some uncommon luck, which was mainly a myth. Yes, at that moment Blackie was in charge and he wanted to savor his territory, his victory, and again he thrust his fist to the heavens. Meantime, the pitcher delivered his pitch and the batter hit it toward the third baseman. At *that* moment Blackie decided to conquer home plate. The third baseman fielded the ball, juggled it, fired to his catcher. They got Blackie by a step. Later, when I explained that had he taken even a dinky two-step lead he'd have been safe, Blackie hung his head like a man who had miserably failed everyone, including his mother and grandmother and the great nineteenth-century national poet Adam Mickiewicz, whose fiercely patriotic verses and plays gave the people hope when Prussia, Russia, and Austria partitioned their country and formally it did not exist, and for whom Adam "Blackie" Ziółkowski was named.

He came to bat now against Górnik with the bases loaded. He was our designated hitter and, Lord, I wanted him to hit one. The first pitch was low, in the dirt. The second was high. "If it's in there, Blackie," I yelled, "whack it to Moscow!" He dug his soccer cleats in the mud; he swung the bat a few times to get loose; he was ready. The pitch came and bounced off his batting helmet. Blackie's fury was so great he couldn't move right away. I reached him just as he raised his fist to the sky—just as a long wailing note declaring filthy injustice left his throat. The umpire pointed to first base and I took Blackie there, telling him if he made one more noise he was on the bench.

Tony trotted in from third base with our third run. The bases were still loaded. Froggy came up and walked on four pitches, forcing in Mariusz, and the Górnik coach had had enough of Five O'Clock Shadow on the mound. The new pitcher—I did a double-take—was a southpaw. And the first batter he faced was July. Lefty against lefty, a very rare sight in Polish baseball. He got two quick strikes on July and I thought, Oh no, the spook. Then a beautiful thing happened. July smacked a sharp single to right field—the first hit of the game—and in raced Marek (who I hoped was no longer nervous) and Blackie (the fist high) with our fifth and sixth runs. And still only one out. I looked over at Dariusz who sat at a small table beyond third base (he and his counterpart from Górnik were keeping score together) and he beamed a big smile at me, as if to say, "What did I tell you? No problem!" George came up again and bounced to the shortstop, who flipped nicely to second base to force July out. Norbert fanned—on high pitches!

In Górnik's half of the first inning, the leadoff batter struck out. July looked slick as snake skin hitting Jake's target three out of four times with his sidearm fastball. I kept my pitchers off the curveball as much as possible. For one thing, they were erratic with it (only big Mark could throw it reasonably well) and for another thing, they didn't need tricks in this league. A good fastball and control, and occasionally a change-up, would win games. Thus, Jake's signs to the pitchers were mainly for fastballs, in these locations: the inside corner of the strike zone, high and low; the outside corner, high and low; and straight down the middle. July walked the next batter on four pitches. He was still basking in that first strike out. He was a good pitcher, but like Blackie, like most of his teammates, and like Stephen Crane's Henry Fleming who was shocked to see the Rebels attacking again after they'd been repulsed once, July did not quite understand yet that one little victory did not automatically assure a second little victory.

Now he was distracted because the runner had stolen second base and Norbert and Mariusz were going through a Cuban number that Tony had taught them, with pencil and paper, on our interminable bus ride the day before. In effect, Norbert and Mariusz were describing a delayed figure 8, with second base the midpoint. Just as July went into his stretch, Norbert took off for a quick circuit around the bag, then Mariusz made a circuit. The idea was to fox the runner into watching Norbert return to his shortstop position—thereby enticing him to take a big lead—at which time Mariusz would be approaching the bag and, theoretically, a throw from July. They'd have the runner dead. The only hitch in all this choreography was that the runner wasn't being foxed, and stayed close to the base. Did this discourage Norbert? No, he continued to make his half of the figure 8, leaving a big hole at shortstop just when July had to decide whether to pitch the ball or attempt a pick-off that was clearly pointless. But Norbert, like Marek who wanted to steal second when the bases were loaded, was nervous, and this was his way of calming down. Finally July threw a very wide pitch to the batter. I yelled at Norbert to forget the runner, damn it, and play shortstop. I yelled at July to throw strikes. He threw two, then the batter flied out to George in right field.

OK, two down. We might get through a first inning yet without mayhem. Górnik's clean-up hitter stepped in. He looked like Mickey Mantle—blond, boyish, good shoulders—and he got hold of July's first pitch just a little late and drove it—foul—over the stand of oak trees behind George. At least three Górnik Juniors raced to search for the ball. (The supply of game balls was a precious two—provided by the home team.) July rubbed up the new ball. I yelled at Jake, "Keep it low, inside. Make him hit it on the ground." July followed through. He jammed this big-shouldered blond perfectly, and the guy hit a routine grounder to shortstop—only it went through Norbert's legs into left field, scoring the runner from second. Norbert made his two usual mistakes on the play: he turned his head and he didn't get his glove down far enough. Since January, beginning in the Gwardia gym, I must have hit a thousand grounders to Norbert, and he almost always turned his head, taking his eye off the ball. But because he was quick, he was successful—in practice—about eighty percent of the time. And because of his superior arm, he looked spectacular when he was successful. In our first three games, however—under pressure—his success rate on grounders dropped to about fifty percent—dismal for any fielder but disastrous at a position where so many balls are hit. When I experimented with Norbert at third base and Tony at shortstop, Norbert performed even worse. And he brooded over there—never mind what I said about his arm being more useful at third—he interpreted the experiment as demotion, defeat, shame. Another Polish prince being deprived of his territory. Yes, yes, he understood about errors, about a team needing to be strong up the middle of the diamond, but *he,* his anguished eyes said, was the shortstop. He and his good arm! From Norbert's point of view, I knew, a spectacular put-out somehow erased the error or errors that preceded it. In fact, one really good play a game, or one good hit, could make the whole game worthwhile to a player, even if the final result was a loss. No one said any of this of course, but in a country where mounted cavalry had ridden out with their sabres to meet Germans with tanks, where an electrician from the shipyards of Gdańsk had stood up to the Communist party and won, briefly, a taste of freedom, no one needed to say it.

The next Górnik batter was the deposed Five O'Clock Shadow, who was still in the game, playing center field. He too hit a grounder that Norbert missed. Norbert raised his hands and face to the sky to argue with an unfair Power, instead of retrieving the ball, and while he argued (and while the ball, resting ten feet behind him in the wet grass, was being chased down by Tony, Marek, and Mariusz), the runner on first went all the way to third and Five O'Clock Shadow reached second. If I'd hit a thousand grounders to Norbert, I'd also told him fifty times that when he took a personal time out to grieve and wail, *the game was still going on.* I yelled that to him now and he pounded his glove, resolved to rise from his ashes.

Tony brought the ball to July, telling all the infielders, softly, "*Spokojnie, spokojnie,* OK?" He patted July on the back and returned to his position. I said, "Two outs, July. Forget the runners. Go after the batter." July nodded and threw a strike. "Do it again!" I said. He did. "All right, baby, one more!" I said. The Górnik batter, their shortstop, ducked from a pitch at his head. Then he ducked from another. "Easy, easy, go easy, July," I said. The batter fouled off one, and then—unbelievably—he fouled off the next five. July threw a ball. The count was 3 and 2. Then July lost him to load the bases. I called time and went out to the mound.

"How do you feel?" I said.

"Maybe I am unhappy," July said.

"You're not sick?"

"No, no, I'm OK that way," he said.

"Is the ball too wet?"

"It's wet. But not too wet."

"You're not tired?"

"No, I'm OK," he said.

"You feel good?"

"I feel good."

"OK," I said, "let's get this next guy."

The next guy, their catcher, was six-feet-three and weighed at least 230 pounds. He stepped into the batter's box and took a few warm-up cuts like a man intent upon making permanent and ugly injury. He looked like Bluto, only bigger. July walked him on four pitches, forcing in Górnik's second run. The bases were still loaded. I looked over to where Mark was warming up. I didn't want to bring him in yet, nor did I want this first inning to get out of hand. I yelled at Pete to get loose, then I yelled at July to bear down, throw strikes. "You can do it, July!"

Górnik's next batter, on a 3 and 2 count, also walked, forcing in their third run. Were we jinxed? Doomed to give up three unearned runs every time we started a game? And things could get worse, I knew. A year ago in Warsaw this same Górnik team defeated the fledgling Sparks 34–3, in a game mercifully stopped after five innings by the knock down rule.

The ninth man in the batting order came up. Surely he was their weakest hitter. I decided to let July pitch to him. "He wants a walk," I said. "Don't give it to him." "OK," July said, but he just stood on the mound looking toward the plate as if he were unsure what to do. "Come on, let's go!" I finally yelled. July looked slowly around at first, second, third—all the runners were standing pat. Then July glanced at Norbert, who seemed to be posing as someone suddenly moved to religious devotion, a brand-new ascetic whose face was saying, "I am not here . . . I have renounced all worldly concerns . . . pay me no mind." I knew that look and I knew what was up—the god damn hidden-ball trick, which the Poles loved as children love candy. If I had let them, the Sparks would have tried to pull it on every runner who reached first base, but I'd made a speech after our first game (in which we had been successful once with the hidden-ball trick, but had also committed nine errors): none of that Little League stuff, I said, until we can throw, catch, and field the ball. At that point, I said, we won't need tricks. Still, it was a habit difficult for some Sparks—like Norbert—to break. I yelled at him now, "Give the ball to July, damn it, and let's play baseball!" Sheepishly he brought the ball to July, and July struck out Górnik's ninth batter on four pitches. We led, 6–3.

In the top of the second inning, Tony led off with a booming triple down the left field line. Mariusz struck out, Alejandro struck out. Tony scored on a wild pitch. Marek flied out to left. In Górnik's half of the inning, July tossed out the first batter on a bouncer back to the mound. He walked the next two batters and I almost pulled him. I was glad I didn't because he struck out their clean-up hitter, and then Tony fielded a sharp smash and threw to Froggy to end the threat. We led, 7–3.

We got another run in the third inning. Blackie singled, stole second, advanced on a fielder's choice, and came home on a wild pitch. (A runner on third base can give a Polish pitcher melancholia.) In their half of the inning—Mark was now on the mound for us—the coal miners sent ten men to the plate. They got two bloop singles to right field and three walks, and two men reached base via errors by Mariusz and Froggy. Górnik had four runs across and had the bases loaded, with only one out, when Mark struck out the last two batters. We now led by one run, 8–7. Dariusz came over from the scorer's table, walking like Chaplin in a hurry, and said to me, "Gary, you listen, no problem. We will win!"

In the fourth inning Mariusz walked and stole second. Alejandro walked. Mariusz stole third, a decision of his own and a foolish one, because Górnik's catcher, Bluto, had a powerful arm; but Mariusz was on his charger. Marek then walked to load the bases. Blackie hit a single to left, scoring Mariusz, but Alejandro, who took time between second and third to whoop it up, was thrown out at the plate. I had to remind myself that he was sixteen and that all of his glands were turned on all the way, *olé*. Marek went to third on the play. Froggy bounced to the shortstop, who tried for a double play but only got Blackie at second. Marek scored. Mark went down swinging for the third out.

Bluto came up to start Górnik's half of the fourth and hit a towering blow to deep center. The ball kept going and going and then there was Alejandro, beyond the yellow flag, robbing the man of a homer. Mark struck out the next batter, and I thought—especially with the number nine man in the batting order coming up—that maybe we'd pull off a rare thing, a three-up, three-down inning. Mark got two quick strikes on the guy, rocking back, kicking his leg out in that wonderfully smooth, big-league motion he had when he got in his groove. Mark stood six-feet-two, weighed 180 pounds, and was only eighteen. He was going to be a real pitcher; already he moved around the mound like one, threw the ball hard, and understood how to use the strike zone, how to go for the corners. All he needed was experience—and to learn *spokojnie*. When he got excited, his big white-blond pompadour seemed to puff out from under his hat like a soufflé. His third pitch to the Górnik batter was very close to a strike, so was the next one. He looked over at me and shook his head in disgust at the umpire's judgment. I said, "This guy can't hit, Mark. Go get him." Mark gave him a fat one down the middle and the guy, swinging late, blooped it to right for a single. Angry at himself, Mark walked the next two batters to load the bases. I called time and went out to visit.

"Umpire is no good," Mark said.

"Take it easy," I said. His cheeks were flaming.

"I throw strikes, he says low, he says high."

"Just settle down," I said.

"I am OK. *He* is not OK."

"It was a cheap hit that guy got," I said.

"Cheap?"

"Worth about ten *złotys*. About what you'd pay to use the toilet in a restaurant."

"What are you saying?"

"I'm saying go get this next guy—forget the umpire."

"I must! He is blind!"

Górnik's number three batter stepped to the plate and, on a 3 and 2 count, blooped yet another single to right, driving in two runs. But their clean-up batter, the guy who looked like Mantle, hit a line drive straight back to Mark to end the inning. We led 10–9. Dariusz again came over, "It's OK! It's OK!" he said. "We will win!"

In the top of the fifth, George walked and went to second on a wild pitch. Norbert struck out and left the batter's box talking to all of his ancestors in heaven, asking them, *"Dlaczego? Dlaczego?"* ("Why? Why?"). Tony fouled out. Mariusz got his first hit, a single to center, scoring George. I said to Mariusz, who was standing on first base burning to run, "*Spokojnie,* OK? Watch me. *Wait* for the steal sign." Not listening, not waiting, on the first pitch delivered by Górnik's southpaw, Mariusz stole second. Talking with Mariusz now was like trying to reason with a man caught up in the flash and flame of battle. Lefty then hit Alejandro on the leg. Lefty was a short, heavy man with a cranklike motion, and his shoulders were sagging. Marek came to bat. I showed him my palm—the take sign—and then I yelled at Mariusz to stay on second base, damn it. Marek had a good eye at the plate; he'd walked twice already and I figured—hoped—with Lefty apparently running out of gas he'd walk again.

Then we'd have Blackie up with the bases loaded—and Blackie was hot. Lefty threw high to Marek, then even higher. His third pitch was almost over Bluto's head. Everything was going perfectly for us—and then Mariusz, who could no longer contain his fire, tried to steal third. Bluto threw him out to retire the side.

When Mariusz came running to the bench for his glove, I grabbed him by the shirtfront, up at his neck, and said, *"Dlaczego? Dlaczego?"* His eyes had a shocked glaze over them—he was confused, then angry. I continued to hold him by the shirt. He wouldn't look at me and wouldn't answer. I said, "Damn it, Mariusz, there was no point to stealing third!" I let him go. He found his glove and raced over to Dariusz. He yelled at Dariusz, threw his glove on the ground, shook his head violently. I didn't know what he was saying, but I could guess he was unhappy. I was unhappy, too. We'd just blown a good opportunity to score some runs. Worse, we were now commencing to fight among ourselves—so many Polish princes and only so much land. Mariusz finally ran out to his position at second base and Górnik came up for their half of the fifth.

We had the lead, 11–9, but that soon changed. Their first batter walked, and then Alejandro, waiting for a routine fly ball, dropped it. A funereal gloom passed over the Sparks, gray as the Rybnik sky we had slept under. Out in center field Alejandro flapped his arms at his sides like a maimed bird. When the next batter, Bluto, smashed a one-hopper at Norbert and the little Praga tough scooped it up and made one of his spectacular throws to Froggy for the out, the team revived. But then the next batter poked one into the oak trees behind George for a double, driving in two runs; and then Tony, of all people, made an error. He picked up a grounder and fired it over Froggy's head, letting another run come in. Mark threw out the next batter and Norbert caught an infield fly to end the inning, but Górnik now had the lead, 12–11. Dariusz came over, his face looking sunburned, and said, "It is no problem, believe me!"

Well, I wasn't so sure. In our half of the sixth—facing a new pitcher, a right-hander—we got the bases loaded on two walks and a hit batter, with only one out. But then Norbert was called out on three straight strikes and Tony, going after the first pitch, popped up. The Sparks returned to the field like men who were sore in body and spirit.

Leading off the Górnik sixth, the blond clean-up batter laid into Mark's fastball and sent it so high and deep to center that I thought, Here's where the roof falls in. But Alejandro caught it over his shoulder, robbing the miners of their second home run. He jumped up and down—no longer a maimed bird—and constructed a string of Spanish syllables that Bizet could have spread around Carmen at her feistiest. OK! The next batter hit a bouncer back to Mark. He dropped the ball, then couldn't find the handle because he kept looking at the runner. He was furious with himself. He tried to pick the runner off first base and threw the ball over Froggy's head. I yelled at him to forget the runner, who now stood on second base. Mark didn't hear me—couldn't hear me for his fury—and tried to pick the guy off second! This throw ended up in center field, the runner advancing to third. "Now will you forget about him!" I said. "OK, OK," Mark said. But his concentration was a mess. He threw two fat pitches to the next batter, who fouled off the first and sliced the second into right-center for a triple, scoring the guy on third. Then Bluto blooped one out toward George that George couldn't quite reach. Another run in. I yelled at Jake to go out and settle Mark down. I told Pete and Adam to warm up. I yelled at Mark to *forget* about Bluto and get the batter. None of us thought the big catcher would try to steal anyway, but he did; on Mark's first pitch he lumbered over to second like a beach bully hugging an inner tube around his middle. We simply watched him. Then the batter bounced to Norbert. Froggy, moving to cover first base, slipped in the wet grass and fell down. Suddenly there was Mariusz, still on fire, sprinting to first to take Norbert's throw. They got the runner on a close, spectacular play, their favorite kind. Two outs, the Sparks were flying. Never mind Bluto moving to third and raising his fist à la Blackie. Well, we weren't quite flying yet. Mark walked the next batter, who stole second and then scored behind Bluto on a single. Finally Mark retired the side on a strikeout. Górnik led, 16–11. Once again Dariusz came over. "I have much happiness," he said, "because I know we will win!"

In the seventh inning neither team scored. The Sparks made a very promising start: back-to-back singles by Mariusz and Alejandro. But then Mariusz, *still* needing to prove something, took a suicidal lead off second base, daring the pitcher to pick him off, and the pitcher did. This was opera, not baseball. If Alejandro, earlier, called up Bizet, Mariusz now, storming back to the bench, was Lieutenant Don José, fuming to get revenge in the last act. Marek then popped up and Blackie struck out. In Górnik's turn at bat, they went down one, two, three: a strikeout, a fly to Alejandro, and a line drive to Mariusz—who, after he caught the ball, slammed it into the wet grass at his feet. Dariusz came over.

Before he could speak, I said, "Do you still have much happiness?"

"Of course!" he said.

"We've only got two more innings, Dariusz."

"All we need!"

Froggy walked to start the eighth. Mark struck out. Górnik's pitcher, smelling victory, was now getting too eager. He walked George and Norbert to load the bases. He was aiming his pitches, trying too hard. I called a quick huddle and said, "Listen—nobody swings the bat unless I say so, OK?" I looked at Mariusz, brooding on the periphery. "OK, Mariusz?" I said. He said, "OK." Tony stepped to the plate then and walked, forcing in Froggy. That made the score 16–12. Mariusz came up. He followed my take sign until the count was 2 and 2. "If it's in there now, Mariusz, hit it," I said. A home run would tie the game, and he was our home run hitter—and overdue. But what he did was hit a feeble fly to the shortstop, and then walk back to the bench like a man who was completely no good. Two outs. Alejandro came up. Taking all the way, he had a 3 and 2 count on him when Tony—dancing a little too energetically off first base, trying to rattle the pitcher—slipped to one knee. Bluto, who had the ball, fired it to first and Tony was dead. We'd had the bases loaded, only one out, our power at the plate, and we got only one run.

To make matters considerably worse, Górnik came up and, slam-bang, got a single, a double, a walk, and a triple. Three quick runs, nobody out, and a runner on third base. They led, 19–12. Here goes your old ball game, I thought. Three more runs and they'll get us on the knock-down rule. But then the Sparks, instead of tossing their sabres in a heap, put on a sharp little show to end the inning: George raced in to catch a blooper to right field, Jake fielded a blunt in front of the plate and threw the batter out, and Mark fanned the clean-up hitter on three straight pitches. Still, we were seven runs behind. As Dariusz made his flat-footed way over from the scorer's table, he did not look like a man who contained much happiness.

"Did you come to tell me we're going to win?" I said.

"Maybe we can!" he said. "Maybe we can!" His voice sounded awfully punished by all the Polish smokes he was going through. Then—desperate—he said, "Maybe George is no good today in right. Maybe Paweł is now OK?"

I said, "It's the ninth inning, Dariusz. We need base runners."

Our first man up should have been Alejandro, I thought, because he hadn't had a chance to complete his turn at bat the previous inning. But the umpire said no, Marek was up. I didn't want to get involved in a discussion that might lead to heat and distraction (when you're behind it doesn't take much, and Blackie, among others, was always primed to join a fray), so I let the matter go. I was sorry I did because Marek promptly fanned. The Górnik players, shouting, raised a finger at the sky. One out! Blackie came up. I hoped he could contain himself and follow my take sign. He did, and walked on four pitches. The Górnik pitcher was aiming the ball again. He walked Froggy on five pitches and lost Mark on a full count. The bases were loaded for George.

George was the smallest and youngest Polish player on the team. He was five-feet-four, weighed 120 pounds, and would celebrate his eighteenth birthday in two days. He wore one of those baseball caps you can buy in the States that are half plastic mesh and have a strap in the back to adjust the size. His strap was on the first hole and still the cap—a New York Mets model—was too big for him. To prevent it from flopping in his eyes, he stuffed some cloth under the sweat band. Like Greg and Jake, he had lived for a while in New York when his father, a chemistry professor, was on a Fulbright grant. George's junior high American classmates gave him the baseball bug, and he still had it. The first time we met—that January at Gwardia—he said to me, "I am Jerzy, Coach, the catcher. Call me George, like George Herman Babe Ruth." On almost every Friday afternoon after that meeting I would run into George at the American Embassy. I was there to collect my mail; he was there for the latest *Sports Illustrated* and any other magazine in the Embassy library that carried baseball news. "Aren't you supposed to be in school now, George?" "Ah," he would say, "school is dull today." Or, "My teachers are all in a bad mood—I don't like to see it." Or, "Hey, Gary, the Mets will start spring training soon!" The Sparks' very early spring practice at Gwardia—which began January 13 and ended March 30—was every Wednesday, Saturday, and Sunday and George never missed. He wanted to be the first-string catcher. He worked hard at it, but Jake, who was six inches taller and weighed fifty more pounds, and had a stronger arm, got the job. George was the back-up catcher. I played him in right field or made him the designated hitter. He was our leadoff batter because he could get on base. He had his own bat—an aluminum model, with red tape on the handle, that he'd bought in Queens—and every time he stepped up to home plate, he would whisper to this bat. "What do you say to it, George?" "I tell it to be good." He stepped up now against the Górnik pitcher who was two outs away from victory.

George had walked five times that day, and I wanted him to walk again. The pitcher threw high. "OK, George, he'll do it again!" I said. But the pitcher didn't do it again—he fired two quick strikes across—and now George had to swing if the pitch was close. On the bus ride back to Warsaw, I would remember the next few moments of the game more than any other. George stepped out of the batter's box and gave his bat two kisses, both in the same place—presumably the spot where he planned to hit the ball. Then he did hit the ball, down the left field line, for a double. Blackie and Froggy came in to score. It was now 19–14, with two runners on and Norbert up.

Lord, I thought, let Norbert crouch down low like a monk with abundant humility on his mind and let him stay there; let him not be tempted by the high pitch of pride or the wide pitch of ambition; let him be cool. Cool was mainly what I hoped for, giving him the take sign. The pitcher threw a strike, and then he threw another strike. Then, trying very hard to finish off this cocky Praga tough—who between pitches swung his bat as if he intended to make big trouble—the Górnik right-hander threw four consecutive balls. We had the bases loaded again, and Tony at bat. The veteran. The Spark, could I have chosen any of them then, I would have chosen. The Górnik coach called time and went out to settle down his pitcher, a guy with thick legs and a boxer's thick neck and a motion a butcher might use to chop meat. I think the coach wanted a new pitcher, but he had no more; and Polish rules forbade him to re-use a pitcher, even if the pitcher were still in the game. Once a pitcher was removed from the mound and sent, say, to play third base, he could not return to the mound. The umpire called, *"Pałka!"*

Tony took two balls. Then he watched a slow, fat pitch float across for a strike. It was like a dollop of ice cream, easy and sweet, but our desperate strategy continued: not to swing unless the pitcher got two strikes on us. The pitcher laid another fat one across. "OK, Tony! It's up to you!" I yelled. The pitcher threw wide, making the count 3 and 2. He delivered another fat one. Tony swung. The ball rose about five stories straight up. When it came down, Bluto had it for the second out. The Górnik players went momentarily nuts, waving two-fingered salutes at each other as if they'd just discovered that number.

Now it was Mariusz' turn. I gave him the take sign, but I was not confident his passion would allow him to obey it. He pulled his Chicago Bears cap down tight and took a slow, measured warm-up cut that said he wanted to *do* something—he'd had too many bad moments that day to live with! The feeble pop-up last inning, getting picked off second base, that humiliating incident following his attempt to steal third! The expression on his dark, handsome face said that he was suffering. If he could sing, he would have made a very good Don José indeed. The pitcher delivered, and Mariusz watched the baseball go past—it was ice cream and pie and the look in his eyes said that he was starving. I gave a cheer. Starving or no, he was playing baseball. And the pitcher walked him, forcing in Mark. The score was 19–15, the bases were still loaded.

If I had Mariusz' passion to worry about, I now had Alejandro's youth.

At the conclusion of my stay in Poland, the Sparks sent me home with a sabre. Crouched in front are Norbert (left) and Krzysztof Jurek (who joined the team near the end). Standing (from left) are Capt. Paweł, Andrzej Stankiewicz (a Junior), Adam, Mariusz, Froggy, George, Dariusz, Henry, and Jacek Demkiewicz (another assistant). George is holding a second gift: a copper plate bearing an embossed mermaid.

Holding my palm up, I said, "Do you see this?" Alejandro nodded, wiggling around in the batter's box hoping to unnerve just a little bit more the already plenty nervous pitcher. And while he threw his hips and elbows around, the pitcher threw wide, he threw low, then he almost threw the ball in the dirt. Bluto was furious. Alejandro was beside himself with joy. All the Sparks were. One more bad pitch and he was on base. The pitch came up—it came straight for his smiling face—and Alejandro bunted the ball. I believe my heart stopped. To bunt at all was madness. To bunt on a 3 and 0 count—and at a bad pitch—well, there was no word for it. The ball was rolling down the third base line. Alejandro, shocked, stood where he was and watched it, jabbering he didn't *mean* to do that. The Górnik pitcher was also shocked, but he soon found his wits and ran for the ball. All he had to do was pick it up, walk about six steps, touch the still-stunned Alejandro or touch home plate—the choice was glorious—and then he could go have a beer. But the ball rolled foul, inches from the pitcher's hand. Alejandro made the Sign of the Cross. The pitcher walked back to the mound, his shoulders slumped, and delivered a fourth ball. Alejandro *ran* to first base and George came in from third, making the score 19–16. On the bus much later,

Dariusz would be drinking a beer and saying to me, *"Chrząszcz brzmi w trzcinie w Szczebrzeszynie,"* Jake would be translating: " 'There is a beetle making sounds in the willow in Szczebrzeszyn." Dariusz would then say, "Yes, and I hear this tiny animal, believe me, when Alejandro tries to make his bunt. I hear no thing in my head, or down where I have my heart, only this tiny animal."

Marek, who began the inning by striking out, came up again and walked on four pitches, scoring Norbert. We trailed by two runs now, 19–17, with Blackie stepping to the plate, the bases still loaded. There was a lot of shouting and cheering from the Sparks' bench for Blackie, and Blackie shot a fist to the sky, shouting with them. This caused Bluto to shout something. Blackie then thrust his bat at the sky like a sword, and the umpire—a man who would brook no displays—rushed out from behind Bluto and made an angry speech directed at both catcher and batter. I ran over and grabbed Blackie's arm (he was so tense his arm felt like wood) and told him in a burble of wisdom that if he didn't play baseball, he wouldn't be playing baseball. Then I assured the umpire everything was OK. He yelled, *"Pałka!"* We all returned to our places. I gave Blackie the take sign. He nodded, fiercely, and then glared at the pitcher. The pitcher, whose thick neck seemed to have gotten thicker—in fact it seemed painful for him to turn his head to look at the runners—met Blackie's glare and raised him. Blackie's head stood up like a rooster's; he took practice cuts that declared manslaughter was on his mind. All I could do was send him a stream of encouraging chatter—"Good eye, baby, good eye; easy does it, *easy* does it"—and hope it would soothe him, hope he would not swing the bat, even though, in my gut, I wanted him to knock one past a yellow flag.

Blackie walked on four pitches, sending in Mariusz, to make the score 19–18. It was the eighth walk of the inning and I was convinced, as Froggy came up, that the law of averages had to turn now in the Górnik hurler's favor. Moreover, Froggy stood very still at the plate; he presented no rattling theatre. All the pitcher had to do was throw two easy strikes, and then all the pressure would be on Froggy. And every Spark knew how chancy Froggy was under pressure.

The pitcher threw two easy strikes, and Bluto was making sounds like a bear who'd finally found the honey hole. Blackie, standing on first base, was quiet. So were his teammates. This was it. Froggy swung at the next pitch and missed. I turned my head, I saw the Sparks on the bench slump like puppets when the master drops all the strings, and then I heard the umpire cry, "Foul!" The Poles had adopted a few terms from American baseball, and this one, at that moment, was the prettiest. Froggy fouled off another pitch, and then, one by one—and they were the most painful and the sweetest pitches I believe I have ever witnessed—he watched four balls go by. Alejandro came in from third with the tying run, hooting Spanish, Polish, and English. Every Spark was jumping up and down except Froggy. He stood on first base like a man who had just given his blood—all of it—at the blood bank.

The Górnik pitcher also looked drained. He'd started this inning with a seven-run lead and now it was gone. And the bases were still loaded. Full of disgust, Bluto walked out to the mound and slammed the ball in the pitcher's mitt. (Bluto had to be plenty mad at himself too: if he'd held onto Froggy's first foul—a foul tip—the game would be over.) Now the pitcher, throwing to Mark, hit him in the ribs. Mark was delighted, the Sparks delirious. Marek came in to give us the lead, 20–19. While the Sparks celebrated his arrival at the plate, the miners of Boguszowice, their heads bowed, walked in little circles at their respective positions like men who had just been told their girlfriends married better prospects. Finally the umpire wanted a batter and George stepped in. George worked the pitcher to a 3 and 2 count, kissed his bat, and then walked, sending Blackie home. Blackie crossed the plate in a handstand, grinning like a kid wearing a false mustache. We'd gone from the opera to the circus. Norbert, our fifteenth batter that inning, stepped in. He too worked the pitcher to a 3 and 2 count, but fanned for the third out. In a way I was grateful for the out. To be seven runs behind in the ninth inning, and then to score nine runs on one hit, one hit batter, and ten walks—and requiring more than an hour to do it—makes for a lot of wear and tear on a guy's personal ebb and flow.

Well, the game wasn't over. The Sparks were up high, but if Górnik got runners on base and we started making errors, started arguing among ourselves, it would be a long, flat ride home. (Going into the eighth inning of our season's opener, we led, 17–14, but lost our cool and lost the game, 28–17.) Górnik held a meeting, which ended with many arms raised to the sky, and then Five O'Clock Shadow stepped to the plate. He worked Mark to a full count. Mark kicked out his leg, fired, and the umpire called, "Strike!" Another very nice borrowing from American lingo. The next Górnik batter swung at the first pitch and popped it up. Mark caught it for the second out. The Sparks in the field were slapping their mitts and the Sparks on the bench were slapping each other. Bluto stepped in, fuming. I yelled, "He's dead, Mark! He's finished! He's too mad to see straight! Blow it past him!" Bluto swung at the first pitch, hit a one-hopper back to Mark, who grabbed it and made a beautiful throw to Froggy. Froggy dropped the ball. Bluto stood safely on first base pounding a fist in his palm, showing *me* who was dead. I yelled out at Mark, "Forget the runner! He's not going anywhere! He means nothing to us!" Mark went into his stretch, threw to the batter, and Bluto took off for second base. I couldn't believe it. Jake had the ball and was cocking his arm to throw down to Mariusz, and I was yelling, "Why! Why!" On the bus later, Jake said, "Coach, when I heard you yelling 'Why!' I almost didn't throw to Mariusz. But I said to myself, 'That catcher is slow and crazy—mainly slow, and I remembered the last time he stole second on us, and I thought, 'He shouldn't be allowed to do it again.' " Dariusz, who had just given me the sentence about the beetle in the willow in Szczebrzeszyn, now gave me another:

"Drabina z powyłamywanymi szczeblami."

"Jake, what does that mean?" I said.

"It means 'A ladder with broken-out steps,' " Jake said.

Dariusz laughed. Then he said, *"W czasie suszy szosa sucha."*

"That sounds like you've got a mouthful of bees," I said.

"No, no, I have *piwo* in my mouth," Dariusz said.

"Give me one of those beers," I told him. Then to Jake I said, "What did Dariusz' mouthful of bees mean?"

"I think he is saying 'A drought makes the road dry,'" Jake said. "But I don't know what he's getting at. Maybe he is just giving you Polish tongue-twisters, for fun."

"That was one hell of a throw, Jake," I said.

"It was easy," he said.

The Demise of the Philadelphia Athletics

BRUCE KUKLICK

The 1950s began an era of change for baseball tradition as franchises shifted for the first time in over a century and expanded to the south and west. Many patriarchal sports businesses crumbled. A simple pattern emerged as the weaker team in the two-team cities moved elsewhere. The Browns left St. Louis, the Braves left Boston, the Giants and Dodgers left New York.[1] This essay analyzes the forces at work in the departure from Philadelphia of the American League Athletics in 1954. The A's were in many respects a much less beloved franchise than, for example, the New York teams, but they were also exceptional in some ways. Their longtime manager and owner, Connie Mack, was the most famous figure in professional sports. Although by the 1950s he had not produced a winner for two decades, he had earlier been responsible for two of the great baseball dynasties, his teams of 1910–1914 and 1927–1932.

* * *

From 1901, financial direction of the A's had rested in the hands of baseball manufacturer Benjamin Shibe. He owned 50 percent of the stock, the franchise and, in 1909, put up the cash to build Shibe Park, the first concrete-and-steel stadium, to house the club. In 1913, Mack became a co-owner, but Shibe and members of his family continued to run "the front office," while Mack was premier on the field. When Shibe died in 1922, the Shibe interest in the A's passed into the hands of his four children but primarily to his two sons, Tom and Jack. They continued to run the business while Mack managed the team. Tom Shibe performed ceremonial duties during his father's later years and was president from 1922 until his death in 1936. His younger brother Jack, always in charge of the money, briefly became president, but Mack took over at the beginning of 1937, shortly before Jack's death.[2] Mack bought Jack's share of the

Athletics from his widow and, with this block of stock, controlled the A's and Shibe Park for the first time, although the Shibes still had considerable holdings in the franchise.[3]

Mack set about dividing his shares among his heirs. He first married in 1887, and his wife had three children before her death in 1892. Mack had long thought that the two sons from this marriage, Roy and Earle, would carry on the business. Earle had played with the A's for a short while and managed in the minor leagues before assisting his dad, sitting next to his father on the Shibe Park bench. Connie assumed he would serve as manager, while Roy, like the Shibes in the earlier period, would run the front office where he had been for some time.

Connie, however, had married again in 1910, eighteen years after the death of his first wife. He had five children by his second spouse, including a son, Connie, Jr., some twenty years younger than his stepbrothers. Because the father had laid his plans when Connie, Jr. was a child, Connie, Sr. did not know how his youngest son would fit into the business. In the 1930s, however, the young man began to devote himself to the club's concessions, then becoming an essential part of the franchise. Connie, Sr. envisioned the three male heirs ruling the franchise in concert.[4]

To this end he split his majority holdings. He kept a block of shares for himself, and apportioned the rest among his wife and his three male children, giving nothing to his four surviving daughters. Perhaps having in mind the Shibe stock, which Ben Shibe's daughters partly owned, Mack did not want the affairs of the club "muddled." He would not include a group of women in ownership. The club, Mack said, would go to his sons so that "the name of Mack," "the House of Mack," would go on.[5]

His wife had other ideas. Mack's plan would empower Roy and Earle, the surviving children of the first marriage. The second Mrs. Mack proposed that her husband distribute stock in equal shares to her, to each of her five children (four of whom were female), to Roy, to Earle, and to the children of Mack's deceased daughter from his first marriage. Controlling interest in the club would go not to the men but to the family of the second marriage (and, indeed, to the ladies).

So adamant was Katherine Mack that the couple finally separated, her husband leaving the house when they could not agree. Mack, well over eighty, had his humiliating estrangement become public knowledge in the winter and spring of 1946 and 1947. The couple were reconciled after several months, although Connie did not compromise on the stock allocation. The feud, however, was just the sort of family quarrel Mack wanted to avoid.

Undistinguished men, Roy and Earle lived in the shadow of their father. Roy was a mediocre executive, given to talking too much. Earle was better known as his father's field lieutenant, but seemed without motivation of his own. The older brothers fought between themselves "like cats and dogs,"[6] one observer said, but a generational bond and a lengthy baseball association that antedated Mack's second family united them. Their stepmother's plan crystalized an alliance between the two. Connie, Jr. and his mother needed allies and turned to the Shibe heirs, who among themselves owned some 40 percent of the Athletics' stock. Now failing, Connie, Sr. was unwilling or unable to settle disputes between the first family and the second family *cum* "Shibe faction."[7]

The prosperity of the postwar period initially masked the problems of the franchise. Baseball attendance soared. Before World War Two, 10 million patrons for all of major league baseball signaled a banner year. In 1946, however, attendance climbed to 18.5 million, and topped 20 million in 1948 and 1949. The Philadelphia franchises profited. In 1946, over 600,000 saw the A's, in 1947 and 1948 over 900,000, and in 1949 over 800,000.[8]

The crowds compared to those in the great twenties era of Athletics prosperity. Connie, Jr. in particular seems to have wanted to move the franchise more surely in the direction of the most successful major league clubs and wished for new managerial and promotional skills for the A's. His brothers, however, were determined to let the fortunes of the franchise rest on the enormous prestige of their father.[9]

From the 1930s, the public doted on Mack, "the Grand Old Man of Baseball" or "Mr. Baseball." His birthdays at Shibe Park occasioned yearly celebrations sponsored by local sports commentators.[10] Writers and players spoke of him—and to him—as "Mr. Mack." Writing in the *Atlantic Monthly* in 1940, John R. Tunis described Mack as "an institution," "the first citizen of Philadelphia."[11] During the war, American G.I.s trapped disguised German soldiers passing through their lines by asking if they'd heard that "Connie Mack pitched a shutout against Brooklyn." What American wouldn't know this was nonsense?[12] In rare disputes on the field, umpires would respectfully come over to the dugout for discussion with the old manager.[13] Later, in the early TV age, when Mack might view a game from his office, A's officials would bluff umps by saying that the elderly owner had seen a play on television and disagreed with the ruling.[14] Mack was, said one analyst, "one of the most popular figures sports has ever known . . . unique in the game's annals."[15]

But this public approbation could not hide from insiders, and in time from the fans, the deterioration of Mack's mind. In 1946, he traded future Hall of Fame third baseman George Kell to the Detroit Tigers. Wish Egan, who made the deal, stated that "I was a little ashamed of myself for taking advantage of the old man."[16] On the field players would ignore incorrect signals, or the coaches would overrule obvious mistakes. "My goodness, yes," Mack would say in acknowledgment. Things got worse. His memory failed, and by the late forties he would call out the names of stars of bygone days—Baker! Foxx!—to pinch-hit.[17]

Sportswriters commented euphemistically on these "mental lapses," and Mack refused to quit. "If I did," he said, "I'd die in two weeks."[18] In a widely read and sympathetic article in *Life* magazine in 1948, Bob Considine wrote that both players and coaches noted their manager's errors of judgment.[19] The same year, Mack exploded in public and fired pitcher Nelson Potter in front of the dugout as he came off the mound. He now occasionally broke into stormy emotions, reduced to tears. The manager was "off the beam."[20] Historian David Voigt described him as "an anachronism."[21] Mack's downward slide and the

Shibe Park, Philadelphia. (Photo courtesy of the National Baseball Library, Cooperstown, N.Y.)

disagreements within his family, wrote a commentator, began to accustom fans "to sudden, sometimes calamitous moves." All sorts of people now knew of his senility.[22]

At the same time Mack constructed a curiously interesting postwar team, assembling draftees, waiver players, and promising youngsters. In 1945 and 1946 they finished last. Yet in 1947, 1948, and even 1949, these bargain-counter discoveries, though they wound up only fifth, fourth, and fifth, respectively, were in the thick of the American League race for much of the season, collapsing in August and September as their lack of reserve strength became critical. To some extent their modest prowess accounted for the high attendance. Nonetheless, Mack overestimated their talents as well as his ability to make up for their deficiencies by clever strategy.

The year 1950 was Mack's fiftieth as A's manager. He was 87, but baseball in April is a siren, and the spring of the sport is a season of eternal youth. Should Mack retire? He would not. His team had shown some mettle, and, as one writer put it, "The will o' the wisp that danced ahead each spring" captivated the old man. Mack would manage, and he predicted a pennant for his "Ath-l-etics." Roy and Earle agreed, and overrode the doubts of their younger brother.[23] The *Elephant Trail,* The A's newsletter, expected the club's attendance to pass the million mark for the first time. The magazine also urged fans to send in ideas to boost the gate to that figure, but asserted that patrons would come out because the A's would be contending for the pennant and because Mack would be receiving nationwide honors throughout the season.[24] Honoring Mack's golden anniversary as manager, a motorcade from City Hall to the park began the festivities on opening day.[25]

Things went downhill from there. The year proved disastrous as the A's tumbled deep into the second division and stayed there. Bill Veeck was asked if a rumored purchase of the A's involved him. "They haven't got a ball club," he said. "All you get is the ball park."[26] In June, the family's internal squabbling, intensified by bad baseball, became more serious and more public. The youngest son and the Shibes failed in their attempt to force Mack's retirement, but they did succeed in removing the nondescript Earle as assistant manager. Voting his faction's stock against his father for the first time, Connie, Jr. made his brother take a job with the franchise's farm system.[27]

The crisis came later in the 1950 season when the A's were in last place. The youngest son agreed to a plan that would permit Roy and Earle to buy out the other shareholders. If they could not come up with the money, Connie, Jr. had the right to buy them out. In either event, the senior Mack would remain as titular head.[28]

Both sides competed to raise money. Local businessmen wanted to buy stock in the team. The newspapers reported that Phillies owner Bob Carpenter refused a half-interest in Shibe Park and its concessions. Connie, Jr. talked to James Clark, president of the Philadelphia Eagles football team, and the press said that wealthy builder John McShain wanted a piece of the franchise.[29]

Roy and Earle triumphed. They needed approximately $1.75 million to buy the 60 percent of the stock of the other side. To finance the transaction, the brothers took a portentous step: they mortgaged Shibe Park, the franchise's single real asset.[30]

Appraisers valued the park at $436,000 and the land at $250,000. But the stadium made money, including a $40,000 rental from the Eagles and 10 cents per head from the Phillies' gates, which in 1950 would generate more than $100,000. Concessions were also important. "Following a careful analysis of the value of Shibe Park and its earnings record," Connecticut General Life Insurance Company issued Roy and Earle a $1.75 million loan over ten years. In addition to the mortgage on the park, the A's turned over to Connecticut General the rent they got from the Phillies. A representative of the insurance company joined the A's board. To raise more cash, Roy and Earle leased the concessions, no longer run by Connie Jr., to Jacobs Brothers, a pioneer food service organization.[31]

These steps changed the club's business. Concessions made big profits and had expanded beyond Shibe Park; a separate Athletics corporation sold wares at the ballpark, at the stadium of Temple University, and at other places. Now the A's got a pared-down amount from concessions at the same time they gave to Connecticut General some of their other income. Thus, in mortgaging Shibe Park, Roy and Earle took on an interest burden—of $250,000 a year—at a time when their cash flow was declining. Much hung on the elder brothers' ability to draw people to Shibe Park. The A's had based their 1950 budget on 800,000 admissions, from which they estimated earnings of $800,000.[32] But when Roy and Earle took over in August, the A's were thirty-five games out of first, "locked in a death battle," the *Bulletin* wrote, "with the St. Louis Browns for last place."[33] The A's won, finishing eighth and drawing 310,000 fans, 500,000 off their budgeted number, 700,000 off the million patrons they had wished for.

To add insult to injury, Bob Carpenter's Phillies won the first Philadelphia pennant in twenty years, drawing over 1,200,000. Part of the A's problem, though not the Phillies', was that baseball attendance began to slacken in 1950 after the postwar rush and did not stop declining until the latter part of the decade. The consequences for the A's were dire. At the end of the season, the Athletics were deeply in debt and mortgaged to the hilt.

The most knowledgeable commentator on the family's fortunes wrote that Roy and Earle forced Connie's retirement in October of 1950. As the abysmal year unfolded, patrons proclaimed with Connie Mack, Jr. that the senior Mack should go. In the seventeen years prior to 1950, the A's had finished in the first division only once. "He should know the parade has passed him by," said one. "Why doesn't he step down and give a younger man a chance?" Philadelphians voted with their feet. Roy and Earle totaled the books and recognized that their younger brother had been right. Their father must retire: "the fans would never be content with any other move."[34]

Sportswriters who had snickered in private about Mack's failings now flooded newspapers and magazines with platitudes about the octogenarian manager. Only the communist *Daily Worker* criticized Mack, a fact that highlighted the vapidity of sports journalism.[35]

* * *

The franchise was sick, but the elder Mack brothers tried to restore its health. Connie remained the nominal president, and Roy and Earle did everything they could to capitalize on his name. In 1951, they opened the Elephant Room under the park's first base stands. The Macks wanted to attract "baseball men," and filled it with memorabilia from the A's great days.[36] To replace Mack as manager, the older sons appointed the popular Philadelphia figure Jimmie Dykes, a stalwart of the dynasty of the twenties and early thirties. Arthur Ehlers, a savvy baseball executive, took over as general manager. In 1951, marginally better results occurred as the A's came in sixth, but then in 1952 they finished a surprising fourth and drew over 600,000. As Roy Mack later commented, however, the middling prosperity of the team did not depend on management. Robert Clayton Shantz made the A's solvent.[37]

"Little Bobby" Shantz was a left-handed pitcher, 5′6″, 140 pounds. Born in Pottstown, Pennsylvania, he played semipro ball after the war in the Frankford section of Philadelphia. In the late 1940s, he recalled, for the price of "maybe a few car tokens to Shibe Park and home," he signed with the A's.[38] In 1949 and 1950 he compiled mediocre statistics, and labored under Connie Mack's suspicion that he was too small to win. In 1951, however, Shantz displayed real ability and compiled an 18–10 record under Dykes' management. The next year he won twenty-four games and lost only seven; the American League named him its Most Valuable Player.

Shantz was a likable and modest young man whose "diminutive stature," as the sportswriters put it, gained him the affection of fans everywhere, but particularly those in Philadelphia. Ray Kelly of the Philadelphia *Bulletin* wrote:

Connie Mack. (Photo courtesy of the National Baseball Library, Cooperstown, N.Y.)

Atop the Shibe Park pitching tee
the village hero stands . . .
the shrimp has muscles in his arms
as tough as rubber bands.[39]

The Year the Yankees Lost the Pennant, later made into the hit musical "Damn Yankees," was an early 1950s novel about middle-aged Joe Boyd, who signs a baseball pact with the devil. Set in the then future of 1958, the novel has Boyd win the pennant for the Washington Senators. In one scene at Shibe Park, Washington faces Shantz in "the late afternoon of a great career." In the ninth inning, Boyd homers over the right field wall to ruin "the diminutive portsider's" no-hitter and win the game for the Senators. But Shantz is such an icon that Boyd spends a miserable, sleepless night turning over what he has done.[40]

Shantz' crowds in Philadelphia in 1952 averaged almost 18,000. When he didn't pitch, the A's drew less than 8,000. His sixteen Shibe Park appearances accounted for almost 44 percent of the Athletics' home gate.[41] In the 1952 All-Star game at Shibe Park, Shantz pitched the fifth inning against the National League and struck out the side: Whitey Lockman, Jackie Robinson, and Stan Musial. The "hometown crowd," said Shantz, cheered as if he had won a World Series game.[42] Then, the inning over, the umps called the game because of rain.

The rain-out left the city's fans believing that Shantz would have gone on to duplicate or overshadow Carl Hubbell's 1934 All-Star feat of striking out five batters in a row. Later in 1952, on August 5, Shantz won his twentieth victory before a packed Shibe Park audience. The *Inquirer* editorialized that the triumph brought to "countless Philadelphians" "the comfortable assurance that no matter what else was happening, the world was a pretty good place to live in. Something about Shantz moved thousands to have some minor part in the occasion." The editorial concluded that "there'll not be another such time in Philadelphia for many days."[43]

The *Inquirer* was right. Shantz won four more games, and then, in late September, a pitched ball fractured his wrist. He never again had a winning record in the city. In 1953 the A's dropped to seventh place and drew 362,000; in 1954 they were last with 305,000. If only Shantz had stayed healthy, said Roy Mack later, the club would have remained in the black.[44] After a few years of precarious profits, Roy and Earle Mack were broke once more.

The problem, again, was not just the team but more family squabbling that hurt the franchise in public. Allied so long as they competed with Connie, Jr. and the Shibes, the elder brothers now feuded openly. When Earle and his wife separated, he moved into the small suite that the franchise provided for him off the A's clubhouse in the stadium. Still in charge of the front office, Roy turned the water off so that his brother could not bathe or use the toilet. They sniped at one another from two different Shibe Park offices, to and from which reporters scurried in their quest for stories.[45]

As early as the fall of 1951, after they took over, the brothers denied tales they would sell the team. In truth, however, only Roy wanted to stay. In the middle of the poor 1953 season, he countered rumors of a sale by saying "we have been here for fifty-two years and will be here for fifty-two more";[46] the club was "part of Philadelphia . . . as much a part of the community as Fairmount Park."[47] But Earle wanted to get out. The brothers never had a united front, and conflicting stories attributed to their father worsened the situation. By the fall of 1953, lack of money and internal strife troubled the Macks; pressure also came from the American League. The A's tiny attendance affected the receipts visiting clubs got from trips to Philadelphia, and other owners demanded change. The powerful voice of the Yankees pushed for the transfer of the A's to Kansas City, where New York had a farm club.[48]

At the start of the 1954 season, knowledgeable sportsmen talked about the A's debts and their failure to meet their Shibe Park mortgage. Then, in the middle of June, the Macks advised Philadelphia Mayor Joseph Clark that they would have to sell or shift the franchise unless the A's attendance leaped dramatically. Roy and Earle hoped that they could turn public feeling to the A's advantage, but the mayor was an insubstantial friend.[49]

Clark was not really interested in baseball, and professional sports in the city held a low priority for him. He did form a "Save the A's" committee. But it had 100 members and fifteen subcommittees. In his July announcement, the mayor also said that he personally rooted for the Phillies and that he was "no socialist"—government would not subsidize sports. Clark vaguely thought that his committee might come up with some long-term solutions to the A's woes. But publicists immediately attempted to encourage more people to turn out to the park.[50] The Macks needed 550,000 patrons to earn the money to meet their obligations and stay in the city. The committee tried to boost attendance for the remaining games.

As "Save the A's" mobilized its forces, the newspapers asked Philadelphians to express their views. The torrential response surprised the papers and yielded arresting insights into the fans' minds.

Appropriately enough, a few letter writers recalled better days. "As a small boy," said one, "we saw the opening of Shibe Park, and we remember the fans, like swarming bees clinging to the outside of summer trolleys." "I learned to love baseball and the A's as a boy following Connie Mack's great team of 1929–32," said another, "I don't want the A's to move from Philadelphia." "Save the team," wrote still another, "that so often brought a thrill of pride in being a Philadelphian"; "it would be like losing something very dear . . ." The most poignant mail noted how significant baseball was "for the kids." "My son is an A's fan," wrote one father now too ill to go to the park. "I took him to his first game when he was five years old to see Babe Ruth. The future of all things are in children."

More often, however, letters displayed the rage and frustration that loyal rooters felt about the Athletics. For the first time the public alluded to the park and the neighborhood. The *Inquirer* reported that parking stirred "bitter complaints." Driving to the stadium "exhausted" patrons. One said, "Get out of that undesirable neighborhood and get a bigger home, where parking will be no problem." Fans wanted "spacious acreage"; motorists did not want to endure "intimidation" or "gangster mob damage" to their cars. Inside the stadium, they demanded "modernistic improvements," escalators, better lighting, roomier seats, more restrooms, and drinking fountains. Finally, fans complained about the concessions, angry about the "ridiculous" price of hotdogs and soda.[51]

To the extent that the stadium and its community were the main issue, Mayor Clark did not help. The city at this time was collecting land and generating construction capital for projects that would revitalize Philadelphia's industrial base and central business district; and other towns interested in the Athletics—Kansas City, Minneapolis, and San Francisco—proposed bond issues to finance new playing fields. But Clark did not think that such bond issues should assist sports facilities. Although he came to accept the principle, he evinced little enthusiasm.

In any event, the stadium was not the main issue. As the A's public relations director asked: if parking kept people away from the A's, why didn't they desert the Phillies (who were drawing twice the fans)?[52] Letters emphasized that the real problem was the Macks and the teams they fielded. "Get rid of the Macks" said the letters. Connie Mack had "surrendered to the years" and a new generation could not "rest on memories" or listen to "sentimental drivel about . . . past glories." The Mack dynasty had "overstayed its welcome by about twenty years." For the preceding two decades, the Macks had run "a bush league circus." One man wrote that he was "tired of watching a franchise made up of second-string ball players . . ."; another said the Macks had done little "to earn the fans' support," consistently fielding second-division teams and selling off good players. Under Bob Carpenter, said one writer, "the Phillies' star" had risen and Philadelphians need not accept the Macks' "take it or lump it" attitude. To the Macks' repeated statement that fans "will not support a winning team," wrote one exasperated rooter, let them compare "the cellar years to the pennant years." "The Macks," concluded one perceptive citizen, "are on the same path as all venerable one-man family businesses." "Family expansion" proves ruinous.[53] A disgruntled father who had faithfully gone to see the A's through thick and thin and had made fans of his children was more blunt: "Roy and Earle Mack ain't worth a shit."[54]

These sentiments affected the "Save the A's" campaign. In early July, the club needed a turnout of 13,000 per game, as opposed to the approximately 6,000 it was then drawing. But as each home date passed with much ballyhoo in the papers, the average draw required for the remaining games climbed as a mere three, four, or five thousand patrons turned out. By the end of July "Save the A's" neared collapse. The committee reported apathy to the franchise in the business community. The Mack family had "a public relations problem to solve," and "a struggle in the family for power" accentuated the problem. The Macks rejected the committee's advice that well-to-do sportsmen be permitted to buy into the franchise and that the team search for playing talent.[55]

Although the Macks did not help in their particular case, the willingness of American cities to aid the baseball clubs they already had was minimal. Urban areas without franchises easily stirred up the civic pride and public funding necessary to entice teams. This combination was equally necessary to rescue existing enfeebled clubs, but it was not forthcoming. Early on in the debate over the A's, the *Bulletin*'s Hugh Brown analyzed the club's "deep-rooted" miseries. The stadium needed "a complete refurbishing" inside, and outside "swifter and more direct transit" and "extensive parking." In examining the Athletics' specific problems, Brown said that "no city, no matter how large and charitable, can be whipped or cajoled into supporting a team that has finished in the cellar eight times in the last thirteen years."[56]

In early August, Chicago businessman Arnold Johnson, who was connected to the Yankee farm team in Kansas City, offered to buy the A's for about $3.375 million and move them to Kansas City. As completed in early November, the deal paid the three Macks, Connie, Sr., Earle, and Roy, about $1.5 million. In addition, Johnson assumed the team's debt, estimated between $400,000 and $800,000, mainly to the Jacobs Brothers concessionaires who had taken over park sales and lent the Macks money. Finally, Johnson liquidated the stadium mortgage, standing at about $1.2 million. The A's had paid off $500,000 of the mortgage, but at the cost of indebting themselves to the vendors.[57]

The transfer of the franchise honored the ability of baseball capitalists to profit from the American commitment to the sport. One cannot help but remark on the contrast between the attractive power of the game for millions of ordinary people and the avarice and imperfection of those who controlled it. What is striking is not that the institutions of baseball were part of an acquisitive society, but that in the affection of fans the game transcended American culture. Roy and Earle Mack took over a weak franchise in 1950 for $2,000 a share. In four years they had run it into the ground, dismissed advice that might have helped them,

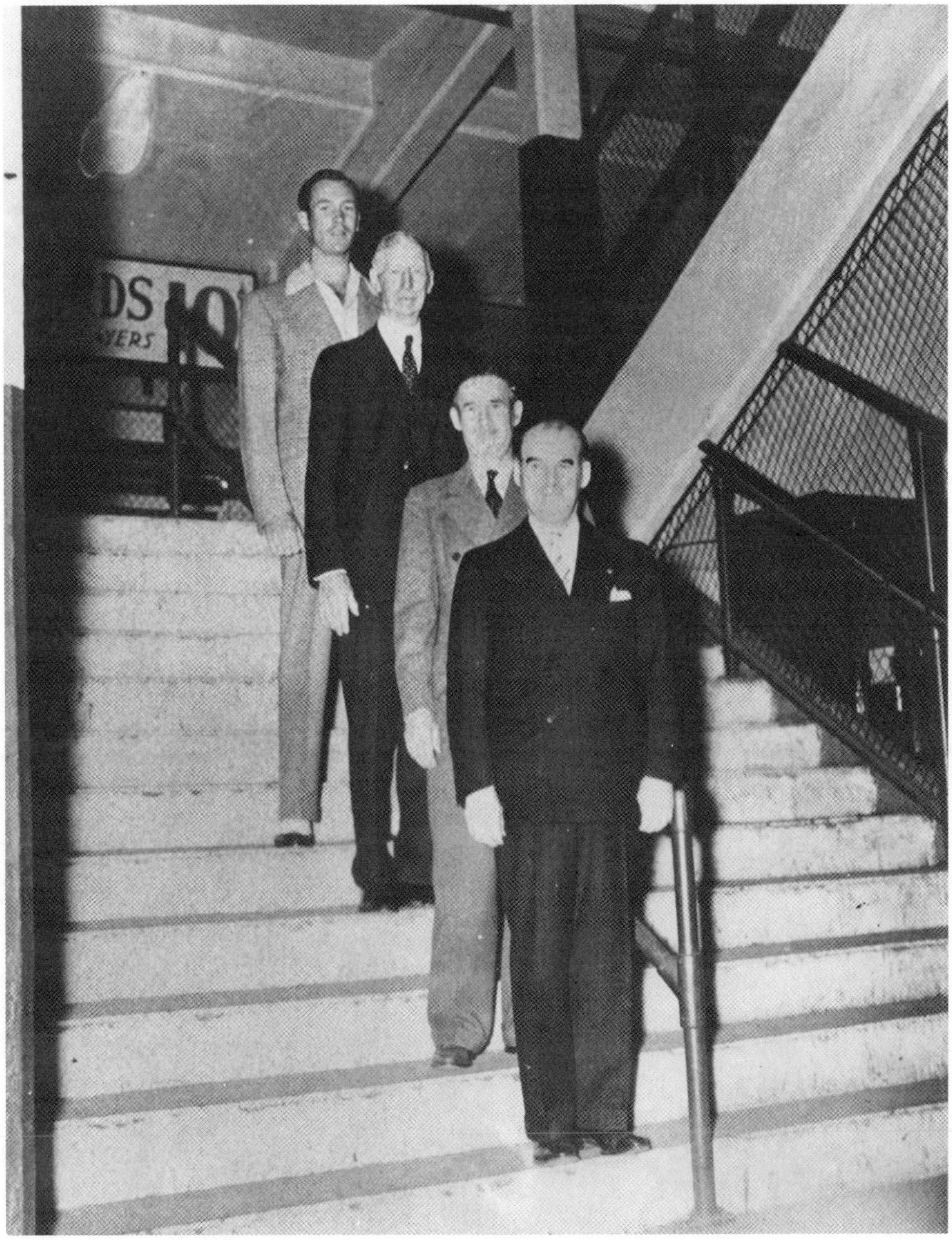

The House of Mack in the late 1940s. In descending order: Connie, Jr.; Connie; Earle; Roy. (Photo Courtesy of Bodziak Studio)

and demanded that someone else save them. Assisted by a spiritless Mayor Clark, however, their incompetence was self-serving. When they sold out to Johnson, they did so at an effective price of $2,250 a share.[58]

Arnold Johnson's even greater gain demonstrated adeptness at joining civic pride to his real estate manipulation of the Philadelphia and Kansas City ballparks, the latter of which was Johnson's major asset. He purchased the

Philadelphia A's with little or no outlay of cash. Stock in the new club paid off Roy Mack. Connie Mack's money came from Johnson's sale of the minor league Kansas City park, to Kansas City. (The city rebuilt the facility to major league standards and leased it back to Johnson.) The new franchise's profits gradually liquidated what the A's owed to Jacobs Brothers.

Bob Carpenter of the Phillies put up the cash in the transaction. After a series of negotiations he bought Shibe Park for $1.7 million. The money satisfied the mortgage on the ballpark and paid off Earle Mack. Carpenter recalled that Johnson was a slick speculator getting by on the skin of his teeth.[59] He picked up the Athletics' franchise on the strength of Kansas City's willingness to underwrite a major league baseball team.

In the summer of 1954, before Johnson made his purchase, Carpenter said he did not want "to buy the park under any circumstances."[60] He let it be known that the stadium was a dubious real estate investment and elaborately looked for land for a new field in West Philadelphia that would have 6,000 parking spaces.[61] No one, said Carpenter, could renovate the present stadium: it would cost $1 million to modernize, and enlarging the seating was impossible.[62] At one point, when it looked as if the A's sale would not go through, he said that purchasing a stadium had not interested him but that he "wouldn't have had any alternative."[63]

The Phillies were leasing the field until 1957, which gave them a short breathing period, and apparently Johnson suggested a new lease. It called for 20 cents a head rental, double the old rate, plus payment of maintenance expenses that the A's had previously carried.[64] Staying in the park without buying would be very expensive. In addition, the value of Carpenter's franchise would leap if the Athletics left. If Johnson would not take the Athletics unless Carpenter bought Shibe Park, was it worth sabotaging the move? He did not covet a ballpark but had few options. Indeed, the price of the property was just what Connecticut General figured four years before, appraising the site as valuable and income-producing. Later, as part of the franchise shift, Carpenter bought the property from the Philadelphia American League franchise.[65]

Johnson's initial offer to the Macks energized Philadelphia business and sports leaders. Harry Sylk, head of Sun Ray Drugs, pointed out that "What we stand to lose is not only the A's but the whole American League."[66] Prominent realtor Albert M. Greenfield added that the "loss of the team would be a blow to Philadelphia's prestige."[67]

In August and September of 1954, before the transaction with Johnson was concluded, various local businessmen tried to purchase the Athletics. They focused on Roy Mack, a weak man who yet seemed determined to keep the team in Philadelphia, as opposed to Earle, who saw no alternative to leaving. No Philadelphia plans had panned out, however, when the American League owners approved the sale of the franchise to Kansas City in mid-October. But Roy Mack wasn't sure. The day before the deal was final, the Macks sold the A's to a local syndicate.[68] Two weeks later, amid a flurry of rumors, charges, and countercharges by various members of the Mack family—including Connie Mack and his wife—the American League met again in New York and vetoed the move to keep the A's in Philadelphia. Led again by the Yankees and conscious of their profits, the owners turned down a plea from Connie Mack himself, whom a chauffeur had taken up from Philadelphia.[69] "The Grand Old Man" was a useful symbol for the sports entrepreneurs, but not a person to listen to in his dotage. Sentiment did not govern the League; the Kansas City move stood.

Ten days later, a remnant of the rejected syndicate raced Johnson to the senior Macks' Germantown apartment to buy Connie's share of the club.[70] Apparently this group wanted to obtain his stock and force the American League to keep the Athletics in Philadelphia. Whether such a move would have worked is doubtful, but it did not as Mack refused four proffered checks from the locals in favor of a single check and some talk from Johnson. "There must be some less excruciating way to spend money," said one of the rejected principals, "than trying to buy the A's."[71] In the end, all the Macks broke down and wept.[72]

New York Times columnist Art Daley wrote that Connie Mack "gave Philadelphia fans a pride in the Athletics. Without him there is nothing left but a dwindling force of habit."[73] The new Athletics spent thirteen years in Kansas City before they picked up again for Oakland, California. Although they drew large crowds and profited their owners, the A's in the midwest performed worse than they had in their last twenty years in Philadelphia.[74] The Kansas City A's were nicknamed the "Yankee Farm Club," as Johnson scandalously traded with his patrons in New York. The transfer assisted the dominance of the Yankees through the 1950s but also upped the league's income.

The removal finally sealed the triumph of New York over Philadelphia during that part of the century when they were the two preeminent American cities. In defeating John McGraw's Giants in the second decade of the century and in battling (sometimes successfully) the Yankees of Ruth and Gehrig, the A's established Philadelphia's credentials as an urban competitor of New York. But by the time the Yankees swept the Phillies in the World Series of 1950, Philadelphia was less significant. The transformation of the A's into a midwestern affiliate of New York ended an era of great rivalry between the two towns. New York writers had good reason for their comfortable, smug feeling that the transfer was an unmixed blessing.

Back in Philadelphia in early 1955, two trucks carried off memorabilia to Kansas City from the Elephant Room at the stadium. Johnson planned to display them for a couple of years. For the time being, Connie Mack was driven to and from his old tower office with the benign consent of Bob Carpenter. But Mack was going downhill rapidly and died just over a year later.[75]

Another, less noticed, death more fully embodied the minor tragedy of the Philadelphia Athletics in the 1950s. "Yits" Crompton lived in the neighborhood of the ballpark and came to the stadium as an A's batboy when he was fourteen. Later he was a fixture as clubhouse custodian. He followed the new A's to Kansas City in 1955 but returned to his old community a year later, disconsolate and unemployed. On August 23, 1956, he hung himself in his home around the corner from Shibe Park. He left a note: "I can't get baseball out of my life."[76]

Some time afterwards, two years before his own death, Roy Mack reminisced: "People always say to me 'I wish the A's were still at 21st and Lehigh.' "[77] Years later many old-time fans agreed when they tried to puzzle out how Philadelphia lost the franchise of the $100,000 infield and of Al Simmons, Jimmie Foxx, Lefty Grove, and Mickey Cochrane and got stuck with the Phillies, perhaps the worst franchise in baseball.

NOTES

1. For changes in baseball traditions see Neil J. Sullivan, *The Dodgers Move West* (New York, 1987). Two counter-examples stand out: the Washington Senators left the District of Columbia, though they were the only team in the city, and Chicago hung on to both the Cubs and the White Sox.

2. On the Shibe family see the clipping files on each of them in the morgue of the *Philadelphia Bulletin* in the Urban Archives of Temple University (hereafter clips, UA).

3. *New York Post,* 20 December, 1940.

4. On the Mack family, clips UA, and, for Connie, Jr., Robert Schroeder clips (Schroeder was head of concessions).

5. Harry Robert, "The Philadelphia Athletics," in *The Book of Major League Baseball Clubs: The American League,* ed. Ed Fitzgerald (New York, 1952), pp. 127–128; Frederick G. Lieb, *Connie Mack: Grand Old Man of Baseball* (New York, 1945), pp. 280–281.

6. Interview with Andy Clarke, 5 April, 1988.

7. See, for example, the report in *Philadelphia Bulletin* (hereafter B), 13 December 1954.

8. David Halberstam *Summer of '49* (New York, 1989), pp. 19–24 vividly treats the excitement of baseball after the war.

9. Roberts, "Athletics," p. 154.

10. Lieb, *Mack,* p. 266.

11. "Cornelius McGillicuddy," *Atlantic Monthly* (August, 1940), p. 212.

12. Richard Goldstein, *Spartan Seasons: How Baseball Survived The Second World War* (New York, 1980), p. 42.

13. Frank Yeutter, *Jim Konstanty* (New York, 1951), p. 87.

14. Jimmie Dykes and Charles O. Dexter, *You Can't Steal First Base* (Philadelphia, 1967), pp. 173–174.

15. Robert, "Athletics," p. 123.

16. Art Hill, *I Don't Care If I Never Come Back: A Baseball Fan and His Game* (New York, 1980), p. 37.

17. Bob Considine, "Mr. Mack: Did He Invent Baseball?" reprinted in *The Baseball Reader* (New York, 1983), ed. Charles Einstein, pp. 75, 79.

18. Ibid., p. 79; Harold Seymour, *Baseball,* vol. 2 (New York, 1971), p. 138; Goldstein, *Spartan,* p. 157.

19. Considine, "Mack" pp. 75, 79.

20. Robert, "Athletics," pp. 126–127, 153–155.

21. David Quentin Voigt quote, *American Baseball,* vol. 2 (New York, 1970), p. 80. For an analysis of Mack in the forties that uses the recollections of his players see Ben Yagoda, "The Legend of Connie Mack," *PhillySport* (August, 1989), pp. 52–62.

22. Robert, "Athletics," pp. 126–127, 153–155.

23. Ibid., pp. 129, 154.

24. *Elephant Trail* (January 1950), p. 3.

25. B, 21 April, 1950.

26. Veeck quoted in B, 26 June, 1950.

27. B, 18 October, 1950.

28. Robert "Athletics," p. 129; B, 27 May, and 28 August 1950, and 22 January, 1951; *New York Times* (hereafter NYT), 11 February, 1960; B, 12 February, 1960.

29. B, 31 July 1950; *Philadelphia Inquirer* (hereafter I), 29 August, 1950.

30. B, 28 August, 1950.

31. I, 9 June, 1950; B, 9 September, 1951: Assignment of Lease, File: Leases, Box 7 and

Jacobs Brothers lease, Agreement. . . , 1 December, 1954, File: Concessionaire Contract, Box 7, Philadelphia Phillies Papers, Eleutherian Mills, Hagley Foundation (hereafter PP); *Philadelphia Daily News* (hereafter DN), 10 October, 1950; B, 11 August, 1954; B, 26 January, 1972.

32. B, 1 August, 1950 (Pollock article).

33. B quote, 26 August, 1950.

34. Robert, "Athletics," p. 129.

35. *Daily Worker,* 20 October, 1950 (On the Scoreboard); for a sampling of other opinion see *The Sporting News,* 1 November, 1950, pp. 11–12, and, in general, *Look,* Tim Cohane, "Connie Mack's Last Year," 14 February, 1950.

36. B, 13 April, 1951.

37. B, 26 February, 1957.

38. Bobby Shantz as told to Ralph Bernstein, *The Story of Bobby Shantz* (Philadelphia, 1953), p. 77; and see Shantz clips, UA.

39. Bernstein, p. 148.

40. Douglas Wallop, *The Year the Yankees Lost the Pennant* (New York, 1954), pp. 91–93.

41. B, 26 February, 1957.

42. Bernstein, *Shantz,* p. 146.

43. I editorial, 6 August, 1952.

44. B, 26 February, 1957.

45. Interview with Andy Clarke, 5 February, 1988.

46. B, 19 July, 1953.

47. B, 29 September, 1953.

48. Ibid., and see all Philadelphia papers for June, 1954.

49. B, 2 July, 1954.

50. B, 9 July, 8 August, 10 September, 1954, and see Lenore Berson, "Philadelphia: The Evolution of Economic Urban Planning, 1945–1980," in John C. Raines et al., eds., *Community and Capital in Conflict: Plant Closing and Job Loss* (Philadelphia, 1982).

51. B, 6, 7, 8, 11, 13, 15, 18, 26 July; I. 13 June, 1954.

52. B, 25 July, 1954.

53. B, 10, 13, 14, 17, 24, July, 1 August, 1954.

54. Quoting my father.

55. B, 29, 30, July, 1 August, 1954.

56. B, 8 July, 1954.

57. Johnson's role is discussed at length in Ernest Mehl, *The Kansas City Athletics* (New York, 1956) but entirely uncritically. Compare his understanding (pp. 130, 191–193) with the one I have adopted from B, 13 October, 1954 and B, 8 April, 1955.

58. My computation of value of stock comes from: B, 3–5, 10 August, and 9 September, 1954; and 21 January, 1955.

59. Interview with Bob Carpenter, 1 April, 1988; and B, 27 September, 1954.

60. B, 18 October, 1954.

61. B, 9 September, 1954.

62. B, 22 September, 1954.

63. B, 18 October, 1954.

64. B, 9 September, 1954.

65. Deeds and Records, City of Philadelphia, Deed to 2000 West Lehigh, 10 December, 1954: 827.323.

66. B, 6 August, 1954.

67. B, 10 August, 1954.

68. All papers, August–November, 1954.

69. Mehl, *Athletics,* p. 98.

70. B, 13–15 November, 1954.

71. B, 9 November, 1954.

72. B, 4 November, 1954, 23 December, 1954

73. NYT, 19 October, 1954.

74. Joseph L. Reichler, *The Baseball Trade Register* (New York, 1984), p. 349; on the New York attitude in general see *New York Herald Tribune,* 11 November, 1954.

75. B, 20 January, 1955.

76. *The North Penn Chat* (on microfilm, Free Library of Philadelphia), 30 August, 1956.

77. B, 11 May, 1958.

Juan Marichal: Baseball in the Dominican Republic

ROB RUCK

AUTHOR'S NOTE: The following essay on Juan Marichal is from my work-in-progress, *The Tropic of Baseball.* The book tells the history of baseball in the Dominican Republic and suggests why it has become this island nation's principal art form in the twentieth century. Research for the book was made possible by grants from the National Endowment for the Humanities and the Social Science Research Council.

Laguna Verde, birthplace of the Republic's most famous sporting emissary, looks like any of the other small farming towns dotting the Dominican countryside. The streets are unpaved and half-clad children fill them. Clumps of soil and vegetation cling to the power lines overhead. Tony Pena points out the house of *Dona* Natividad, Juan Marichal's 86-year-old mother. Her son no longer lives there. These days, Juan Antonio Marichal Sanchez splits his time between a house in San Francisco and his home in the posh El Millón section of the capital.

On this January day, Marichal is in the States, where he directs Latin American scouting for the Oakland Athletics. Six months later, I track him down at *Estadio La Normal,* an aging ballpark in downtown Santo Domingo. It's late June and I've been trying to make contact with him for several days.

The day before, I had set out in the morning for a small complex that Epy Guerrero runs for the Toronto Blue Jays in Villa Mella, on the outskirts of Santo Domingo. I was to talk with Marichal there as he evaluated talent in the Dominican summer league that had just begun play.

One wrong turn and I find myself lost in the city dump instead. Smoke from mountains of burning garbage envelops an army of scavengers picking through the refuse. Most have rags covering their mouths and noses. Many are children, others gnarled and gray. They separate reusable sheets of plastic, rags, and pieces of cardboard from the decay. A few carry their prizes back to the collection of stick and cardboard hovels on the edge of the site where they live. With a quarter of the Republic's citizens unemployed or underemployed, these dump denizens are far from the worst off of Santo Domingo's poor.

Epy Guerrero's complex might as well be in a different time zone than the dump. Well off even the un-beaten path (all the better to hide his prospects, Guerrero's competitors say), the Villa Mella complex was the most advanced effort of its kind when Guerrero began building it a decade ago. With a dormitory for players, a weight area, and two well-manicured ballparks, Guerrero offers Dominican teenagers a chance to strengthen their bodies and prepare their minds before venturing off the island. Those who make it will never again smell the stench of the dump that lies hidden behind the hills only a few kilometers away, beyond the thick scrub vegetation shielding the complex.

"Latin players need more time to develop," offers Guerrero, a 46-year-old former Dominican pro who has become the island's foremost scout, as he explains the purpose of his operations. "They are not as physically mature as young North Americans. They are not as big, they haven't had the nutrition. And going to the States to play is tough when they don't speak the language and are away from home for the first time. We give them a chance to get a summer of play in here first, and see if they can make it. We teach them a little English and feed them good. Some go home after a few weeks, but others you will see in the United States in a few years. You can count on it."

Guerrero's employers, the Toronto Blue Jays, have savored the offerings that he has heaped upon their plates in recent years. The Blue Jays of the 1980s frequently fielded four, even five, Dominicans at a time, with all-stars like Alfredo Griffin, Damaso Garcia, George Bell, and Tony Fernandez pushing them to the brink of championship play. Griffin and Garcia have since been traded, replaced by representatives of the seemingly endless flow of middle infielders from San Pedro de Macoris. Overall, a third of the 200 ballplayers in the Toronto organization comes from the Dominican Republic or elsewhere in the Caribbean basin.

"But Marichal?" Guerrero says. "He is not here today. They changed the schedule. Maybe tomorrow, he will be here."

He's not. I find him instead at *Estadio La Normal,* not far from where the Ozama River drains into the Caribbean, watching the Oakland A's summer league team play a club composed of Yankee minor leaguers. Tiers of houses that look no more substantial than those built of playing cards line the ravine down to the river. When it floods, many wash out to sea. Outside the park, boys sell hubcaps by the curbs of the pitted streets and women crouch on the sidewalk to fill plastic jugs with water from an underground spigot.

Now 51, Marichal is more than the "Dominican Daddy" than the "Dominican Dandy" as five-year-old Juan Antonio Marichal, Jr. climbs all over him. Dressed in charcoal slacks, an Oakland A's cap, and a gray and black checked shirt with purple and pink threads running through it, Marichal's sanctified status is reflected only by the gold *Salon de Fama* medallion around his neck and the attention he draws from the other men who gesture his way as they talk to their own sons.

"I played here once," Marichal says. "In fact, when I first came to Santo

Domingo to play for *Aviacion* in 1956, I lived for awhile in the locker room inside this stadium with some other ballplayers. We were training for a youth tournament in Mexico that year."

Juan Jr. throws his arms around his father, imploring "Papi?" Marichal fishes some *pesos* out of a brown leather bag and calls to the small boy circulating through the stands with roasted peanuts for sale. The child shows his *estufa* (a stovelike contraption of two cans, the upper one with peanuts, the bottom with charcoal) to Juan Jr., who sits and shares his purchase with his new acquaintance.

"We had a farm," the tall, still sturdily-built Marichal resumes. "We called it a *parcela,* a parcel of land, a few kilometers outside Laguna Verde, when I was growing up. It was small, something like 60 acres, and we grew mostly rice, *platanos,* and beans. Now it's bigger, because when I started making a little money, we started buying more land and I bought a tractor for it. It's over a thousand acres now."

Juan's father died when he was three, but *Dona* Natividad held the family together with the help of relatives. "I don't think my father played baseball, but I know that he used to live for the *gallos,* for cockfighting. I think that's why I've got that in my blood. I love roosters. I'm a member of a club that has an arena for *pelea de gallos,* cockfighting. In the Dominican Republic, *gallos* come right after baseball."

Laguna Verde numbered about four hundred residents then and is only up to two or three thousand 50 years later. While the *casa de Marichal* was comfortable by peasant standards, with indoor plumbing and a tank of water that could be filled by hand for bathing, like the other homes in Laguna Verde, it lacked electricity. "We had propane gas for cooking, just like most people still do. And we had a battery-powered radio on which I listened to the ballgames. There was a player then from Laguna Verde, "Gallo" Martinez, and when he did something in a game, his father would shout '*Ese es mi gallo!* (That's my rooster!) I would tell my mother that some day she would listen to the radio and shout '*Ese es mi* Juan!' "

During the morning, Juan worked the *parcela,* before walking eight kilometers to school in *El Duro* each afternoon. "We didn't have any money but we had a lot of food. Almost everything that we needed to eat we had right there. My mother had a herd of goats that one of my brothers and I used to take care of. I grew up on goat milk." (Could that be the source of Marichal's incredibly high leg kick?) "Later on, I used to send my mother five hundred dollars every 15 days and when I got back here I see she has been buying cattle and more goats with it."

As Marichal recounts the saga of his youth, he misses little on the field. When a player slides at home and misses the plate, Marichal is on his feet, shouting "He missed the plate!" to the catcher. The umpire, who had not yet made his call, waits until the catcher follows the runner into the dugout and tags him to signal out.

"In 1947, when I was nine years old, I almost died," Marichal continues. "We had been working on the farm, doing what we called *en junta.* That is when you invite all the families around you to help when you are doing something that needs lots of hands. You would feed them for their efforts and go to their farm when they needed help. We were harvesting and cleaning rice. After the work was done, my mother fed all the children first so that they would go away and not bother the adults while they ate.

"We started swimming in the canal right away after eating and I got cramps. The next thing I knew it was a week later. When the doctor looked at me after they fished me out of the canal, I'm told he said 'I don't see too much chance. But be sure to give him lots of baths with very hot water.' They sent me to the house of one of my uncles where they gave me lots of baths, but nothing happened. On the seventh day of my coma, the doctor looked at me and told my mother that if I did not come out of it by midnight, I was not coming back. At fifteen minutes to midnight, I awoke. . . .

"It seems like all I did as a boy was work on the farm, go to school a little, and play ball. We swam in the canals, and hunted and fished some, but mostly it was baseball.

"All the boys in my town played baseball. I used to love baseball and dream of playing it. And I will tell you, I feel very proud that, coming from that little community, I went all the way to Cooperstown."

A persistent five-year-old interrupts the reveries of the only Dominican in the Hall of Fame. Extracting a few more pesos, Marichal calls "Tito, *por favor,*" to a handsome young man concentrating fiercely on the field of play. Tito Fuentes Jr., son of the former Cuban major leaguer who played with Marichal on the Giants, swoops down on Juan Jr. and carries the boy off to find him a mango. After completing high school in San Francisco, Tito has come to Santo Domingo to play ball and to see if he can interest a major league organization in his services.

Fuentes, like Stanley Javier, Ivan Calderon, Danny Tartabull, Roberto and Sandy Alomar, and Moises Alou, is the son of a Latin major leaguer. But while their fathers grew up in dirt-floored, thatched-roof homes in the countryside, these sons have known little but the affluence of suburban life in the States and an elevated status in their homelands. "They are not as hungry as their papas, they don't have the same drive, but some of them can play. . . .

"Tito still has to learn just about everything," Marichal muses. "He is almost a man, but he hasn't played that much. He's just starting, compared to a kid here at that age."

By the time Marichal was Tito's age, he had been playing ball for a living for several years. "Baseball was strong around *La Linea.* And we seemed to produce more pitchers than anything else, then. There was a ballplayer in the 1920s and '30s from there, Pedro Alejandro San, who pitched for the Cuban Stars in the Negro Leagues. And there was Bombo Ramos, who I will tell you a story about, and the Olivos, and Juan Sanchez. These days, this part of the country is producing some hitters, too, like Tony Pena, and this boy, Junior Felix, who plays with Toronto.

"All we wanted to do then was play ball. We made our own bats, from branches that we cut from the *guasima* tree and dried in the sun. For gloves, we would take a piece of canvas, the kind of stuff they used to cover trucks, and fold it around a piece of cardboard and then sew up the sides. And for balls, we would get some golf balls from the golf course at Manzanillo and wrap nylon

Juan Marichal. (Photo courtesy of the National Baseball Library, Cooperstown, N.Y.)

stocking or tape around them, and then take them to the shoemaker, who would sew a leather cover around them. And then we would play! Later on, my brother, Gonzalo, would give me spikes or a glove."

Laguna Verde was too small to have a team in the DGD-organized amateur network, but it did have a town team for the men and a youth club for the boys.

"We played all day, every day, whenever we were not in school or working. We played on a field that we made ourselves, but now we're planning on building one there. Laguna Verde had a team for the boys that would play youth teams from other *bateyes*. We traveled to those towns on horseback or on the back of a dumptruck or they would come to Laguna Verde, every Sunday. If they came to Laguna Verde, we would have a meal for them after the game, with goat meat, enchiladas, rice, and beans. Sometimes we would go from house to house, asking for contributions so that we could feed the other team. Often, Ramon Villalona, who was a bit better off and helped coach us, would give us money so that we could have a little *fiesta* after the game."

While Juan played for the town's youth team, his older brother Gonzalo, campaigned for a team in Monte Cristi. "Gonzalo was the best ballplayer in our family," Marichal swears, slipping back into the hero worship of his youth. "I became a baseball player because of all the help he gave me." Seven years older than Juan, Gonzalo frequently returned to Laguna Verde to play for its adult team. Juan would ride to Monte Cristi on a horse to watch Gonzalo play Saturdays for his team there and the two rode back together on Sunday mornings for the game in Laguna Verde, Juan interrogating his brother on baseball the entire way. "He played all the positions then, while I was a shortstop—until I saw Bombo Ramos play. That's when I became a pitcher.

"I think I was 11 or 12 years old. *Los Caballeros* from Santiago were playing against Monte Cristi. The game had been announced in the area for a long time. There were posters for it up everywhere. My brother-in-law got me permission to go. Even today, I remember watching Bombo Ramos pitching. I get goose bumps thinking about that day. He pitched for Monte Cristi, and you see that man over there, the groundskeeper—he was the catcher that day. Bombo would turn all the way around, like Luis Tiant, but he never used to raise his head up like Tiant. He would throw sidearm, too. He was something to watch! He shut out *Los Caballeros* that day. That was what converted me to pitching. When I went back home I told my friends that I was not playing shortstop anymore—that I had to become a pitcher like Bombo Ramos. He inspired me and I tried to pitch just like him."

The horseback seminars with Gonzalo turned to the art of pitching. On the mound, Juan imitated his new hero and delivered the ball sidearm, turning his back to the plate during his windup. Under Gonzalo's guidance, and with an arm strengthened by years of farm work, Marichal developed a good curve and was soon trying a screwball. "I had control, too," Marichal remembers with the trace of a smile.

Only fifteen, he was ready to play for the adult town team, but *Dona* Natividad was none too pleased with that. "I was always getting in trouble with her when she found out I was playing ball instead of being in school. And she thought I was too young to be playing with the men." But Juan did play with the town team, and almost always pitched them to victory.

Marichal completed the primary school in *El Duro* when he was fifteen but could not afford to continue his studies in Monte Cristi. Instead, Juan went to the capital for a visit with Gonzalo, who had moved there to operate a small fleet of dump trucks for their uncle. The visit turned into a stay of a year, and Marichal did not return to school. "I never finished school, and that was something that my mother reminded me of even when I was in the major leagues. I regret not finishing," he admits.

In Santo Domingo, Gonzalo taught Juan how to drive a truck and arranged for him to play on the Esso Company team. When he returned to Laguna Verde in 1955, Marichal joined a team called *Las Flores,* that the Bermudez Rum Company sponsored, in time for a tournament in Monte Cristi. *Las Flores* won and the best players in the city, including Marichal, were selected to represent Monte Cristi in the regional tournament. That was Marichal's first encounter with the Grenada Company's Manzanillo team.

Sweeping through the sub-regional tournament, Marichal led Monte Cristi to victory in Santiago, and then to the national amateur championship tournament in Santo Domingo. "We played the best amateur teams from all over the country—from San Pedro de Macoris, Santo Domingo, and, of course, from the armed forces. I cannot remember, though, how we did. I'll ask Gonzalo. He'll remember." The Bermudez Rum Company covered the team's expenses, but provided no stipend for the players. "It was typical that a tractor driver tilled the soil Saturday night so that work could be done early Sunday morning. On Saturdays, I would go around to the bigger farms until I found a tractor driver who wanted to carouse instead of work that night. I would drive his tractor from six in the evening until six in the morning, and then clean it, lubricate it, and fill it with gas. All that for five *pesos!* Then I would wash up in an irrigation ditch, go home and get my uniform, and wait on the road for a ride into Monte Cristi."

Marichal did not stick with the Bermudez Rum team for long. His pitching attracted the attention of the manager of the Manzanillo club, which offered work, meals, a little bungalow to live in, and 25 *pesos* a week.

"It was an easy job," Marichal recalls. "All the players used to do was to go down to the docks when they loaded a ship with bananas and check to see if there was a mashed one. I didn't really consider it a job. They just had us do it so that they could say we were working. They treated the players first class, like the way a nice lady was to be treated.

"When there weren't ships to be loaded, I drove a tractor to water the trees and flowers in town, because Manzanillo doesn't get much rain. Sometimes, when it did rain a lot, I drove my tractor all over the golf course, cutting the grass."

Manzanillo had a core of veteran players and traveled across the Republic in a bus. "It sure was more comfortable than the dump truck in Laguna Verde," Marichal says. Winning the regional tournament in 1956, the club picked up a few of the best players from other teams, including Danilo Rivas from Puerto Plata, and then swept through the national tournament.

"Soon after that, *Aviacion* came to Manzanillo to play. I threw a four-hitter and we beat them 2–1. That night we celebrated. The next day, I was drafted."

A sudden downpour sends the fans scurrying for cover. Marichal clasps his son's hand in his own and asks, "Why don't you come to Las Palmas when the Oakland team plays there next week? We can talk more. It's near San Isidro, where I served with *Aviacion*."

* * *

Las Palmas is a swath of Dodger blue in the multihued green Dominican countryside. A first class, first world operation, the Los Angeles Dodgers' state-of-the-art baseball academy opened in the spring of 1987. About an hour's drive from the capital, Las Palmas abuts Batey Mojara, a group of dilapidated huts where Haitian cane cutters from the nearby *Ingenio Rio Ozama* spend the hours they are not sweating in the fields.

It's July 4th and the United States flag flutters in the languid breeze over center field, alongside the banners of the Dominican Republic and the Los Angeles Dodgers. *El Campo* Las Palmas might be dedicated to the youth of the Dominican Republic and their love for baseball, but it pays homage to a pantheon of Dodger heroes. The thirty or so young Dominicans living there emerge from the Roy Campanella locker room to play ball on Manuel Mota field. Evenings, they study English in the Al Campanis classroom. While Campanis has fallen into disrepute since his confused, conceivably racist comments on "Nightline" regarding the capacities of blacks to manage and hold front office positions, the former Dodger general manager is still respected in the Dominican Republic. There, his image is that of a man free of racial prejudices and more than willing to accommodate Latin ballplayers. And the players eat in—where else but the Tommy Lasorda dining room?

Like Epy Guerrero's complex in Villa Mella, the Dodger academy offers youngsters the chance to make the transition to organized baseball without adding culture shock to the complexities of hitting curveballs. More than a dozen pro organizations run some sort of complex in the Dominican Republic, at which they can host a prospect for several weeks before they must either sign him to a contract or tell him to hit the *calle*. But none of the other organizations can offer facilities that compete with *Las Palmas,* complete with dish antenna and VCR.

"Look at this," Juan Marichal commands with a wave. "There is nothing like it in all of the Caribbean." The Dodgers, who have occupied baseball's *avant garde* since Branch Rickey came aboard in 1942, broke baseball's color line in 1947, but were slow to jump into the Latin market. The club utilized former Negro League talent better than any other in the 1950s, as Jackie Robinson, Roy Campanella, and Don Newcombe led them into the World Series in six of the first ten seasons after integration. But only a few Latins stuck with the club, until the 1980s when their major league roster began to carry at least three or four Latins annually, including Mexican Fernando Valenzuela and Dominicans Pedro Guerrero (since traded to the Cardinals), Alfredo Griffin, Alejandro Pena, Mariano Duncan, and Ramon Martinez. Overall, one-fifth of its players at all levels were Latin in 1989. "It's awfully tough to compete with this," Marichal says, as much to himself as anyone.

A few Haitian children from the *batey* watch impassively from the shade of the palm trees that ring the field. Several snazzily-dressed motorcycle cowboys with punkish sunglasses perch on their scooters nearby. Marichal takes to the mound and throws a few pitches before making the ceremonial toss that opens official summer play at *Las Palmas.* Afterwards, he stands in the shadow of the dugout talking shop with prospective pitchers from both rookie teams. He emphasizes control and timing, rather than sheer velocity or an array of pitches.

When play begins, Marichal joins the Dodger brain trust in the shade behind the backstop. One Dodger coach takes copious notes, while another evaluates the pitchers' velocity with a JUGS speed gun. Rafael Avila, who administers Las Palmas, talks with Marichal about Pedro Guerrero's brother, Ramon Guerrero, and his half-brother, Domingo Michel, two prospects in the Dodger organization.

Like Avila, the other Dodger coaches are transplanted Cubans, men who made the jump from their island to the major leagues and stayed with the latter when their homeland embarked on its revolutionary adventure in 1959. Havana-born Chico Fernandez, who played briefly for the Orioles, shakes his head dolefully as he contemplates Cuba since Fidel. "They've fucked everything up there. It once was a beautiful place. You could get everything you wanted—women, gambling—anything. And the *beisbol* was almost as good as in the United States. But now, it's shit." Like Fernandez, Avila has since settled in the Dominican Republic. There, he runs Las Palmas, coaches *Licey,* and has won acclaim as one of the most capable and astute baseball men in the basin.

Marichal settles into a lawn chair and accepts a soft drink from one of the Dodger groundskeepers hovering nearby. Clad in blue jumpsuits with Dodger patches, the attendants are the most enthused fans at the game. For Marichal and the coterie of expatriate Cubans, the game is an opportunity to evaluate talent, to see if any of these youngsters has a legitimate chance. "Once the Dodgers sign a boy," Avila says, "we try to keep him at least two years. We want to be fair to them. If they are released before them, it is usually because of something they did off the field, not because of their performance on it."

Most of the players on these rookie teams received between $3,000 and $25,000 to sign with a major league club. During the season, they make about $700 a month, a little less than what the Dominican minimum wage would pay a worker for an entire year. And if they make it to the majors . . .

The road from Santo Domingo to Las Palmas skirts the San Isidro air force base, the primary air force installation in the country and long a pillar of Trujillo's power. In the 1950s, Trujillo's favorite son, Ramfis, commanded the *Aviacion* and took special interest in its ball club, which competed in the amateur network organized in the 1940s.

And beating *Aviacion,* as Marichal discovered after pitching Manzanillo to victory in a 1956 encounter with Ramfis' team, had its consequences. "We beat *Aviacion* on a Sunday in Manzanillo. I remember that we had quite a *fiesta* after that, but early the next morning, there was a lieutenant from the Manzanillo installation at the door of my bungalow. He had a telegram for me from Ramfis saying *'Favor de Reportarse de inmediato al Equipo de la Fuerza Aerea.'*

"I told him that I had to talk with my mother." The officer and his conscript got in a jeep and drove to Laguna Verde. *Dona* Natividad might not have been an aficionado of the game, but she was politically savvy enough to know that her youngest son's success on the ball field would attract Trujillo's attention. Almost anything out of the ordinary did.

"She didn't have much to say at first. I didn't want to pressure her and kept quiet myself. At four that afternoon, another military man showed up with a second telegram asking whether I had left yet for Santo Domingo. My mother looked at it and finally said, '*Bueno,* my son. You know that to these people you cannot say no.' "

Even at 17, Juan knew that one did not turn down a summons from God. After a cry with *Dona* Natividad, the new recruit returned to Manzanillo to pack up his belongings and was soon riding the highway that bisects the island from north to south. Before dawn the next day, he was at the San Isidro base.

"The next morning, they took me to meet General Fernando Sanchez, Ramfis' assistant. He gave me a hundred *pesos,* and remember that a hundred *pesos* was worth a hundred dollars then, and told me to go to *Estadio La Normal* in Santo Domingo where they were having tryouts for a youth team for a tournament in Mexico. I lived under the stands there for a few weeks while they picked the team and then I was off to Mexico."

Joining Marichal in Mexico were Danilo Rivas, Manuel Mota, Manuel Emilio Jimenez, and Mateo Alou. It was the Laguna Verde youth's first airplane trip and first time out of the country.

"It was something, I'll tell you. Sometimes you tell this story and people don't believe it. I started against Puerto Rico and beat them, and was used to close another game that we won. Finally, we were playing Mexico for the championship. The stands there were low, like in Dodger Stadium, so the fans were right on top of you. And these Mexican fans had guns and knives and were threatening us with them. Our manager sent us to the bullpen to warm up, but it was impossible. We didn't want to come out of the dugout. Those people were crazy the way they rooted for the home team. It is not fair dealing with kids that way."

Mexican police guarded the dugout, and stood alongside the relievers as they warmed up in the bull pen, but Mexico won the game.

Returning to the island, Marichal reported to the air force base at San Isidro. Like other draftees, he had his head shaved and was handed an ill-fitting khaki uniform. But unlike the other new recruits, whose salary was 27.50 *pesos* a month, Marichal was making 52.50 *pesos*. "We were specialists," he grins.

Nor did Juan don his military threads very often. "That was for when we were off the base. At San Isidro, I mostly wore a baseball uniform."

And he mostly played baseball. "That was my job in the air force, playing ball. We played inter-squad games every day of the week on the base. If we played in the morning, we practiced in the afternoon. If we practiced in the morning, we played in the afternoon." And on Sundays, this more than amateur but not quite professional team traveled into the interior or hosted other clubs at the San Isidro base.

Although Nestor Gonzalez Pomares managed the team, Marichal's mentor was Francisco "Viruta" Pichardo. Viruta, as he was known throughout Dominican baseball, was the team's trainer and probably the best instructor in the country during the 1950s. He had answered Ramfis' call to make *Aviacion* the best "amateur" squad in the nation.

He did it, with equal parts of tough discipline and astute instruction.

"Viruta trained us to be winners," Marichal explains, "and we beat everybody in the country. We even flew in an air force plane to Puerto Rico and Curacao to play. In the fourteen months I was on the *Aviacion* team, we hardly ever lost."

The *Aviacion* club was made up of two groups, a contingent of young prospects like Marichal, whose potential had yet to be reached, and a number of veterans in their late 20s, who would never play at a higher level. Viruta put up with these "lifers" while focusing his unrelenting effort on the younger players.

Among that group were Marichal, Manuel Mota, Pedro Gonzalez, Danilo Rivas, and the Jimenez brothers. Each starred in Dominican winter ball and all but Rivas, who played in the Giants organization, played major league ball, too.

Gonzalez, Jompy Jimenez, and Manny Jimenez were from sugar mill *ingenios* in San Pedro de Macoris, an advance guard of the army that surged out of the cane fields in the 1970s and '80s. Manny hit .301 as a rookie for the Kansas City Athletics in 1962, sixth best in the American League. Manuel "Geronimo" Mota, a native of Santo Domingo, played 20 seasons in the majors, mostly with Pittsburgh and the Dodgers. He hit .304 over his major league career and totaled 150 pinch hits, the most ever, before retiring in 1982, to become a coach with the Dodgers. In winter ball, the three-time batting champ holds the best career batting average (.333), hit over .300 a record 11 times, and retired from active play in 1981 with 800 hits, then the third highest lifetime total in Dominican ball. After that, Mota managed *Licey,* the Dodgers' Dominican affiliate, to consecutive championship in the 1983–84 and 1984–85 seasons.

In the air force, Marichal ate better than the other servicemen, and was given vitamin supplements, too. Most nights he spent at Gonzalo's home in Santo Domingo, which was still named *Ciudad Trujillo* at the time. At five each morning, he would grab a ride in a truck to the base.

Despite the relatively soft treatment off the field, Marichal and his *compadres* never worked so hard on it. "Viruta had us running wind sprints from foul line to foul line, and doing calisthenics to build up our endurance. And he insisted that we practice something until we did it the way he wanted us to do it."

When players tried out for the team, Viruta hit them grounders and flies until they dropped. "If an infielder missed a ball and said, 'Viruta, it took a bad hop,' Viruta would say 'Then why didn't you take a bad hop with it?' I saw a guy miss two ground balls in a row during a tryout and say to Viruta, 'I don't know the field too well.' Viruta walked over, grabbed him, and pulled him down so that his face was touching the dirt and said, 'Ground, this is so and so. I want you to get to know each other.' "

If a player feigned illness, Viruta marched him over to the clinic and stood there while the doctor diagnosed and treated him, and then usually brought the player back to practice.

He brooked little interference with the sport. Not long after Marichal arrived, a few of the veterans persuaded him to go drinking with him one payday. "They taunted me, saying I was a *niño de faldas,* a mama's boy. I was only 17, and had never really been drunk before, but I was unable to tell them no. We drank rum, straight. You had to down the glass and then turn it over with a slap to show that there was nothing left in it.

"The next day, Viruta ran us from foul line to foul line in the sun, until most of these guys were puking their guts out. I didn't do that, but I assure you, I felt sick. But Viruta didn't say anything about the drinking the night before."

He didn't say anything to Marichal the entire next week. Finally, as Juan was putting on his uniform to play a game at San Isidro, Viruta confronted him.

"He said, '*Mira,* look, Juan, you see those star players on the team, these veterans? The North American scouts don't want to sign them. They have no future in baseball, and it was with them that you drank last week!'

"He told me that he thought that I had a real future in baseball and that if I wanted to, I would pitch in the major leagues. I don't know if I was ready to hear that then, but I listened to Viruta. I listened to everything he said and tried to pitch like he told me to—with attention, above all else, to control. He said that control was more important than velocity."

After Marichal had been with *Aviacion* for a year, he returned to Manzanillo to play against his old teammates. Marichal started the first game of the doubleheader and lost 1–0. Danilo Rivas, who had pitched for Manzanillo against *Aviacion* the previous year, pitched the second game for *Aviacion* against Manzanillo. The banana company boys won that game, too.

Ramfis was beside himself. "I don't think he ever played baseball, but he loved to watch us," Marichal recalls. Twenty-eight at the time, Rafael Leonidas Trujillo Martinez, whom everyone knew as Ramfis, was the son of *Dona* Maria, Trujillo's mistress and lifelong companion. They wed in 1935. Ramfis was made a colonel in the Army at his fourth birthday, a festivity that the entire cabinet attended, and advanced to the rank of Brigadier General by the age of nine. Taller and more handsome than the father who adored him to the brink of idolatry, Ramfis fancied himself a sportsman. Like papa, he had boundless sexual appetites. But unlike the elder Trujillo, Ramfis had little interest in politics. Captain of the *Ciudad Trujillo* polo team, which he led on forays abroad, Ramfis took a special interest in the *Aviacion* ball club.

After the astounding double defeat to the Grenada Company team, Ramfis ordered a special commission to go to Manzanillo and find out why his squad had lost both games. While the commission interrogated the players and investigated the events preceding the games, the *Aviacion* players were confined to base.

"The commission declared that the players had been drinking before the game and that was why we had played so poorly. But you must remember that Manzanillo was a good club, and the truth is not that we were drinking, but that the water had made many of the players sick. I had a very high fever that day."

Despite their protestations, the players were fined and jailed for five days. The manager and team captain were confined for a month.

"But we never lost a doubleheader again while I was there," Marichal concludes.

In 1956, while Juan was playing for *Aviacion,* Monte Cristi native Ozzie Virgil became the first Dominican to play major league ball. Like a host of dark-skinned Cubans, Puerto Ricans, and Venezuelans, Virgil's debut had been made possible by Jackie Robinson, whose 1947 voyage across major league baseball's color line irrevocably altered the sport.

Major league scouts descended upon the Caribbean, eager to sign ballplayers they had coveted during countless winter seasons past. Cuba, long the center of basin baseball, sent the first and most players northward; but during the 1950s, the Dominican Republic began to follow suit.

"By the time I was with *Aviacion,*" Marichal says, "Virgil was playing for the

Giants and winter ball was strong again on the island. I knew I wanted to become a professional, but I was only 17."

The first scout he met was Carlos "Patato" Pascual, brother of Washington Senator pitching star Camilo Pascual. Carlos had only had a sip of coffee in the majors, and was scouting the Caribbean for the Senators. He saw Marichal strike out sixteen when *Aviacion* played in Aruba and spoke to him afterwards about signing with the Senators, but didn't follow up.

Back in the Dominican Republic, *Licey* president Ignacio Guerra approached Ramfis about signing Marichal and second baseman Pedro Gonzalez. He wanted Gonzalez to play winter ball for *Licey* that season and for both players to then sign with the New York Yankees. Ramfis, a *fanático* of *Escogido,* granted Guerra permission to sign Gonzalez but refused to let him have Marichal.

By then, Mota, Mateo Alou, and Danilo Rivas had turned professional, signing with the New York Giants. Marichal was not long in joining them.

For some time, Horacio Martinez had been talking to Gonzalo Marichal about signing his younger brother to a contract with *Escogido* for winter play and the New York Giants for major league ball. Martinez, the Santiago-born shortstop who Dominicans still revere, was bird-dogging for Alejandro Pompez, the New York Giants scout.

The Cuban-born Pompez had barnstormed a team called the New York Cubans through the Negro Leagues during the 1930s and '40s. With one foot in the numbers rackets (which likely had its origins in the Caribbean game of chance called *la bolita* and gave sustenance to independent black baseball in those decades before Robinson) and the other in Caribbean ball, Pompez jumped into organized baseball after integration. As a scout for the Giants, he helped recruit Monte Irvin, the Giant's first black player and future Hall-of-Famer, and signed Manuel Mota, Danilo Rivas, and Felipe and Mateo Alou.

Martinez, along with Tetelo Vargas, had played for Pompez's New York Cubans, and while coaching for *Escogido* in the 1950s, he scouted the island for Pompez. He talked to Gonzalo, Gonzalo talked to Juan, and they both sought Ramfis' approval. With that final hurdle cleared, the brothers Marichal got in a Lincoln Continental on the afternoon of September 16, 1957 and went to the home of Francisco Martinez "Paquito" Alba, *Escogido*'s president and Rafael Trujillo's brother-in-law. There he signed to play for the *Leones* of Escogido. The next day, he signed to play for the New York Giants. His bonus was $500.

That night, a team of touring major leaguers led by Willie Mays played in *Ciudad Trujillo.* Marichal watched in awe from the *Escogido* dugout but caught up with Mays a few seasons later, in San Francisco.

In March, 1958, Marichal flew to the Giants' spring training camp in Sanford, Florida, along with countrymen Mota, Mateo Alou, Danilo Rivas, Julio Cesar Imbert, and Rene Marte. Alejandro Pompez was there to greet them and ease the transition to both the majors and a new culture.

"Like the other Latin players, I had problems with the food and got homesick. There was a group of us from here that would play *merengue* after practice. But that made me so sad that I finally took my records and broke them one by one and stopped listening to any Dominican music at all."

When camp broke, Marichal was assigned to Michigan City, Indiana in Class

D ball. After two days in a bus riding north, Marichal met racism, North American style, for the first time. Along with Rene Marte, Jose Tartabull and Julio Santana from Cuba, and a few black American players, Marichal encountered hostility on the street and an unwillingness to serve him at restaurants in the town and on the road.

"I didn't speak any English at all then," Marichal frowns. "I used to eat a lot of fried chicken because a restaurant there gave a meal of fried chicken to the pitchers for every game they won. They only gave us $2.50 for meal money and I won lots of games that year. Sometimes, I would see what someone else was eating and point to his plate."

On the field, Marichal blocked out the racial and cultural indignities of his new venue and led Michigan City to the championship. Pitching to his compatriot, Rene Marte, Marichal won 21 games and lost only eight, with a 1.87 ERA and 246 strikeouts. He won two more games in the championship series.

That won him a promotion to Class A ball the following year, where he pitched for Springfield, Massachusetts. His salary jumped from $250 to $450 a month. He was also reunited with Mota and Alou, and shared an apartment with them. "That's where I learned how to cook," he recalls proudly.

Although his record slipped to 18 and 13, Marichal helped pitch Springfield to their league championship with two postseason victories and continued to please the Giant organization. When Giant Hall-of-Famer Carl Hubbell had observed Marichal during his first spring camp, the former screwballer noted that Marichal possessed a poise rarely seen in players that young. Unbeknownst to Marichal, Hubbell directed Giant pitching coaches in the minors to keep their hands off the young Dominican and let him develop on his own. He did, picking up an extraordinarily high leg kick and a screwball along the way. The leg kick became Marichal's trademark in the majors.

In addition to the two hundred plus innings he worked each of his first two years in the minors, Marichal was throwing another hundred innings during the winter season. He began his third season in the minors in Tacoma, Washington in AAA ball and showed he could win there, too. Mid-season, the 5′11″, 160 pound, 21-year-old received a telegram from the parent club requesting he report to San Francisco. "That was better than the telegram from Ramfis!"

Marichal's totals for two and a half seasons in the minors were 54 wins, 26 defeats, an ERA of 2.35, and 575 strikeouts in 655 innings. And true to Viruta, he only allowed an average of 1.8 walks per game.

A week after being called up, Marichal debuted on July 19, 1960 in Philadelphia. He no-hit the Phillies into the eighth inning, when Clay Dalrymple singled with two outs. It was the only Philadelphia hit. Four days later, Marichal tossed a four-hitter to beat the Pirates, who would win the World Series that fall, and in his next start, he beat Warren Spahn and the Milwaukee Braves. The league quickly began to take notice of this latest Latin import. Marichal finished the season with a 6–2 record, his play marred only by a shoulder injury that would plague him throughout his career.

The Giants, who had followed the Dodgers into the black American and Latin talent markets, already had Felipe Alou and Puerto Ricans Orlando Cepeda and

Jose Pagan on their roster. Mateo Alou and Manuel Mota would soon join them, followed by the youngest Alou brother, Jesus, in 1963. Felipe, the senior Dominican on the team, arranged for Marichal to room with Blanche Johnson, a black woman who lived near Candlestick Park. Mateo Alou did the same when he was called up.

Marichal won 31 games and lost 21 over the next two seasons. In 1962, the Giants came from behind to beat the Dodgers in a West Coast reprise of the 1951 pennant playoffs and went to the World Series. Marichal pitched shutout ball through the first four innings of the fourth game, but as he tried to bunt a runner up in the top of the fifth, the pitch smashed into his fingers and he was forced to leave the game. He did not return to play in the series and the Giants succumbed, losing the seventh game 1–0 when Bobby Richardson snagged Willie McCovey's line drive with two out and two on in the bottom of the ninth.

For the rest of the 1960s, Marichal compiled a simply astounding record, winning more than twenty games six of the next seven seasons, leading the National League twice in victories, shutouts, and complete games, and once in ERA and winning percentage. Overall, he had an ERA below 3.00 nine times, struck out over 200 batters six seasons, and won at least 25 games three times. In 16 seasons, Marichal won 243 games, lost 142, and had a career ERA of 2.89. He completed over half of the games he started and struck out 2,303 batters. An eight-time All-Star, he won two of these contests and no-hit the Houston Colt 45s on June 15, 1963.

Marichal was the best Latin pitcher of his time, and perhaps any time. His celebrity was dimmed only by the brilliance of a trio of stellar National League pitchers with whom he shared the stage during the 1960s—Koufax, Drysdale, and Gibson.

Dodger lefty Sandy Koufax was considered even better than Marichal during these seasons. Few could argue against the two-time Cy Young award winner who pitched four no-hitters and won 111 games against only 34 defeats between 1962 and 1966 as he led the Dodgers to three pennants and two World Series triumphs. But Koufax's career totals were only 165 wins and 87 losses, as arthritis shortened his brilliant career. Joining Koufax on the Dodgers was the intimidating right-hander, Don Drysdale, whose 58 consecutive innings of shutout ball set a record that lasted over twenty years. Right-hander Bob Gibson, who hurled St. Louis to three World Series appearances and also won the Cy Young award twice, posted career marks that approximated Marichal's stats. During this trio's tenure, the Dodgers and the Cardinals appeared in seven World Series. Marichal's Giants, meanwhile, came up empty in 1962 and the club did not return to the fall classic until 1989. Each of these men wound up in the Hall of Fame, although Marichal's route to Cooperstown was the most tortuous.

In 1959, during the winter season, Marichal met Alma Rosa Carvajal, a pretty 15-year-old neighbor of the Alous in Santo Domingo. Her father, a pensioned army officer, was a good friend of General Jose Garcia Trujillo, who was the Secretary of the Armed Forces, a cousin of Rafael Trujillo, and an aficionado of the game.

"The General used to send for me every morning during the winter season just to talk about baseball. He followed Cuban baseball as well as major league ball. I was nervous, a young kid talking to a general, while he would sit back and drink vodka while we talked.

"Alma's family lived near the Palace of Trujillo, and her father's relatives had a lot of money and land. That made them very, very close to Trujillo.

"I didn't know anything about politics as a kid. The only thing I knew was that Trujillo was the biggest man in the country. It wasn't until I went to the United States and lived there for six months that I started learning what had been happening in my country. I didn't know the things Trujillo used to do to people—the political repression and murder—because Trujillo controlled the media here.

"When I started playing with lots of Puerto Ricans, they used to know more about what was happening in Santo Domingo than I did. They called the Dominicans *chapitas.* A *chapita* is a bottle cap. They said that Trujillo's medals were only bottle caps that he wore to make him look like a big man. They called Trujillo a *chapita,* too." Indeed, by then, Rafael Trujillo had accumulated a chestful of decorations and several pages worth of titles, collecting such honorifics the way a latter-day autocrat, Imelda Marcos, collected shoes.

As Marichal's career was ascending, Trujillo's reign was coming to an end. An increasingly isolated figure in the Caribbean, the man they called "the goat" went down to a hail of assassins' bullets on May 30, 1961.

"I was afraid at what was going to happen to my country. After 31 years with the same man, I didn't know what to think. I was engaged to Alma by then and extremists were threatening to bomb her family's house. After I went to spring training with the Giants in 1962, I got worried about her. I asked Alvin Dark, who was my manager, if I could go back to get married and he said yes."

They wed on March 28, 1962 and made their first home together in San Francisco, where they shared a house with Felipe Alou and his wife, Maria. The next year, Mateo and his wife, Teresa, moved in, too. "We got along very, very well together," Marichal remembers. Mateo, who had caddied at the Santo Domingo Country Club as a boy, taught Felipe and Juan the game in San Francisco while the three women helped each other adjust to the trials ballplayers' spouses encountered on foreign shores. "Felipe is godfather of my oldest daughter, Rosie, and I am the godfather of a daughter of his. And Mateo is the godfather of my second girl, Elsie, while I'm the godfather of his daughter. That is a serious obligation for a Dominican, to be a godfather."

Marichal and his housemates returned each fall to the island, where winter play began on October 24th, Trujillo's birthday, and lasted until the play-offs in January. The winning club then played in the Caribbean Championships the first week of February.

During the 1960s and '70s, Dominican winter play flourished, in part due to the collapse of Cuban league play following the revolution. As North American and Cuban major leaguers joined the growing numbers of Dominican major leaguers on winter team rosters, the calibre of baseball soared. Imports such as Frank Howard, Gaylord Perry, Steve Garvey, Dave Parker, Phil Niekro, and Willie Stargell made Dominican ball frequently as competitive as summer play.

Marichal played eight seasons of winter ball, all for *Escogido,* the club most associated with the Trujillo family. Joining him were Giant teammates Willie McCovey, Andre Rogers, Manny Mota, Tito Fuentes, and all three Alou brothers. *Escogido,* which had established a relationship with the Giants, got first pick of the club's players for winter ball, while *Licey* threw their lot in with the Dodgers, *Aguilas* with the Pirates, and *Las Estrellas* of San Pedro with the Braves.

After signing with *Escogido* in 1957, Marichal struck out the side in his first appearance, a relief stint in late December. He threw over a hundred innings each of the next three seasons.

"It wasn't easy doing that," Marichal protests. "After pitching for two or three hundred innings in the States, it was hard to come down here and be expected to play winters. There was a lot of pressure on you to play. But there was also pressure from the Giants not to play, because they wanted me to rest my arm.

"But if you don't play, the whole country gets on you."

Marichal compiled a 36–22 won-lost record in winter ball, a career winning percentage second only to that other Manzanillo hurler, Guayubin Olivo. His cumulative ERA of 1.87 is still the best among all pitchers with over 300 innings of work, and his 32 complete games behind only Guayubin and his brother, Chi-Chi.

But because Marichal did not play every season, he became the focus of criticism in the press and by fans. Nor did his injuries or heavy workloads for the Giants fend off the constant nagging as to why Marichal was not playing winter ball. While his spectacular success in the United States was appreciated, Dominicans wanted to see Marichal play on the island. And there, the game's *fanáticos* were even more demanding than their counterparts in the States.

Injuries, the need for rest, and the four daughters born during his playing days, however, were enough to keep Marichal away. "I finally built a house in San Francisco and stayed there one winter so that I would not have to go home and listen to them asking on the radio as to when I was going to pitch. They were having a rough time with baseball then, anyway. After Trujillo's death, and then the military's overthrow of Juan Bosch, they didn't play winter ball for awhile."

While Marichal skips over the shoulder and back injuries that plagued him, these ailments made playing a painful process and sometimes hospitalized him. Often, the only comfortable place he could sleep was the floor.

Marichal even tried bathing in the *Rio Sanate,* near the shrine of the Virgin of Altagracia, a pilgrim's destination in Higuey that looks like a huge McDonald's Golden Arches. "Mateo Alou had a dislocated shoulder and would go to the *Sanate* to bathe. If you did that on the way to Higuey, it was supposed to heal you. It seemed to work for him, and with all the problems I had, I went to that river every year."

In the 1980s, as salaries escalated in the major leagues to the point where most established Dominican ballplayers did not need the relatively small pay that winter ball provided, fewer and fewer Dominican major leaguers continued to play. "I cannot criticize them," Marichal says. "Look at Tony Pena, playing almost every inning in the majors and then most of the season here. I don't agree with what he is doing. I don't care how much he loves the game. When a team starts paying you over a million dollars in salary, they want you to produce for them. I don't think a guy who plays that much can be ready for the whole season."

A pitch sends an Oakland rookie sprawling and when he takes a few steps towards the mound and shouts at the pitcher, Rafael Avila quips, "Juan, show him how it's done."

The oblique reference to the darkest moment in Marichal's career brings a grin to Chico Fernandez's face and the hint of a smile to Marichal's.

That the Dodgers and Giants were waging war between the lines in the summer of 1965 was little surprise. This Brooklyn versus the Bronx rivalry in the senior circuit had reached new heights with the Giants' come-from-behind victory in the 1951 pennant playoff and then traveled west as both clubs deserted New York City in 1958. The Giants bested the Dodgers again, in the 1962 play-offs, with Los Angeles rebounding to win the World Series in 1963.

By late August 1965, the two teams were virtually tied for first place when the Dodgers visited San Francisco for a four game series. Both clubs were known for their aggressive approach to the game, with pitchers laying claim to the inside portion of the plate, *caveat* batter. A batter who crowded the plate would invariably be knocked down. In the 1950s, Giant pitcher Sal Maglie, a.k.a. the Barber, for the close shaves he gave batters at the plate, set the tone. In 1956, Maglie was traded to Brooklyn, where he tutored a Dodgers staff in the art of intimidation. Among his eager disciples was Don Drysdale, who went on to set a major league record by hitting 154 batters in the course of his 14-season career.

Earlier in the summer, Drysdale had decked Mays twice, prompting Marichal to respond that, "If he keeps that up, somebody's going to find out we can protect our hitters." Such payback was *de rigueur* and batters expected that their pitcher would retaliate when they were thrown at. Willie Mays had made a point of telling Marichal that early in his career. After Marichal's intemperate remarks to the press, National League President Warren Giles tried to halt the escalation by threatening to impose a thousand dollar fine if Marichal or anyone else retaliated.

In the final game of the August series, Marichal came to bat with the Dodgers leading 2–1 in the third inning. Marichal had decked Maury Wills and Ron Fairly in the second inning, and Sandy Koufax, on the mound for the Dodgers, had sent Willie Mays sprawling in the bottom of the inning.

John Roseboro, who stepped into the void created by the car crash that ended Roy Campanella's marvelous career, was catching. Neither he nor Marichal could have been immune to events off the field that spring and summer. In late April, constitutionally-minded junior officers in the Dominican military had backed the protests of the supporters of deposed president Juan Bosch, who had been ousted in a 1963 coup. A bloody civil war broke out, with aerial bombing and house-to-house fighting in Santo Domingo. President Lyndon Baines Johnson, seeing Red, sent in 23,000 U.S. troops, with the backing of the Organization of American States, to support the anti-Bosch forces, and thousands more died as the summer played itself out. Roseboro, meanwhile, was a black man living in Los Angeles in the midst of that summer's Watts uprising, the worst outbreak of racial rioting since World War II. Thirty-four died, and

Watts, a neighborhood where sixty percent of the people were on relief, went up in flames.

Koufax's second pitch to Marichal was low and inside and Roseboro dropped the ball. According to Marichal, when Roseboro fired the ball back to Koufax, it clipped his ear. Marichal whirled and shouted, "Why did you do that?" Later, Marichal said, Roseboro replied "(expletive-deleted) you!"

As Roseboro moved toward Marichal, the Dominican pitcher clubbed him three times with his bat, gashing the Dodger catcher's scalp.

A small brawl erupted. After the umpires restored order and ejected Marichal, Koufax retired the first two batters before walking the next two. Figuring that under these circumstances, Koufax was not going to jam him, Willie Mays stepped into the batter's box expecting a pitch over the middle or outside of the plate. He got one and hit a three-run homer that won the game for the Giants.

Marichal subsequently argued that Roseboro had deliberately tried to hit him with the ball, but did not try to defend attacking him with a bat. League president Giles fined Marichal $1,750 and, more important, suspended him for eight playing days. The Giants staggered through the suspension, and reclaimed the league lead in mid-September, before folding in the stretch.

Marichal's record was 3–4 the remainder of the season, and the incident haunted him the following year. "I didn't throw inside to anybody the remainder of that season, and into '66. I didn't even realize that was happening until Tom Sheehan, the pitching coach, pointed it out to me. That's bad enough for any pitcher, but especially for a control pitcher, and that was what I was."

Far worse than the immediate effect on Marichal's pitching was the impact on his image, and, by extension, that of all Latin players. That it was a Latin player on the Giants, who had more Latins on their roster than any other team, probably made the attack seem even worse.

Marichal's teammate, Puerto Rican-born Orlando Cepeda, had battled Giant managers repeatedly, holding out each spring and drawing the charge that he was a lazy, undisciplined player. In 1958, the Pirates' Bob Friend and the Giants' Ruben Gomez, also from Puerto Rico, threw repeatedly at each other's batters in a game at Forbes Field. Bench jockeys, including Pirate manager Danny Murtaugh, and his Giant counterpart, Bill Rigney, tossed further invective at each other from the dugout. Gomez decked Friend and, later in the game, Friend returned the honor in kind. Feeling the need to come to Gomez's defense, Cepeda grabbed a bat and went on to the field after Danny Murtaugh. Only a shoestring tackle by Willie Mays saved the Pirate skipper. But the image of Latin players as hotheads had been firmly imprinted on the sporting public.

"They call us hot-tempered and say that we don't play under control—that we are too emotional," Marichal protests. "But there are a lot of American players that do the same. It's part of the game. It's excitement that makes you act like that."

Marichal had waged a few hold-outs with the Giants over his contract, too, but what irked him the most about his relationship with the club was manager Alvin Dark's questioning of his courage.

"Alvin Dark to me was one day the best man in the world and the next day, he was the worst. I love the guy, I love him, but I think you have to love people with all the defects that they have. He did things for me that I still appreciate, like when he let me come back to get married during spring training. But I saw Alvin Dark do things that hurt me deeply."

The problem, Marichal explains, was that Dark did not believe him when he said his back hurt too much to pitch. Dark charged Marichal with not wanting to pitch and not having the guts to play with a little pain.

Dark, a Barry Goldwater supporter and fervent Christian, had difficulty keeping his political and religious views out of the clubhouse. During the 1964 season, communications deteriorated with his players. In late July, Dark was quoted by *Newsday*'s Stan Issacs as having said that the problem with the Giants was the presence of so many black and Latin players who ". . . just are not able to perform up to the white ballplayer when it comes to mental alertness. You can't make most Negro and Spanish players have the pride in their team that you can get in the white player. And they just aren't as sharp mentally. They aren't able to adjust to situations because they don't have that mental alertness."

Dark's comments came at a time when the Giants not only had Marichal as their ace, but fielded a team that started three American-born blacks and three Latins. Dark did not return to manage the Giants in 1965; he was replaced by Herman Franks, a Spanish-speaking, former Puerto Rican winter ball manager whom the players found a great deal more *simpatico.*

The image of Latin and black players as malingerers was not an uncommon one. What Marichal encountered in San Francisco, Roberto Clemente confronted in Pittsburgh. The graceful Pirate right-fielder from Puerto Rico had a medical history that rivaled Marichal's and both were devotees of chiropractic medicine. And both were viewed as hot-headed showboats on the field.

"Roberto Clemente was beautiful to watch," Marichal attests. "He was something getting to that ball, even if it meant hitting the wall. Roberto used to go to the field to beat you. But look at how he was treated!"

The stereotyping of the Latin ballplayer lingers in the late 1980s, with Dominicans Joaquin Andujar, George Bell, Julio Franco, and Damaso Garcia, a few of the latest to be castigated in the press for their alleged shortcomings.

After splitting his time between two societies for thirty years, Marichal offers one last thought on cultural conflict. "I have always thought that food is a great thing in life. With the Giants, Alvin Dark would sometimes come into the clubhouse after a loss and kick the spread of food set out for the players onto the floor. It was as if he couldn't stand the sight of us eating after we had been defeated. I remember Felipe Alou bending over after Dark did this one night, picking up some of the food off the floor, and eating it while looking Dark right in the eye. I think that is why Dark approved of trading Felipe. He couldn't understand that for us, even if you lose, you don't kick food on the floor. You just don't do that."

Marichal recovered from the Roseboro incident on the field, and was the National League's winningest pitcher between 1963 and 1969. He could not quite, however, recoup the loss that his persona had suffered. The Giants remained a first division team until 1972, when the club fell to fifth place in the National League West. Management decided to revamp the club. They traded Mays, the club's icon, to the Mets, largely so that the Say Hey Kid could salvage a bit of financial security from the game, and Marichal and future Hall-of-Famer Willie McCovey were next to go.

Marichal had dropped to 6–16 in 1972, his first losing record. After he went 11–15 in 1973, the Giants shipped him to Boston in the junior circuit. Marichal was 5–1 for the Red Sox, but pitched in only 11 games.

The Dominican Dandy finished his career the next year in, of all places, Los Angeles. "Not many people know this, but I was a Dodgers fan for awhile when I was a kid," Marichal reveals. "They came to Santo Domingo in 1948 during spring training, with Jackie Robinson, Pee Wee Reese, Gil Hodges, and Duke Snider. I was nine then and it made an impression."

Dodger fans seemed to have forgiven Marichal his transgressions now that he was wearing Dodger blue. But sixteen seasons in the majors and eight in winter ball had taken something off Marichal's fastball. He pitched only twice for the Dodgers in April, 1975 before deciding to call an end to his career.

The rookie game is over and Marichal talks to some of the players before walking to his car. "I stayed in San Francisco for about two years, then came here in November, 1977. I played golf, made a few investments, and traveled some. Then, almost four years ago, I got a call from Oakland to see if I was interested in working in their organization. Bill Rigney, who had managed the Giants when I came up, recommended me to them. And since then, I've worked for the A's. I spend more time here, but I also have to travel a lot, to Oakland and throughout their minor league system. And I'll tell you, I don't like to fly anymore.

"Baseball has come on real strong here the last ten or fifteen years. I don't think it has peaked yet, either. It's better organized every year and the players are better prepared. There's better instruction all the way up the line. I'm afraid that some day they will stop so many Dominican players from coming to the United States. There is already a visa system. Oakland has only twenty visas for Latin players for the entire organization."

(Major league baseball, the United States Department of Labor, and the Immigration and Naturalization Service have developed a quota system over the last fifteen to twenty years that limits the number of foreigners eligible to work as professional ballplayers. Most teams get between twenty and twenty-four work visas each year, using them for foreign-born players who will hold positions that they argue can not be filled by U. S. citizens. The total of these visas represents the ceiling on the number of foreigners [mostly *Latinos*] who can play either minor or major league ball. Some years, there are not enough visas to go around.)

Marichal leaves Las Palmas behind and returns to Santo Domingo. The visiting players board the bus, while the Dodger rookies head for the showers.

In 1981, five years after Marichal retired, he became eligible for election to the Hall of Fame. His affirmative vote total fell short of the 75 percent of the ballots cast by members of the Baseball Writers of America needed for election. Also on the ballot for the first time that year was Bob Gibson, who was voted in, with 100 more votes than Marichal. Gibson told the press he didn't think that he was a hundred votes better than Marichal, whom he called the best pitcher during the years that they, Koufax, and Drysdale were playing.

The Roseboro incident had clearly hurt Marichal. Protests were raised across the Caribbean and by some writers in the States as well. The following year, 68 additional yes votes were cast, but the Dominican Dandy still came up seven votes short.

More and more voices in the baseball world decried the refusal of the electors to decide for Marichal. In a moment fraught with symbolism, Roseboro and his wife, Barbara, came to the Dominican Republic in late October, 1982. Marichal had invited his old nemesis for a golf tournament he hosted in Puerto Plata. Roseboro told the press that the events of 1965 should be forgotten and urged Marichal's election to the Hall of Fame in the January 1983 vote.

As the island held its collective breath, the Baseball Writers of America announced on January 12 that Marichal had finally won election, with 83.6 percent of the votes cast.

Marichal said he didn't believe that there existed a man happier than he was anywhere else on earth and dedicated his honor not only to all Dominicans, but all Latinos. They share in my triumph, he said, because it is their triumph, too.

Congratulations came from Venezuela, Mexico, and Puerto Rico as well as throughout the United States. But nowhere was the jubilation greater than on Hispaniola. Marichal had become the foremost Dominican ever, beating the *Yanquis* at their own game.

"For three years, they didn't want to give, how you call it, the *merito,* to be in the Hall of Fame," Marichal had said earlier in the day. "After I made it, I told them that if they had come to my country and seen where I grew up and how I grew up, and then thought about how far I went in baseball, I would have made it a long time ago."

Herman Goldberg: Baseball Olympian and Jewish-American

LOUIS JACOBSON

Berlin. 1936. Nazi Germany. Hitler.

Not exactly the situation in which you would expect to find an American Jew—unless, that is, your name is Herman Goldberg. Herman Goldberg: member of the American delegation to the 1936 Berlin Olympics, a catcher and outfielder on the team that would play a demonstration game of baseball in front of 125,000 spectators.

Few had an inkling of the impending Final Solution: the death camps, the six million. Goldberg certainly didn't. "Nothing had come to my attention as a nineteen-year-old youth," he says. "Perhaps if I had dug more, I might have known more. I was unaware as a young man of all the things that, perhaps, I should have been aware of."

But Goldberg did know that things weren't right, both before he left for Germany and in his experiences there. A boycott movement was on. Many influential Americans—such as Henry Sloane Coffin, Al Smith, Charles E. Coughlin, Heywood Broun, Reinhold Niebuhr, Norman Thomas, Oswald Garrison Villard, Francis Biddle, Westbrook Pegler, and Paul Gallico—and institutions—the NAACP, the American Federation of Labor, *The New York Times, The Nation, Christian Century,* and *Commonweal*—supported the idea of boycotting the 1936 Olympics for fear of "supporting a Fascist country with professed racist policies that included open hatred and open discrimination of Jews and other 'non-Aryan' people."[1]

Still, this support didn't concern Goldberg.

> There were five or six Jewish athletes out of the three-hundred-plus on the team, and some of us were considering whether we would boycott. We came to the conclusion that if the entire team would boycott, we would also do so.
>
> But we were really American athletes of Jewish religion. It didn't make sense to us to be the only ones to boycott. We were not Jewish ballplayers (Herman

> Goldberg); we weren't Jewish sprinters (Sam Stoller and Marty Glickman); we weren't Jewish basketball players (Sam Balter); we weren't Jewish pistol shooters (Morris Doob); we weren't Jewish weight lifters (David Mayor). We were American athletes, selected by the team to represent our country.

Their decision not to boycott did not go unnoticed by at least one (Jewish) reporter, as Goldberg relates:

> There began to be some inquiries by newsmen, especially a writer, Bernard Postal, from Seven Arts Feature Syndicate, who inferred, in conversations to me, that he would be very much interested in writing stories about how poorly I was going to be treated in Berlin as a Jewish athlete.
>
> I did not answer his letters. He continued writing to me. When the U.S.S. *Manhattan* was leaving the New York harbor for Germany under the guidance of a harbor pilot, he managed to get on the pilot boat and then the U.S.S. *Manhattan*. He sought me out and reminded me that I should be very sure to take good notes of any anti-Semitic feelings that were developing against my being on the team, as a Jewish athlete.
>
> He wrote me several letters that arrived in Berlin's Olympic Village; I did not answer them. When we were on the U.S.S. *Theodore Roosevelt,* the ship on which we returned, he was on the harbor pilot's boat and sought me out again. He asked, "Why haven't you written to me? What happened? I still would like to write a story. Were you treated badly?"
>
> I politely replied, "There are no episodes I can report. Nothing happened. And I wish you wouldn't bother me any more."

Goldberg was not treated badly. But some of the things he saw and experienced had a profound impact later in his life . . . and a profound impact on a lot of other people's lives, as well.

* * *

Herman Raphael Goldberg was born on November 20, 1915, in Brooklyn, New York. His mother, Rose Saltser Goldberg, a Russian Jew, did something rather unusual for a woman at the turn of the century: she graduated from Hunter College in 1905, received a master's degree in social studies from Columbia University, and went on to become a teacher in the New York public schools and later an acting principal. Her field of work and her success and achievement would be something that Herman would emulate.

Goldberg's father, Isidore Baruch Goldberg, was trained as a wood-carver in London. When he arrived in the United States, he went directly to Grand Rapids, Michigan, to become an artistic designer and pattern-maker for a furniture manufacturer. He later moved to New York City, where he met Rose. He opened a hardware store there and remained in that business until his death.

"I had a normal orthodox, but not ultra-orthodox, upbringing in my home as a child," Goldberg says. "Though I was raised in an orthodox home, it was difficult to abide by all the regulations all the time. My parents were very active in the synagogue, and we enjoyed a good relationship with the local rabbi and staff."

The importance of education was obvious in the Goldberg home, as it was in many other Jewish families at the time. "My Jewish education was what I obtained from the synagogue. My parents, however, wanted me to have a more intensive program, so both my sister and I worked with a private teacher of Hebrew who came to my home twice a week. We studied Hebrew, conversational Yiddish, and Yiddish writing."

Later, his mother encouraged him to prepare for a career in education, which he did. He took the required college courses in education to qualify as a teacher in the New York City schools. Yet he says that his parents were not only tolerant but rather supportive of his athletic interests—from amateur youth baseball in Brooklyn (1925 to 1929) to semipro teams in Queens and Long Island (1927 to 1931) to Boys High School (1927 to 1931) to Brooklyn College (1931 to 1935).

"My mother was very much interested in my developing career," Goldberg says. "As for my father, he expected me, even as a young boy, to help out in the hardware store, but he never objected when I played ball for eight hours a day on weekends and didn't show up for meals on time."

In fact, as a surprise, his father appeared at the ballpark one day when Herman was playing in the minor leagues for the Rome (New York) Colonels of the Canadian-American League. It happened to be the day the club was taking the team picture, and clearly visible in the background of that picture, waiting in the stadium to see his son, is Mr. Goldberg.

Still, Herman's mother did have one pet peeve that adds a new twist to the stereotypical "Jewish mother" stories. Herman enjoyed football as well as baseball as a boy, so when the neighborhood kids formed a semipro football team, he joined eagerly.

> My mother didn't mind my playing football so much, even though I got banged up plenty. My mother came to one game, and the thing that greatly annoyed her was seeing a ten-quart, galvanized water bucket with a ladle in it. The whole team drank out of that ladle, and she harped on that. She couldn't get it out of her mind that we were drinking from the same ladle. That was her concern, of health—not so much that we win the game.

"But they backed me," he concludes. "If I wanted to play ball, they said, 'Go ahead.' Secretly, I guess, they wanted me to do something else. But they never pushed me away from it."

Before he tried out for the Olympic team, Goldberg played briefly for the Paducah Indians of the Kitty (Kentucky–Indiana–Tennessee) league. After playing a couple of games with the Indians, Goldberg received a phone call from a local resident:

> I got a phone call from a resident of Paducah, Mr. J. J. Sabel. I remember the name very well. He told me on the phone how happy he was that there was a Jewish ballplayer in the league, finally, and would I be good enough to say yes to an invitation to have dinner at his home on Saturday night. Since we played day games, he said he could pick me up at my hotel about 6:30 on Saturday. I accepted; I was delighted. I got to his home and found all his friends and relatives were there. I was presented as the one Jewish ballplayer in the league at the time.

Herman Goldberg as a member of the 1936 United States Olympic Team, Hakenfeld, Berlin, Germany, August 1936. (Photos courtesy of the author)

> But I later found out that one of the real purposes of his invitation was the fact that he had a daughter of marriageable age, and that what he really wanted was to have me become acquainted with her and perhaps take her out. I kept in touch with Mr. Sabel the rest of the time I was in Paducah, but I didn't accept any further dinner invitations.

The mother of Herman's eventual wife, Hariette Balacaier, had no qualms with Herman's baseball-playing, either. "She approved of me from the first," he says. "She felt that it was an episode in my life that their daughter should not be too concerned with." Mr. Balacaier was "somewhat disturbed" when his daughter told him of Herman's profession, however:

> He figured that it wasn't a good idea for his daughter to get married to a ballplayer. She said, "But he's taking his master's degree and he's teaching at Columbia."
>
> He said, "But he was a ballplayer," and that equated in his mind with being a bum.

After my father-in-law understood what my goals were and my various skills and the background I had had, his earlier feelings were wiped out, and we became fast friends.

While Goldberg says that the Jewish boys in his neighborhood favored roller hockey and ice hockey to baseball, New York in the time he was growing up was very aware of the special needs of Jews playing youth baseball. "As far as the conflict between the High Holidays and baseball, it never crossed my calendar, and I didn't have to resolve it," he says. "The neighborhood teams, the high school teams, the college teams did not play on Jewish holidays. In fact, the New York City colleges were very cognizant of the Jewish holiday calendar, and I don't think they ever violated that."

* * *

Goldberg's success in baseball led him to try out for the 1936 U.S. Olympic baseball team. He was sent to tryouts in Baltimore, Maryland, and was one of twenty-one players ultimately selected from the three tryout sites (the others were in Palo Alto, California, and Kalamazoo, Mcihgian).[2] Being Jewish didn't matter one bit.

"Work at the Olympic tryouts in Baltimore carried the same spirit throughout," says Goldberg. "The coaches—Harry Wolter from Stanford, Leslie Mann from the Boston Braves, and Judson Hyames from Western Michigan College—showed me no favoritism and no antagonism. It was hard work; it was getting down behind the plate every day; it was my hitting and throwing that led to my selection on the team, not my name."

He would be in for a shock when he arrived in Germany:

In the first place, when we arrived in the Olympic Village, we were assigned to different houses. The baseball team stayed at a house called Brandenburg, which housed 28 people. In the Olympic Village—*Olympischen Dorf* (*Dorf* meaning village)—instead of housing the athletes in college dormitories or in huge, high-rise apartments which could be turned into low-cost public housing after the games, Germany taxed every city fifty percent of the cost of erecting smaller buildings that would hold twenty to forty athletes. The city of Brandenburg put up fifty percent of the cost of our house, and Hitler's *Reichstag,* or parliament, put up the other fifty percent. The buildings were called by the donor city's name, and the mayor of Brandenburg came to visit us one day.

I was curious about a door in the hallway of our home which did not open into a hall closet. I opened it and saw a big chain across the staircase. I looked around; I shouted, "Anybody down there?" No answer. I dropped the chain and I walked down to the basement. I saw a cavernous cement floor with nothing on it. There were enormous overhead garage doors, almost the size of half a tennis court—huge doors and huge ramps leading to the doors. Then the *Hausmann* and the *Hausfrau,* the couple in charge of the building, making the beds and cleaning up the rooms, saw that the chain was down and they both shouted at me, "Get out of there!" I came upstairs. Later I found out that the *panzer,* or tank, units were going to move into this house and several others after the Olympics, and the oversized basement was where big tanks were going to be stored. The floors were about a foot deep of

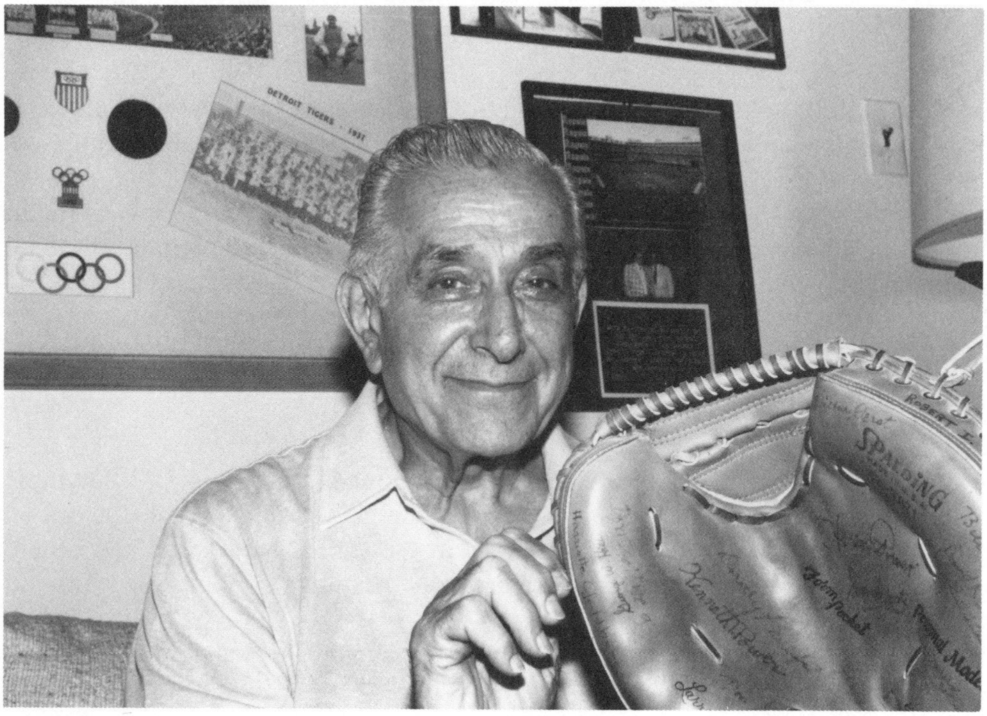

Herman Goldberg in 1988.

concrete; they were very solid. As soon as the American athletes and other athletes left the Olympic Village, it became the military academy of Germany.

But Goldberg adds that his being Jewish did not make him a target of the *Hausmann* and *Hausfrau.* "I do not think it mattered that I was Jewish and went to investigate an absolutely vacant basement," he says. "It could have been done by any one of the athletes, but I was the one who went down and got shouted at. I don't think they even knew my name."

It was not only the house and its basement that troubled Goldberg. In each of the players' rooms was left a book called *Germany.* In an insert at the beginning of the book was a welcoming message—from Field Marshal Von Blomberg, the *Reich* Minister of War. "It seemed unusual to me," Goldberg says, "that the Minister of War would be welcoming us to the games. To me, that would be the equivalent of Caspar Weinberger, when he was U.S. Secretary of Defense, welcoming the athletes of the world to the 1984 Los Angeles Olympics representing the Department of Defense of the United States."

But parts of the book beyond this welcome on the first page struck Goldberg as threatening:

> This book was a massive propaganda production showing Adolf Hitler in his search for *Lebensraum,* "more room" for Germany and for Germans, and the development of the *Luftwaffe,* the air force, the German navy, the German army—the whole history of his push of developing Germany into a world power—not mentioning anti-Semitism, but developing all the instruments of war: their ship-

building, their merchant marine, and their activity relating to the *Graf Zeppelin,* the *Hindenburg.*

Various proclamations of the *Führer* were detailed in the book, including the one of March 16, 1935, in which he announced that, "According to the German belief, a people without protection is a people without honour. The German army is the expression of the common will of the people and the supporter of the national standing and honour." The assignment of the brightest children in the German schools to the Hitler Youth Corps was detailed.

Taking the time to read this book carefully, I could sense the beginnings of their war machine, epitomized on one page by the red white and black Nazi insignia, the swastika, winning allegiance from the German people. They were telling us, throughout this book, that they were getting ready for war, although they didn't call it that. They just called it the "preparation of Germany for expanding its borders." It went on and on, and we were somewhat disturbed by it. This, along with a second book showing Hitler's activity at the Olympics—complete with his photograph and autograph—demonstrated the glorification of Germany as his primary goal, rather than serving as host country for the youth of the world.

* * *

Despite these threatening elements, Goldberg himself was treated well at the Olympics. He did, however, have some trouble assuring that his name—commonly Jewish—was spelled correctly. "I remember when the scoreboard in the Olympic stadium was lighted up," he says. "The big game was played at night, before the largest crowd ever in the history of baseball, 125,000. My name was spelled G-O-L-D-B-U-R-G-H, the German spelling, as opposed to the usual Jewish spelling G-O-L-D-B-E-R-G."

Later, after he injured two fingers severely in batting practice, Goldberg was taken to the X-ray department of the Olympic Village. "The medical department was run by the German army," he continues. "The doctors were all in military uniforms with white half-smocks over them. They recorded my name and badge number—the things they needed to identify me—and they also spelled it G-O-L-D-B-U-R-G-H. But there were no other episodes at the time. I guess they were on their good behavior."

One incident that has received notice in the press decades later, specifically in *Parade* magazine, is the report that before the game the American baseball team entered the field and gave the Nazi salute. Goldberg (and the other members of the team), however, vehemently dispute that. "Those reports were not true at all," he says. "We marched in in our dress uniforms: white slacks, blue coat with an Olympic shield on the breast pocket, a white straw hat, a red-white-and-blue striped tie, and white shoes. We did not salute. We put our hands over our hearts when we passed the reviewing stand, because the American flag was leading our path. People could have misintepreted that in other ways."

Regardless of the Nazis' "good behavior," Goldberg says the anti-Jewish sentiment of the German government was evident. "When they listed the house of worship in some of the publications, there was no mention of Jewish synagogues. They had all the others, but never these. I was especially concerned when I read in an American newspaper that Hitler had forbidden the use of the word *hallelujah* at all religious services in all churches because it was a Hebrew word."

A few times Goldberg had contact with Germans:

> Sprinter Marty Glickman, one of my Olympic teammates, and I were hitching a ride downtown on what turned out to be a German army jeep, with machine guns stowed under the rear seat. I asked the driver, in fairly decent German, if he knew whether a certain boxer was fighting that night. But instead of using the German word *heute* for "tonight" I substituted the Yiddish word *heint,* by accident. The driver game me a startled look and corrected me, but did not become angry or impolite. That could have developed into an incident, but it passed quickly. Before we got out of the jeep they asked for our autographs.

Years later, Goldberg was invited by Paramount Pictures to become a technical advisor to *The Jesse Owens Story,* a four-hour, two-part TV movie about the life of sprinter Jesse Owens. He reviewed the script and made suggestions to the directors to help them portray the scenes at the 1936 Olympics.

Goldberg himself is portrayed in one of the scenes, which was created with some artistic license by the directors. In the scene, David Levitt, a fictional U.S. sprinter, was inserted to portray another Jewish athlete. Goldberg is seen with Levitt and Owens, who won four gold medals but was snubbed by Hitler because he was black. They get out of a bus in Berlin to look at a sign that says, *"Juden und Hunde verboten!"* or "Jews and dogs forbidden!" Levitt considers going home, but Owens and Goldberg convince him to stay and prove their strength by beating Hitler's Aryan athletes.

In real life, Goldberg met Hitler at a swimming meet: "He was constantly grinning and raising his hand, obviously wanting to make the most of the Olympics to promote his cause."

* * *

Cut to 1980. The Olympics are about to be held in Moscow, but President Jimmy Carter announces that the U.S. team will not attend because of America's disagreements with the Soviet Union, specifically its invasion of Afghanistan. Herman Goldberg is now an Assistant Secretary of Education for the United States Department of Education. And, with his experience at a politically-charged Olympics, he plays a vital advisory role in the U.S. boycott. Liz Carpenter, former press secretary for President Lyndon Johnson and his wife Lady Bird, was working with Goldberg as a fellow Assistant Secretary of Education. She knew he participated in the 1936 Games, and before long, people in high places found out about it.

> The propaganda books distributed to the athletes by Germany at the 1936 games, with other books and papers I had, were brought to the White House. Mr. Carter and Vice President Mondale put them on display near the Oval Office and invited members of the House of Representatives and the Senate to come by to examine them. When they saw these books their concern intensified, leading Mr. Mondale to make speeches against our participation. He referred to me in the speeches and identified his feeling that propaganda materials would probably be developed and distributed in Moscow, as well.

The boycott, of course, was controversial, and remains so today. But Goldberg still feels, given the circumstances and the climate of the time—the Cold War, the invasion of Afghanistan, and the Soviet Union's refusal to allow Soviet Jews to emigrate—that it was the right thing to do. "I feel that my growth in going to the Olympics and the things that resulted from it may have helped hundreds of young people," he says. "Later, having the experience of maturity and [having] my story [related] to Vice President Mondale and President Carter intensified my feelings that what I had done was important. And I feel that a contribution was made, although there were many people who thought we should have gone."

Would he say the same thing today, with Soviet president Mikhail Gorbachev's *glasnost* and *perestroika?* "Perhaps not," he says. "But in 1980, Mr. Carter, Mr. Mondale, and Secretary of State Cyrus Vance were very much concerned [about] what was going on in Russia.

* * *

The Olympics put Goldberg on the road to the major leagues. The chief umpire of the Olympic baseball demonstration—George L. "Tiny" Parker—was watching Goldberg carefully, without his knowing it. He had connections with "Wish" Egan, the head scout for Detroit, and with Hank Greenberg, the Tigers' star Jewish first baseman. After he returned home from the Olympics, Goldberg received a letter from Hank Greenberg saying that "Tiny" Parker had tipped him off. Goldberg was "a promising, young Jewish ballplayer," the letter said, and Greenberg "wanted very much" to see him make it.

Though the Olympics was over, Goldberg was not yet done with Bernard Postal. When Goldberg went to training camp with the Detroit Tigers in 1937, there were phone calls and letters from Postal at the hotel in Lakeland, Florida, where the Tigers trained. One letter dated March 10, 1937, requests that Goldberg write about 1,000 words entitled, "A Jewish Rookie Speaks." "Such an article under your name in our papers throughout the country would be valuable publicity for you," Postal writes. "If we keep you in the limelight you'll be back bigger and better next year. Good luck to you."

> I brought the letters to Hank Greenberg and had a long discussion with him about it. He advised, "Don't grant him any interviews. If anything happened to you—not necessarily as a Jew, but as an individual ballplayer and there were Jewish overtones—talk it over with me. We'll see what we can do."
>
> I never had any trouble on that score. I let my bat speak for me, and I let my behavior speak for me. Later that day, Greenberg said to me, "This afternoon I'm going to a local hospital for crippled children. Want to come with me? We can talk some more." We drove there together. He talked with the kids, gave out some baseballs, and he kept talking to me, saying, "Make your mark as a human being. Your name is Goldberg, mine is Greenberg. Don't let it bother you. don't talk to these guys. Just play ball as hard as you can." I was very grateful for the advice.

Spring training with the Tigers in 1937 "was vey buoyant," Goldberg says. "The 1937 team was a very busy, active, fun-loving team. Manager Mickey

Cochrane inspired everybody—he got everybody moving. It was an exciting time. Those were my fondest memories of baseball."

Goldberg clearly recalls the moment the equipment manager handed him his own Tigers' uniform, the one with the Old English "D" that his heroes had worn. "To have started off with the Tigers instead of some obscure minor league was a great thrill. Perhaps if it had been the other way around I would have been better off. But you can't begin to feel the thrill that I had as a young player to be putting on a major league uniform."

Goldberg says that he never did experience any anti-Semitism on or off the field. Though some Jewish major leaguers in earlier decades changed their surnames to ones that didn't sound Jewish in order to avoid being known as Jewish. Goldberg says that, despite his obviously Jewish surname, he would never have done that himself, citing as role models a number of other people who kept their Jewish-sounding names: Hank Greenberg, his mother, and his sister Harriet Goldberg, who was a soprano at the Metropolitan Opera House.

Since he didn't hide his being Jewish, he was identified as such in the press.

> When I was transferred from the Detroit Tigers to the Buffalo Bisons, I remember very specifically that I was identified as a "stocky, young Jewish catcher from Brooklyn who is being loaned to the Buffalo Bisons." As I read that in the Buffalo papers and in the Detroit papers, I sort of wondered why they did it. But I accepted it because that's what I was: I was a young, stocky catcher who was Jewish. And I was aware of the fact that teams were looking hard for players with ethnic names, probably Italian, Polish, and Jewish players, because the fans in particular cities of the leagues would flock in.
>
> Because I understood that, it didn't bother me. I had no feeling that I was being used by the ball club; as a matter of fact, when I was beaten out for the third catching spot on the Tigers by Birdie Tebbetts—he became the third catcher after Mickey Cochrane and Ray Hayworth—it was because he could hit the curveball better than I could; he could throw to second base better than I could; he was a better catcher than I was. At no time did I feel I was being promoted or kept back in my career because it would satisfy the box office for Jewish fans. It all had to do with ability.

Occasionally the press mis-identified him, too—once as "Sammy Goldberg," in the *Buffalo Courier Express.* " 'Sammy' sounded even more Jewish than 'Herman,' " Goldberg jokes today.

According to legend, New York Giants' infielder Andy Cohen—one of the first Jewish players to be open about his ethnic background in the 1920s—was playing for the New York Giants one day in Boston. The game was a homecoming for teammate Shanty Hogan, and before the game Hogan was presented with numerous gifts. In the last inning, Cohen was told to pinch-hit for Hogan. The umpire—who used a megaphone in those days to announce lineup changes—yelled, "Cohen batting for Hogan!" Legend has it that a fan replied loudly, "Flanagan leaving the park!"

Years later, the *Ottawa Journal* reported an anecdote that might be of sociological interest. In the ninth inning of a game against the Ottawa Braves, Goldberg pinch-hit for Rome Colonels' teammate and pitcher Jimmy O'Rourke.

When the umpire announced the switch, the *Journal* reported, "Contrary to the old . . . baseball yarn of a similar situation, not an Irishman left the park."

* * *

Forget that Hank Greenberg was Jewish, Goldberg says. Greenberg was simply the best player he ever saw. "He worked so hard at whatever he was doing," says Goldberg—even volunteering to move from first base to the outfield when rookie Rudy York was brought to the Tigers. The manager, Cochrane, thought that York's fielding would do less harm at first base, so the solution to keeping both bats in the lineup was to move Greenberg.

"He never rested on his laurels," Goldberg says. "Greenberg, very, very loyally, agreed with Cochrane's suggestion. To master left field after many years at first base, Greenberg worked hard. He got up early in the morning, he used me as a batting-practice catcher, and as a fungo hitter he had some rookie pitchers—7:00 A.M. at League Park, every single day until he mastered ground balls, fly balls, liners." The strategy worked. York hit 18 home runs in the month of August—a record. And Greenberg would later in his career be voted Most Valuable Player in his new position.

Herman Goldberg's career was not as glorious as his role model's. He severely injured the cartilages in his left knee at a crash at home plate. In the days before arthroscopic surgery, the doctor gave him two choices: surgery, in which there was only a fifty-fifty chance of being able to walk or play sports again, or rest. "I had some real hard thinking to do," he says. He chose rest.

There is an old story about a bush leaguer who writes home to his mother explaining why she should expect him soon. "I'll be home soon," the letter goes. "They're starting to throw the curveball now." To a certain extent—even without the injury—such was the career of Herman Goldberg. "I guess the most difficult thing for me to do was to learn to hit the curveball, a very difficult procedure for ballplayers—one that turns out to be their Waterloo very often," he says. "I did change my batting stance from time to time, with the advice of batting coaches and managers and just wasn't able to settle down to one style of hitting, although I hit comfortably well during my short career. I guess my desire to hit over .300 was not realized, and that was the thing I was always working on."

He never did play in a regular season major league game. "Perhaps," he reflects, "if I had wanted to stay at it for several years, enduring the long bus travels, the poor hotels, and the meager meal and laundry money, I would have tried to stay on and extend my career. I have given much thought to having ended my baseball career as quickly as I did, because of the knee injury. But I had begun to think, 'Do I want to live in a hotel half the year! Was I going to live on a bus? Was I going to live on a train? Was I going to eat hamburgers every night? What was I going to do for a career in later life? Was I going to make it? Did I want to be part of the daily, small-time card-playing in the clubhouse?' "

The answer was clear. "No."

* * *

Having foregone the buses, hamburgers, and cards, Goldberg went back to school for his master's degree in education of the deaf at Columbia University's Teachers College. It was there that he met his wife Harriette. "I had been teaching there in the winter of 1941 when my father died," he says. "The Columbia authorities appointed a substitute for me, Harriette Balacaier. After she took over the courses for me, curiosity got the better of me and I went up to Columbia and saw who was teaching my course in my room. There was this young lady, and six weeks later we got married."

From 1939 to 1948 Goldberg was a classroom teacher in New York, as well as a baseball coach at the New York School for the Deaf. From there he went to Rochester, New York, where he was Coordinator of Instruction, Director of Special Education, and, finally, Superintendent of Schools from 1963 to 1971. He was so well respected that he received offers to be the superintendent in the St. Louis County Special Education District, the Chancellor of the New York City Public Schools, and the Superintendent of Schools in Philadelphia and in Detroit.

"Oh, what a thrill I thought it would be," he says. "If I didn't make it as a regular with the Detroit Tigers, I could now become their superintendent of schools." Better yet, two members of the city council were former Tiger teammates, Billy Rogell and Charlie Gehringer. "When the job offer came, I sort of dreamed for a few days about realigning myself with some of my former teammates. They would control the budget of the Board of Education in Detroit. What a great feeling that would have been."

In the end, though, he decided not to accept any of the offers, because the Rochester schools were in a large expansion program. Then, in 1971, he got a job offer that he wouldn't turn down: to be the U.S. Associate Commissioner for Elementary and Secondary Education for the Department of Health, Education and Welfare (later the Department of Education). He remained with the government for seventeen years, eventually becoming an Assistant Secretary of Education, Office of Special Education and Rehabilitative Services. Goldberg worked at the Department of Education during the civil rights era, and one of his assignments had to do with handling the funds for desegregation of segregated school systems.

Goldberg speculates that some of the traits that made him a success in the classroom and within the school system first appeared on the baseball field, when he always took the most "cerebral" position.

> I never from my youth days on wanted to be anything but a catcher. My teammates sometimes used to laugh at me because they said, "You're going to get hurt—that's the worst place. You sweat, you work too hard. Why don't you go for second base or outfield or pitcher or something else?"
>
> I always thought as catcher I could learn more, I could teach better. Maybe some of the innate traits in me to be a teacher started early from my family, which included several teachers. I was able to impart, even as a young player, some of these ideas. I read voraciously on baseball. I had nobody to coach me until I really got to high school.

> On the semipro teams and the amateur teams I played with, when I was still in high school, I pretty much served as catcher and also the advisor to the rest of the team. I didn't think I knew a lot more than the others, and I wasn't necessarily a better player, but they trusted me to call the shots. That was kind of fun, too, to run the team from the catcher's spot. I think that catchers still make good managers, because of their knowledge of the game, and because 50 percent of the game is pitching and you really work with the pitchers so closely.

Goldberg now is semiretired, working as an educational consultant for ERGO Associates, Inc. He spends much of his time writing reading textbooks for junior high and high school students, using a special process he developed. His process allows the teacher to teach the same material to a class with different levels of reading ability by using easier or more difficult words to describe the same ideas or actions. Each textbook centers around one topic relevant to the students. For instance, in one textbook, there are stories dealing with street crime, drugs, parental relations, and jobs. His next "concept" book is one about truckers. He has worked on it with his wife Harriette, traveling all over the country to truck stops and talking with drivers. In fact, Harriette even took a truck-driving course to learn more about the subject—and to learn firsthand how to handle a "big rig."

* * *

When Goldberg went to Bologna, Italy, as a Fulbright professor in 1960 and 1961, he couldn't resist bringing baseball along with his intellectual baggage. Fluent in Italian, Goldberg taught courses—in the native language—at the University of Bologna. While he was in Rome, he visited the 1960 Olympics where he caught up with an old friend from twenty-four years earlier.

> I was very friendly with Jesse Owens—especially friendly—for many years. We didn't spell out the reasons, but I guess he may have been very much aware I was Jewish and that Germany was a hotbed of anti-Semitism and anti-black emotion.
>
> We arrived early in the summer of 1960, in order to attend the games. My older son, Robert, sold newspapers in the Olympic stadium in Rome, wearing my Olympic sweater.
>
> Jesse Owens saw him and asked, "Young man, where did you get that sweater?"
>
> He said, "It's my father's."
>
> "Who is your father?"
>
> "My father's Herm Goldberg."
>
> "Herm Goldberg! Is he here?"
>
> "Yes he is."
>
> "How do I get in touch with him?"
>
> "Well, he's at the Hotel Universo."
>
> "OK, let's make a date for lunch."
>
> And, so, wearing the same sweater that Bob had worn when he was selling newspapers, I met Jesse Owens for lunch at the Olympic Village dining room.

When they arrived in Italy, his two sons brought their baseball equipment. They had played Little League and Babe Ruth League ball in Rochester, and their father had coached Little League there for fourteen years. In Italy, Gold-

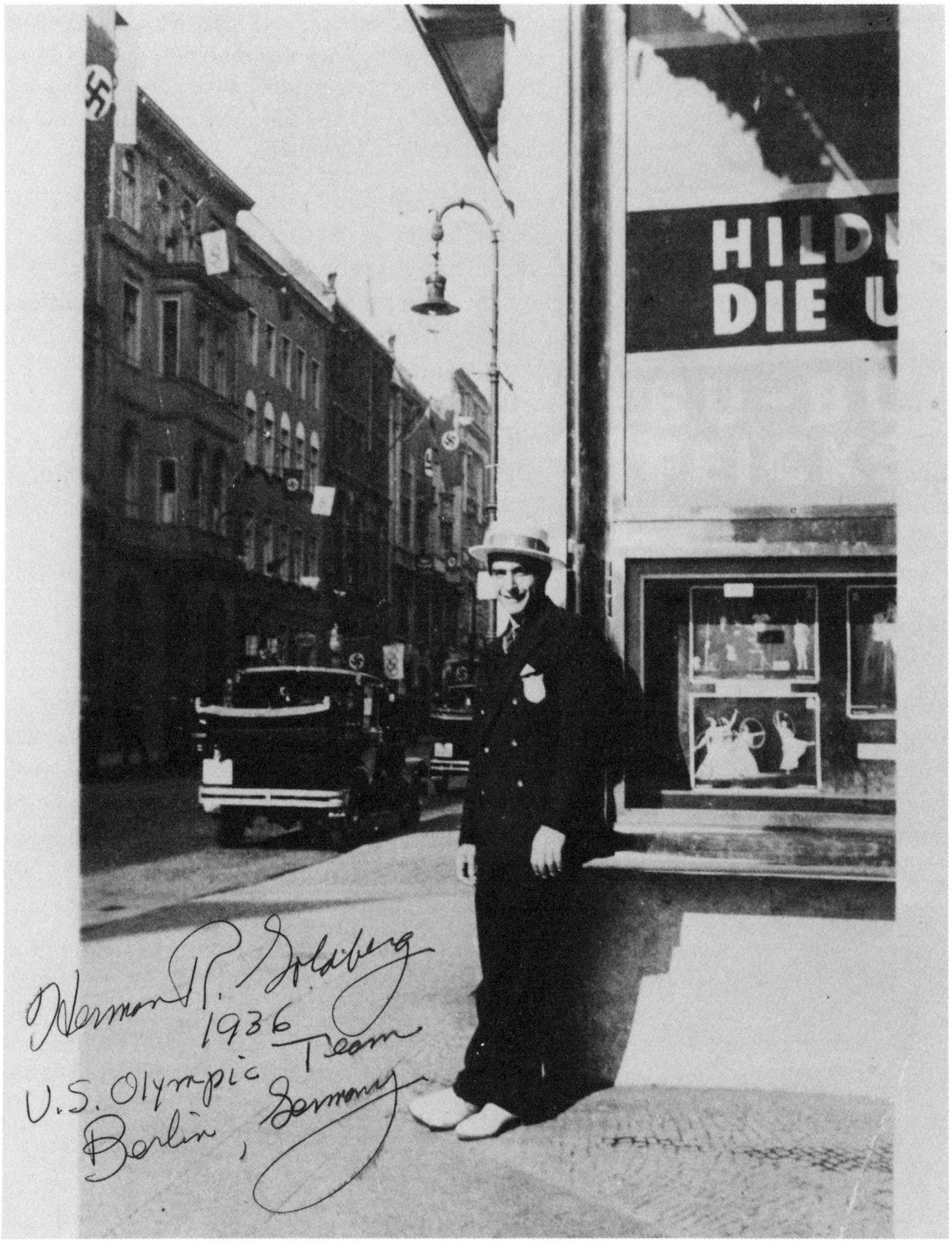

Goldberg on a Berlin streetcorner.

berg says, "we found that there were a great many young people who were interested in learning to catch and bat, not just kick a soccer ball around."

Goldberg took advantage of this burgeoning interest. In Bologna, he met Angelo Zara, a police lieutenant who was a sportswriter in his spare time. "He was looking for ways in which more Italian youngsters could learn to play baseball, even in the United States," Goldberg says. "He too may have had the feeling that some people have, that use of an ethnic name and use of the ethnicity of certain backgrounds would attract the fans of those backgrounds in major league parks. But that never came out in our discussions."

Zara gathered hundreds of Italian youth in different squads; Goldberg coached kids in Bologna and trained Italian athletes to help him. That led to the formation of a semiprofessional league throughout Italy, with teams in Bologna, Milan, Turin, Pisa, Perugia, and other cities traveling on weekends to play games. At the end of the year, a surprise opportunity came Goldberg's way: the offer to become commissioner of the Italian National Federation of Baseball Clubs. "It seemed like a very exciting prospect, but it meant moving permanently to Italy," he says. "I decided I was not ready to do that. It was a very genuine feeling on their part. It didn't matter that my name was Herman Goldberg, and not somebody with an Italian name."

Today in Italy the sport has grown dramatically in popularity, but in those early days, Goldberg still had to learn a few things about some of the idiosyncrasies of the game's Italian version:

> When we traveled by bus to Milan or Turin to play against the Alfa-Romeo team or the Fiat team or the Pirelli tire team, we stopped for lunch en route. When my players ordered lunch, they ordered wine with it. I asked the assistant manager how they could be drinking so much wine two hours before game time. He said, "If they drink milk or coffee, they will vomit. They're used to wine with the pasta, and that's what their bodies are set for. All teams in the league drink wine with their meals, not milk."
>
> When I got to the field in Milan, we went out for infield practice. I was hitting grounders to my team, and I noticed that there was only one batter's box around home plate instead of two—for right-handed hitters, on the left side of the plate. I said to the opposing manager, "Where's the other one?" He said, "Oh, it's lovely grass. We don't want to spoil the grass. We have no left-handed hitters on our team." And I thought that was typical Italy. It was just a beautiful kind of returning to nature, a refusal to tear up what nature had produced.

His experience in Italy had not actually been his first experiment in international baseball. The Olympic team, when in Germany, had tried to spread the popularity of the game by going to different cities to teach baseball and showing baseball films to the German athletes. "Many of them were army personnel. That annoyed us, but our mission was to get American concepts over to them," Goldberg says.

Though these original efforts failed when World War II began, today many European countries outside Italy are becoming increasingly interested in baseball. Ironically, one of the most recent of these is the country that Goldberg suggested the U.S. boycott: the Soviet Union. "They are a long way from rapid development, but it's a start," Goldberg says.

In 1984, the Los Angeles Olympics included an international competition in baseball, the first time it was part of the games since Goldberg played in 1936. (Another Olympic competition was held at the 1988 Seoul Olympics.) In honor of the return of baseball in the 1984 games, the surviving members of the 1936 squad were invited to Los Angeles and were hosted at California Angel and Los Angeles Dodger games.

One of the teams to compete in the Olympics in 1984 was Italy. "I have kept in touch with Mr. Zara over the years," says Goldberg. "And I have a feeling that their Olympic team was made up of the younger brothers of the ones I may have introduced to baseball in 1960 and 1961."

In fact, when Goldberg returned to Italy in April of 1989—as a lecturer invited for the 900th anniversary of the founding of the University of Bologna—baseball again crossed cultural and language barriers.

> After a good give-and-take in one session, one of the assistant superintendents reviewed with me his responsibility in heading up the project involving mainstreaming of handicapped children. He reviewed all his charts, tables, and staff directives and took an additional half-hour to explain the details of his important work. As the meeting was about to end, after the last *arrivederci,* he shook hands with me and blurted out, "I AM SHORTSTOP!"
>
> Pleased as I was to have him announce his apparent proudest title, I was puzzled. He explained. He remembered me from earlier days of introducing youth baseball to Bologna. He was one of the kids who was part of my first training program in 1961, and later grew up to continue playing baseball—instead of *calcio,* soccer. He went on to play with one of the semipro teams in the Italian National Baseball Federation. I guess he figured that if he hadn't registered with me as a top school administrator, he could rebuild his bond with me through the phrase, "I AM SHORTSTOP." I was touched.

* * *

Herm Goldberg lives outside Washington and in recent years has attended services at Temple Sinai in D.C. He says that he's an active Jew, interested in learning more about Jewish affairs and participating as a donor in Jewish fund-raising every year.

In some ways, his sons have followed in his footsteps. They played baseball in high school, but were even more active in soccer, which they had learned in Italy. His younger son, Arnold, was named as an honorable mention All-American soccer player at American University; he later played semipro soccer in St. Louis. Like his dad, Arnold became a superintendent of schools, first in Merrick, New York, and now in Hauppauge, New York. Robert, the older son, is in the advertising business in New York. Both became interested in instrumental music, something that Herman had not been, although he had been interested in vocal music. "They were interested in things that I had not been interested in," he says, "and I was proud of them for that. I had no need for my boys to become baseball players just because I was a baseball player."

* * *

As one of the relatively small number of Jews to play in the minor leagues—much less the major leagues—Goldberg speculates on why there are few like him.

> The career goals for sons in many Jewish families do not include professional athletics as a major drive. The career could be curtailed because of an injury. It

Goldberg in Bologna, Italy, in 1960 coaching Italian youth.

could be curtailed because of a lack of super skills—although the person may have a great many skills, he may not have enough to compete in the very competitive world of major league baseball. Then there's the drudgery of the game, along with the fun; the long schedule; the airplane rides now, formerly the train travel or bus rides; the temptation, perhaps, that's in the mind of some families, that all the free time that the professional athletes have can lead to gambling or, perhaps, other unacceptable activities, including alcohol or drug abuse.

In baseball, your mind is not on a long-term career. You're in a fresh competition every single day. Your accomplishments are reported in the press every day, unlike a lawyer, who might win a big case and get some publicity, but he might win a great many cases and not get in the papers. The heroics of certain physicians and others are not always reported in the daily paper. But in baseball, the box score indicates whether you made it or didn't make it the night before.

Goldberg was impressed by a work he read in the UNESCO library by the late Dr. Harry I. Shapiro, chairman of the Department of Anthropology at the American Museum of Natural History in New York. Shapiro was asked, "Why is it that Jewish families have worked so hard for success in the professions?"

Goldberg says that Shapiro "identified the Jews not as a super, bright people, but one with an insistence on literacy, that the tradition of the Jewish family is to learn, to read, to understand, to relate to other people, in medicine, in law, in education, in architecture, in business, in finance, in writing, and in music."

Looking back on his career, Herman Goldberg muses about what makes a great leader, the role he has so frequently taken.

I have the feeling that, regardless of the times, and while there would be hurdles set in the path of any human being because of prejudices of whatever sort, that the common denominator is integrity, talent, and demonstrated skill—a feeling of caring for other people, a demonstration of the skill you have, not just to beat others, but to show you have leadership quality, and use it in a way that brings out the best in people. One of the objects of leadership is to remove the obstacles so that creativity in others can go forward.

NOTES

1. For more on the movement to protest the 1936 Berlin Olympics, see the following works:

• Moshe Gottlieb. "The American Controversy Over the Olympic Games." *American Jewish Historical Quarterly.* LXI (March 1972). pp. 181–213.

• Edward S. Shapiro, "The World Labor Athletic Carnival of 1936: An American Anti-Nazi Protest." *American Jewish History.* LXXIV (March, 1985). pp. 255–273.

• Peter Levine. " 'My Father and I, We Didn't Get Our Medals': Marty Glickman's American Jewish Odyssey." *American Jewish History.* LXXVIII (March, 1989). pp. 399–424.

The quote immediately preceding the note reference is taken from Peter Levine's article. Material on Herman Goldberg's life, including the quotations in this article, originated from several interviews conducted by Louis Jacobson in 1988 and 1989.

2. For more on the 1936 U.S. Olympic baseball team, see:

• M.E. Travaglini. "Olympic Baseball 1936: *Was es das?*" *The National Pastime.* Society for American Baseball Research. Winter, 1985. pp. 45–55.

Tom Zachary's Perfect Season

JIM SUMNER

Pity the poor baseball goat. The national pastime has a way of immortalizing him as surely as it does its heroes. Consider Fred Merkle. For all but the most devoted baseball historian, Merkle's sixteen-year major league career has been reduced to the single 1908 baserunning blunder that led to his enduring nickname "Bonehead." The strike that Mickey Owens didn't put away, the ground ball Fred Lindstrom didn't catch, and the throw Johnny Pesky didn't make have been immortalized in baseball lore and have distorted the careers of its victims. It is likely that Bill Buckner will share this fate. Nor are pitchers immune from this phenomenon. Mention Ralph Branca, Mike Torrez, Tracy Stallard, Ralph Terry, or Al Downing to a knowledgeable baseball fan and he or she will automatically think of the home run pitch thrown to Bobby Thompson, Bucky Dent, Roger Maris, Bill Mazeroski, or Hank Aaron.

Another pitcher best known for the pitch that didn't stay in the ballpark was Tom Zachary. On September 30, 1927 the Washington Senators southpaw hung a curve near Babe Ruth's head in an otherwise meaningless late-season game. Ruth hit the pitch into the right field stands for his 60th 1927 home run, breaking his own single-season record by one. As generation after generation of sluggers chased this record in vain, until Roger Maris broke it in 1961, it became one of the most famous home runs in baseball history. It also became a millstone around Zachary's neck. Long before baseball trivia contests became popular, Zachary was remembered only as the man who threw Babe Ruth's 60th home run. This was particularly unfortunate since Zachary was a fine pitcher who completely bypassed the minors on the way to a nineteen-year career in the big time. Almost totally forgotten is the exceptional season Zachary had in 1929. That year, pitching for the New York Yankees, Zachary won twelve games without a single defeat. Sixty years later this remains the major league record for most wins in a season without a loss.

Jonathan Thomas Walton Zachary was born in rural Alamance County, North Carolina on May 7, 1896. He was the seventh of eight children of farmer Alfred Zachary and Mary E. Zachary.[1] Rural North Carolina was a hotbed of baseball during the early twentieth century. Wes Ferrell, raised about the same time on a farm in nearby Guilford County, recalled that they "raised hay, wheat, corn, and tobacco" on the Ferrell farm. However, he continued "more than anything else we raised ballplayers on that farm. We'd go out into the fields after harvest time and hit for hours."[2] Zachary recalled knocking squirrels out of trees with rocks at an early age but no doubt he played the game as often as the Ferrells or anyone else.[3]

Zachary attended Guilford College, a small Quaker-supported school located near Greensboro, not far from Ferrell's home. Small school or not, Guilford had developed an enviable baseball reputation and was highly competitive with larger southern schools by the time Zachary enrolled in 1913. Ernie Shore preceded Zachary at Guilford before joining the Boston Red Sox, while Zachary's teammate and fellow pitcher Tom Murchison had cups of coffee in the big leagues both before and after World War I.[4]

Zachary was both a football and a baseball star at Guilford and made all-state football as a guard in 1917. His forte was baseball, of course. Zachary led Guilford to a 12–1 record and the unofficial state championship in 1917. The highlight of his college career, however, came in 1918, his senior season, when he pitched five times in a six-day swing into South Carolina, winning three and saving two. Guilford finished 11–2–1 in 1918.[5]

After he graduated from Guilford in the spring of 1918, Zachary made plans to join a Red Cross unit on the way to France. While awaiting departure from Philadelphia, Zachary wrangled a tryout with Connie Mack's Athletics, supposedly by telling Mack "I have been watching your pitchers for two days, and if I can't do any better than they, why, I'll send you the first German helmet I can grab over there."[6] He pitched two games for Philadelphia under the pseudonym Zach Walton. Although hit hard twice, he was able to post two wins. He then went to France where he served until the summer of 1919. When he returned he signed with the Washington Senators because "I just got tired of waiting for Mr. Mack . . . to make up his mind."[7]

The North Carolina left-hander quickly became a mainstay of an outstanding Washington pitching staff in the early to middle 1920s. He won at least ten games every year from 1920 through 1925, including 18 wins in 1921. His best year for the Senators was 1924. His 15–9 record helped Washington to the American League pennant, while his 2.75 earned run average was second in the league, narrowly trailing only his teammate, the immortal Walter Johnson, at 2.72.[8] Zachary then excelled in the 1924 World Series against the New York Giants, winning twice. He won game two 4–3 with ninth inning relief help from Firpo Marberry. Yet the Senators trailed three games to two when Zachary took the mound for game six. He proceeded to even the series with a masterful 2–1 complete game victory. Washington then won game seven and the series.[9]

Zachary slumped somewhat in 1925. Although his 33 starts led the league, his 12–15 record and 3.85 ERA were not quite up to his previous standards. He also worked ineffectively in the World Series, losing game five to the Pirates in relief. The next February he was traded to the St. Louis Browns, along with Win Ballou, in exchange for Joe Bush and Jack Tobin. He was reacquired by Washington in the summer of 1927 in a trade for fellow North Carolina pitcher Alvin

Crowder. It was this trade that put Zachary on the mound for Ruth's famous home run.[10] Zachary later recalled that "I gave Ruth a curve, low and outside. It was my best pitch. The ball just hooked into the right field seats and I instinctively cried 'foul.' But I guess I was the only guy who saw it that way. . . . If you really want to know the truth, I'd rather have thrown at his big, fat head."[11] On another occasion Zachary grudgingly admitted that "I don't see how he did it. He never hit a worse ball in his life."[12]

Ironically, Zachary was acquired by the Yankees the following season. In late August, Washington tried to sneak Zachary to Minneapolis as part of a waiver deal for pitcher Ad Liska. With ace left-hander Herb Pennock sidelined with neuritis, the Bronx Bombers were desperate for pitching help. Consequently Yankee manager Miller Huggins claimed Zachary for $7,500.[13] He went 3–3 down the stretch as New York held off the resurgent Athletics for the American League title. In his third World Series, Zachary threw a complete game 7–3 victory in game three, as New York swept the St. Louis Cardinals in four straight.[14] Zachary no doubt felt that he would see more World Series action in future years with the Yankees. The 1928 American League pennant was New York's third straight, while their four-game sweep in the series gave the Yanks eight consecutive wins in the fall classic. Featuring such stars as Babe Ruth, Lou Gehrig, Earle Combs, Bill Dickey, Waite Hoyt, and Pennock, and managed by Miller Huggins, New York was a prohibitive favorite going into the 1929 campaign. However, some observers recognized that the American League had a new bully on the block. For years Connie Mack had been assiduously rebuilding his Philadelphia Athletics. They had finished a close second to the Yankees in 1928 and were picked for the runner-up slot going into the 1929 campaign. Their list of stars, which included Al Simmons, Jimmie Foxx, Mickey Cochrane, Lefty Grove, and George Earnshaw, equaled that of the Yankees, or indeed any other team. The 1929 American League race figured to come down to these two powerhouses.[15]

Perhaps overstating his value to the Yankees, the 32-year-old Zachary was a brief holdout in the spring before coming to his senses. He made his first appearance in spring training in Pensacola on March 31.[16] The veteran was ready to go by opening day, however. This was not the usual opening day, for the Yankees had something new to offer their fans. For the first time, the players would wear identifying numbers on their backs.[17] Opening day was twice delayed by rain. Indeed, four of New York's first seven scheduled games were rained out, an ominous harbinger of things to come. Zachary's first regular season appearance was inauspicious. On April 21 he pitched the last 4⅓ innings in a 7–4 loss in Philadelphia in a game plagued by rain delays, a biting wind, and approaching darkness.[18]

Although Pennock was still sidelined by neuritis, the Yankees made little use of Zachary in the early going. His first start came on April 30 against his old Washington team. New York jumped out to a big lead before "old Tom Zachary began to feel his years and falter."[19] He left with a 9–4 lead, only to see the bullpen allow the Senators to gain a 9–9 tie before an eventual 10-inning, 10–9 New York win.

Zachary's first win came on May 7, his 33rd birthday. He won in relief against

St. Louis and Crowder. Zachary pitched a hitless eighth and ninth inning as the Yanks scored twice in the top of the ninth for a 6–5 come-from-behind victory. The game winner was a dramatic two-out, two-run double by Bob Meusel. Zachary's victory put New York in first place with a 10–4 record, one-half game ahead of 10–5 Philadelphia. The win came in the midst of an eight-game New York road winning streak that gave early, if misleading, evidence of their ability to withstand the Philadelphia challenge.

It was several weeks before Zachary posted his second win. On May 11 he pitched ineffectively in relief in a 13–7 loss to Detroit, retiring none of the four batters he faced. Three days later the Yankees were rained out again and dropped out of first place for good. The bad weather that had plagued New York all spring took a tragic turn on May 19. A sudden thunderstorm led to a stampede in Yankee Stadium's right field bleachers by shelter-seeking fans. The chaos resulted in 2 deaths and 62 injuries, many serious.

The Yankees' early season winning streak would be their high-water mark for 1929. In late May, they slipped further and further behind Philadelphia. A May 25 doubleheader split with Boston at Fenway Park left New York 18–13, in fourth place, 5½ games back. Zachary won the nightcap 8–3, scattering 13 hits in a complete game performance. Five days later New York lost twice at Washington. Although not charged with the loss, Zachary allowed two inherited runners to score in the ninth inning of game two. He entered the game with a 3–2 lead, the bases loaded, and one out. A bunt single tied the game and a clean single by Sam Rice won it for the Senators. At the end of May, New York was in third place with a 20–16 record, already eight games behind first place Philadelphia.

The Yankees made little progress against Philadelphia in June. Ruth missed much of the month with a bad cold. In late June, Philadelphia won three of five at Yankee Stadium to go up by 8½ games. At the end of the month, New York was in third place with a 38–26 record. Philadelphia was in first at 43–17, while St. Louis was in second at 41–26. Zachary pitched several times in relief during the month but had no starts, no decisions, and no saves. His best outing was on June 18 in a 7–4 loss to Boston, when he allowed only one hit in five innings.

At the beginning of July, Zachary was 2–0 and apparently on the way to an ordinary season. Perhaps a close brush with defeat on July 3—his closest of the year—turned his season around. He gained a starting nod against Boston but was hit hard and knocked out of the box early. He trailed 5–0 after five innings. New York got Zachary off the hook with 5 runs in the seventh, including a grand slam home run by Ruth, his 17th homer of the season. A single run in the eighth won the game for New York 6–5.

After this close call, Zachary's season took off, with four victories in July. On July 9 he won 8–7 in relief against St. Louis, pitching 1⅓ innings in a come-from-behind win. On July 13 he went nine innings in game one of a twin bill sweep over Chicago, posting a 4–2 win. His fifth victory, and one of his best performances of the year, came on July 19 when the Yanks split with Cleveland. Zachary threw a complete game three-hitter to win the opener 7–2. On July 28 Zachary defeated St. Louis at the stadium 7–6 in 12 innings. He garnered the victory with 7 scoreless innings in relief. Babe Ruth won the game in the bottom

Tom Zachary as a Yankee. (Photo Courtesy of the National Baseball Library, Cooperstown, N.Y.)

of the twelfth with his 24th homer. Earlier in the game, Gehrig had hit his 25th round-tripper. By this time Zachary was beginning to attract some media attention. After the win over St. Louis one paper acknowledged that "Zachary, for the past month, has been the topnotch pitcher in the Huggins ensemble."[20] He ended the month 6–0. Nonetheless, at the end of July New York was 9½ games behind the A's.

Zachary continued his good work in August. On the 4th the Yankees split a doubleheader with Cleveland. He won the first game, a 12–0 romp, pitching a complete game, allowing just 7 singles. The Yankees scored 6 runs in the first, 4 in second, and coasted to an easy win. Six days later Zachary posted a less impressive, although still solid, 4–2 victory over the Indians. Zachary carried a 3–0 lead into the sixth before losing his stuff and allowing 2 runs. Wilcy Moore picked up the save. Ruth hit his 29th homer in this game, the 499th of his career. His 500th came the next day. On the 14th Zachary pitched 3⅔ innings in an exciting 17–13 loss to Detroit, but was not involved in the decision.

On August 20 Zachary won his ninth game, 5–4 over the White Sox in Chicago, again with relief help from Moore. This equaled the 9–0 season compiled by Joe Pate of the Philadelphia Athletics in 1926, an unpublicized record to be sure. It was also one of the most unusual victories of Zachary's season. The game was designated Red Faber Day in honor of the veteran Chicago pitcher, a future Hall-of-Famer. Hundreds of Faber's Iowa friends and neighbors helped swell the crowd to 20,000 at Comiskey Park, where the White Sox ace was presented with an assortment of gifts, including a pot of gold worth $2,750 and a diamond ring. One Chicago paper noted that "Manager Miller Huggins cooperated in the day by sending forth another old warhorse" to face Faber.[21]

Late in August the slumping Yankees suffered the ignominy of being shut out in three consecutive games against the Browns. Quite a humiliation for baseball's most feared sluggers. By this point the Yankees were playing not for the pennant but for second place. Zachary had several no-decisions during this period and picked up his first save of the season on the 29th for Herb Pennock against Washington. At the end of August New York was in second place with a 73–51 record, 12½ games behind Philadelphia.

The Yankees played out the string in September against the backdrop of an unfolding tragedy. Zachary won his tenth game on the 1st, beating Boston 6–4. This moved him ahead of Pate. Zachary scattered 14 hits in 9 innings, while Ruth hit his 40th home run. New York jumped to a 6–0 lead after 5½ innings. The Red Sox pounded out 10 hits in the last 4 innings "but the distinguished southpaw thwarted every rally." He also singled three times. Zachary was no doubt pleased by his promotion from the faltering "Old Tom" to "the distinguished southpaw."[22]

Philadelphia dispelled whatever mystery still remained in the race on the second and third of September when they swept a three-game series against New York, leaving their rivals a distant 14½ games behind. On the 10th Zachary was hit hard in relief in an exciting 10–9 win over Detroit and was not involved in the decision. Ruth's three-run homer, his 44th, tied the game 9–9 in the ninth, after which New York scored the winning run. Zachary defeated Cleveland again on the fifteenth in game one of a doubleheader split. This performance was his best of the season. A throwing error by Cleveland catcher Luke Sewell led to an RBI single by Bill Dickey that gave the Yankees a 1–0 lead in the third. Zachary made the lone run hold up in a masterful performance. He allowed only four hits and 2 walks, and permitted no Indian runner to advance past second base. In the third, with runners on 1st and 2nd and 2 out, Zachary saved his shutout with a superb stop of a line drive off the bat of Luke Sewell. He also escaped a jam in the eighth created when an error and an infield single left runners on first and second with only one out.

Zachary's quest for an undefeated season was gaining some attention. After the eleventh win one paper wrote that "The callused knuckles of Old Uncle Tom Zachary . . . rapped insistently on the mythical door of baseball's Hall of Fame. . . . [He] thereby stands ready to be the only regular major league pitcher in history who ever went through a big time season without a defeat."[23] Three days later Zachary notched his second and last save of the season, getting the last out in the ninth in a 9–7 win over Cleveland, saving the victory for Fred Heimach.

As the Yankees played themselves out of the pennant in August and September, the health of manager Miller Huggins began to deteriorate. Despite his successes, the slightly built but intense Huggins had not had an easy tenure in New York. His periodic feuds with the difficult Ruth took their toll as did the widespread perception that almost anyone could have won with the material given Huggins. As a result, Huggins suffered from nerves, bad teeth, indigestion, headaches, and insomnia.[24] These problems, especially the headaches, were pervasive during the summer of 1929. Consequently when he entered New York's St. Vincent's Hospital on September 20 with "influenza," it was viewed as simply another in a long line of Huggins illnesses. It turned out not to be influenza at all, however. Rather it was a serious infection under his left eye. The infection led to blood poisoning and an uncontrollably high fever. On September 24, as Zachary defeated Boston 5–3 for his twelfth and final win, Huggins was undergoing two blood transfusions in a desperate but unsuccessful attempt to stem the tide. Huggins died at 3:15 P.M. on September 26. The same day, the Yankees clinched a bittersweet second place with an 11–10 victory over the Red Sox.[25]

Whatever acclaim Zachary might have received for his splendid record was lost in the Yankees' disappointing season and the life-and-death struggle of Miller Huggins. One tribute to Zachary came from the *Sporting News* sportswriter John Drohan, who observed that "for the most part, ol' Tom has rendered the enemy bats as mute as a stuffed cornet . . . his curves would turn a bathing beauty Nile green."[26] A close look at his 12–0 season shows that Zachary relied on more than just good luck and the big bats of the Bronx Bombers. His 2.48 earned run average would easily have won that title had he pitched a few more innings.[27] Only once, on July 3, did a late Yankee surge get Zachary off the hook and turn a loss into a no-decision. Despite an ill-defined role that saw Zachary variously wearing the hats of a spot starter—frequently in doubleheaders when pitching staffs became thin—long reliever, short reliever, and mop-up man, Zachary set a record in 1929 that has endured for six decades. The most formidable challenges occurred in 1937 when Cleveland's Johnny Allen posted fifteen wins before losing a 1–0 heartbreaker on the season's final day, and in 1959 when Pittsburgh relief pitcher Elroy Face won his first 17 decisions before finishing 18–1.[28]

Zachary did not pitch again in 1929 after his September 24 victory. Although it is possible this was an attempt to protect his perfect record, a more likely explanation is that the Yankees felt a need to rebuild and used the season's final games in the time-honored tradition of looking at young arms. That "Old Tom," despite his 12–0 season, did not figure in the Yankees' future became apparent when he was waived the following May. He was 34. Yet if the Yankees thought Zachary was over the hill he fooled them again. He pitched effectively, this time in the National League, until the middle 1930s. His mediocre won–lost records during this period were more a result of playing for second division teams than any decline on Zachary's part. Indeed, after leaving New York, Zachary played for a first division team only once: in 1932 for the fourth place Boston Braves.[29] Zachary hung up his spikes in the 1936 season after being acquired by the Phillies because he "always said if I ever get stuck in that Baker Bowl it would be time to quit." His 19-year career totals included 186 wins, 191 losses, and a 3.72 earned run average.

Zachary retired to Graham in his home county of Alamance where he made a comfortable living farming and dealing in real estate, and became a member of the North Carolina Sports Hall of Fame. A genial, good-natured sort, Zachary did resent somewhat the attention given to Ruth's 60th home run at the expense of the rest of his career. In 1961 he told a correspondent of a New York newspaper: "I used to get sort of annoyed because people didn't remember anything else. I used to wonder why nobody ever asked me how many times I struck out the big fellow, but I guess it's just because nobody gives a damn."[31] Sure enough, when Zachary died on January 24, 1969, his obituary in the *New York Times* was headlined "Tom Zachary, Pitcher, Is Dead; Served Ruth's 60th Home Run: Veteran of 19 Years Was Known Chiefly as Victim of Historic Smash."[32] *The Sporting News* likewise confirmed that his chief claim to fame was "something he always wanted to forget but couldn't. He served up Babe Ruth's 60th home run."[33] Yet the record suggests that this is an incomplete legacy. Zachary's baseball epitaph should be broadened to include the year he couldn't lose.

NOTES

1. Twelfth census of the United States, 1900, Alamance County, North Carolina, Population Schedule, Vol. 1, Enumeration District 8, Sheet 12, Line 65; Zachary file, National Baseball Library, Cooperstown, New York.

2. Donald Honig, *Baseball When the Grass Was Real* (New York: Coward, McCann, and Geoghegan, Inc., 1975), p. 15. The Ferrell farm, of course, also housed Wes Ferrell's older brother Rick, a member of baseball's Hall of Fame.

3. *New York Herald Tribune,* February 19, 1961.

4. Herb Appenzoller, *Pride in the Past: Guilford College Athletics, 1837–1987* (Greensboro: Guilford College, 1988), pp. 6–18. According to Appenzoller, 25 former Guilford players had turned professional by 1920, including 8 members of the 1914 team.

5. Appenzoller, pp. 18–21.

6. *New York Telegram,* August 21, 1929.

7. *New York Herald Tribune,* February 19, 1961.

8. Shirley Povich, *The Washington Senators* (New York: G.P. Putnam's Sons, 1954), pp. 100, 113, 117–119; Joseph L. Reichler (ed.), *The Baseball Encyclopedia: The Complete and Official Record of Major League Baseball,* Seventh Edition (New York: Macmillan Publishing Company, 1988), pp. 279–298.

9. Povich, *The Washington Senators,* pp. 121–129; Joseph L. Reichler, *The World Series: A 75th Anniversary* (New York: Simon and Schuster, 1978), p. 208.

10. Reichler, *The Baseball Encyclopedia,* pp. 299–300, 2707; Reichler, *The World Series,* p. 209.

11. *The Sporting News,* February 8, 1969.

12. John Tullius, *I'd Rather Be a Yankee: An Oral History of America's Most Loved and Most Hated Baseball Team* (New York: Macmillan Publishing Company, 1986), p. 94.

13. *New York Times,* August 24, 1928; *The Sporting News,* August 30, 1928; *New York Telegram,* August 21, 1929.

14. Reichler, *The Baseball Encyclopedia,* p. 2246; Reichler, *The World Series,* p. 213.

15. *New York Times,* April 13, 1929.

16. *New York Times,* April 1, 1929.

17. *New York Times,* April 16, 1929; Marshall Smelser, *The Life That Ruth Built: A Biography* (New York: Quadrangle, 1975), p. 391. The regulars took numbers according to their batting order. Thus Babe Ruth became 3, Lou Gehrig 4, and so forth.

18. *New York Times,* April 22, 1929. Unless otherwise indicated, all game accounts come from the *New York Times* and the *New York Herald Tribune* of the day following the game. Direct quotes will be footnoted.

19. *New York Times,* May 1, 1929.

20. *New York Times,* July 29, 1929.

21. *Chicago Tribune,* August 20, 21, 1929. Ironically, Pate never won another game in the majors after his 9–0 season in 1926.

22. *New York Times,* September 2, 1989. Zachary was a better than average hitting pitcher. His lifetime average was .226 with 6 home runs. Reichler, *The Baseball Encyclopedia,* p. 2246.

23. *New York Herald Tribune,* September 16, 1929. The real Hall of Fame was still years from opening, of course.

24. Smelser, p. 402.

25. Smelser, pp. 402–403.

26. *The Sporting News,* September 29, 1929.

27. Zachary's earned run average was 2.48 in 120 innings. Lefty Grove led the league with a 2.81 ERA. Reichler, *The Baseball Encyclopedia,* pp. 315–316.

28. Allen's final day loss came from his desire to equal the then American League record of 16 consecutive wins in a season. Ironically, both Allen, from Lenoir, and the pitcher who defeated him 1–0, Detroit's Jake Wade, from Morehead City, were also from North Carolina. Wade threw a one-hitter at Cleveland.

29. Reichler, *The Baseball Encyclopedia,* pp. 2246, 2707.

30. *New York Herald Tribune,* February 19, 1961; Reichler, The Baseball Encyclopedia, p. 2246.

31. *New York Herald Tribune,* February 19, 1961.

32. *New York Times,* January 26, 1969.

33. *The Sporting News,* February 8, 1969.

Baseball and the Reconstitution of American Masculinity, 1880–1920

MICHAEL S. KIMMEL

All boys love baseball. If they don't they're not real boys.
ZANE GREY

Baseball is sport as American pastoral: more, perhaps, than any other sport, baseball evokes that nostalgic longing, those warm recollections of boyhood innocence, the balmy warmth of country air, the continuity of generations. More than this, baseball is a recollection of the America we have lost—languid and rural. The ballpark itself is a bucolic patch of green nestled in the burgeoning urban landscape. Baseball expresses the contradictions that lie at the heart of American culture.

And baseball is about both remaining a boy and becoming a man. Like other sports, baseball fuses work and play, transforming play into work and work into play, and thus smoothing the transition from boyhood to manhood. Play as work (the "professional" athlete who gets paid to play sports) generates adult responsibility and discipline; work as play (the incorporation of sport either literally, as in corporate softball leagues, or as metaphor as assembly lines compete with one another) allows one to enjoy the economic necessity of working. Some contemporary studies suggest that men who were successful as boyhood athletes become more successful in business; many cutting-edge corporations have introduced team sports among managers on the premise that such teamwork will increase productivity.

But unlike other sports, baseball inspires a literary eloquence that is unmatched, perhaps because it is so delicately poised between boyhood and manhood. No other sport has produced a Roger Angell or a Donald Hall, each of whom is preoccupied with the link between baseball and family memory. For Angell "going through baseball record books and picture books is like opening a family album stuffed with old letters, wedding invitations, tattered newspaper clippings, graduation programs, and curled up darkening snapshots," so that, for writer and fan, baseball players "seem like members of our family, or like trusted friends" (Angell, 1982: 10, 199). And Hall underscores how baseball "connects American males with each other, not only through bleacher friendships and neighbor loyalties, not only through barroom fights, but, most importantly, through generations"; he continues:

> Baseball is fathers and sons. Football is brothers beating each other up in the backyard, violent and superficial. Baseball is the generations, looping backward forever with a million apparitions of sticks and balls, cricket and rounders, and the game the Iroquois played in Connecticut before the English came. Baseball is fathers and sons playing catch, lazy and murderous, wild and controlled; the profound archaic song of birth, growth, age, and death. This diamond encloses what we are (Hall, 1985: 49, 30).

In this essay, I will examine one of the ways in which "this diamond encloses what we are," by looking at the historical links between baseball and masculinity in the United States. Focusing on the rise of baseball at the turn of the century, I will explore two themes, well developed by others, in order to make a third thematic argument. Looking back at the ways in which the rise of organized participatory sports was offered as a corrective to a perceived erosion of traditional masculinity in the late nineteenth century, and how the rise of mass-level spectator sports was part of the shift from a culture of production to a culture of consumption, I will argue that baseball was a key institutional vehicle by which masculinity was reconstituted and by which Americans accommodated themselves to shifting structural relations. Specifying the terms on which sports reconstituted American masculinity, I shall link participation and spectatorship, and explore how baseball provided an institutional nexus for a manhood that could be experienced as personally powerful while it simultaneously facilitated the emergence of a docile and disciplined labor force.

I. STRUCTURES AND FORCES

The early nineteenth century provided a fertile environment for an expansive American manhood. Geographic expansion combined with rapid industrial and urban growth to fuel a virile optimism about social possibilities. The Jacksonian assault against "effete" European bankers and the "primitive" Native American population grounded identity in a "securely achieved manhood" (Rogin, 1975: 162). But by mid-century, "the walls of the male establishment began to crack" as social and economic changes eroded the foundations of traditional American masculinity. Westward expansion came to an abrupt end at the Pacific coast, and rapid industrialization radically altered men's relationship to their work. The independent artisan, the autonomous small farmer, the small shopkeeper, were everywhere disappearing. Before the Civil War, almost nine of every ten American men were farmers or self-employed businessmen; by 1870, that figure had dropped to two of three, and by 1910, less than one of three American men were as economically autonomous. Increased mechanization and routinization of labor accompanied rapid industrialization; individual workers were divorced from control over the labor process as well as dispossessed of ownership (see Braverman, 1974).

Simultaneously, social changes further eroded American men's identities. In the burgeoning cities, white Anglo-Saxon native-born men felt threatened by waves of immigrants. In 1870, for example, of the nearly one million people who lived in New York City, 4 of every 9 were foreign born (Adelman, 1986: 21). The rise of the women's movement in the late nineteenth century spelled the beginning of the end for men's monopoly over the ballot box, the college classroom, the professional school. The "New Woman"—single, upwardly mobile, sexually active, professionally ambitious, and feminist—exacerbated men's insecurity and malaise.

The "crisis" of masculinity in the late nineteenth century emerged from these structural and social changes, as "the familiar routes to manhood were either washed out or roadblocked" (Hartman, 1984: 13). This was not a generic crisis, experienced by all men in similar ways, but a crisis of middle-class white masculinity, a crisis in the dominant paradigm that was perceived as threatened by the simultaneous erosion of traditional structural foundations (economic autonomy, the frontier), new gains for women, and the infusion of nonwhite immigrants into industrial cities. It was a crisis of economic control, a struggle against larger units of capital that eroded workplace autonomy, and new workers (immigrants and women) who were seen as displacing traditional American men. And it was also a political crisis, pitting the traditional small town and rural white middle-class masculinity against new contenders for political incorporation. It was a crisis, in this sense, of gender hegemony, of whether or not the traditional white middle-class version of masculinity would continue to prevail over both women and nonwhite men. And therefore to understand how baseball articulated with these various dimensions of crisis in hegemonic masculinity, we will need to draw on analyses of the relations among various social classes, the relations between whites and nonwhites, and the relations between women and men.

Responses to the turn-of-the-century crisis of masculinity varied tremendously, especially given the simultaneity of the forces that seemed to be affecting middle-class white men. One reaction, the *antifeminist backlash,* sought to restore traditional gender arrangements in an effort to preserve a threatened masculinity. Antifeminists believed that if women would get out of the public sphere and go back to the private sphere, where, antifeminists argued, they belonged, the adverse impact of these social changes would be eliminated. A second reaction, the *profeminist reaction,* saw feminism as auguring important positive changes for men as well as for women. Thus profeminist men supported those reforms—coeducation, woman suffrage, women's entry into the labor force, birth control, higher education for women—that antifeminists opposed (see Kimmel, 1987 and Kimmel and Mosmiller, 1991).

A third group believed that the problem lay not among women but among men, and specifically in the enervating effects of modern society on the nation's collective manhood. This *masculinist* response sought to revitalize masculinity, to return to men the vitality and strength which had been slowly draining from American men.[4] Masculinism, both interpersonally and institutionally, articulated with other turn-of-the-century social currents, among them a rejection of the city as a den of corruption where healthy country men were transformed into effete dandies as hordes of unwashed immigrants threatened the racial purity of the nation. "Get your children into the country" one real estate advertisement for Wilmington, Delaware urged potential buyers in 1905. "The cities murder children. The hot pavements, the dust, the noise, are fatal in many cases and harmful always. The history of successful men is nearly always the history of country boys" (cited in Jackson, 1985: 138). Frank Lloyd Wright's antiurban tirade in *The Future of Architecture* captures this sentiment, and links it to the perceived feminization of American culture:

> A place fit for banking and prostitution and not much else . . . a crime of crimes . . . a vast prison . . . triumph of the herd instinct . . . outgrown and overgrown . . . the greatest mouth in the world . . . humanity preying upon humanity . . . carcass . . . parasite . . . fibrous tumor . . . pig-pile . . . incongruous mantrap of monstrous dimensions . . . Enormity devouring manhood, confusing personality by frustration of individuality (Wright, 1970:167).

Antiurban sentiments were also fueled by a nativist racism that saw cities as the breeders of an immigrant threat.

Institutionally, the masculinist effort to stem the tide of feminization of American manhood included the development of the YMCA and the Boy Scouts, in which young boys could experience the remedial effects of the wilderness away from the feminizing clutches of mothers and teachers. If consumer society had "turned robust manly, self-reliant boyhood into a lot of flat-chested cigarette smokers with shaky nerves and doubtful vitality," as Chief Scout Ernest Thompson Seton had it (cited in Macleod, 1983: 49), then the BSA could "counter the forces of feminization and maintain traditional manhood" (Hantover, 1980: 293).

Masculinism included the Muscular Christianity movement, in which, through texts like Thomas Hughes' *The Manliness of Christ* (1880) and Carl Case's *The Masculine in Religion* (1906), the image of Jesus was transformed from a beatific, delicate, soft-spoken champion of the poor into a musclebound he-man whose message encouraged the strong to dominate the weak. Jesus was no "dough-faced lick-spittle proposition" proclaimed itinerant evangelist Billy Sunday, but "the greatest scrapper who ever lived" (cited in McLoughlin, 1955: 179). A former professional baseball player turned country preacher, Sunday drew enormous crowds to his fiery sermons where he preached against institutionalized Protestantism. "Lord save us from off-handed, flabby-cheeked, brittle-boned, weak-kneed, thin-skinned, pliable, plastic, spineless, effeminate, ossified three-karat Christianity" (cited *Ibid.:* 175). Masculinism also promoted a revived martial idealism, and found a new hero in Theodore Roosevelt who believed that "the greatest danger that a long period of profound peace offers to a nation is that of [creating] effeminate tendencies in young men" (Thompson, 1898: 610). Perhaps masculinity could be retrieved through imperial expansion, since, as General Homer Lea put it, "[as] manhood marks the height of physical vigor among mankind, so the militant successes of a nation mark the zenith of its physical greatness" (cited in Roszak and Roszak, 1975: 92; see also Levine, 1985; Mrozek, 1983; and Lears, 1982).

And masculinism also found institutional expression in the sports craze that swept the nation in the last decade of the century. The first tennis court was built in Boston in 1876, the first basketball court in 1891. The American Bowling Congress was founded in 1895 and the Amateur Athletic Union established in 1890. Sports offered a counter to the "prosy mediocrity of the latter-day industrial scheme of life," as Thorstein Veblen put it in *The Theory of the Leisure Class* (1899: 208), revitalizing American manhood while it replaced the frontier as "the outlet through which the pressure of urban populations was eased" (Green, 1986: 215). Nowhere was this better expressed than in the rapid rise of baseball, both as a participatory sport and as a spectator sport. Baseball became one of the central mechanisms by which masculinity was reconstituted at the turn of the century, as well as one of the vehicles by which the various classes, races, and ethnicities that were thrown together into the urban melting pot accommodated themselves to industrial class society and developed the temperaments that facilitated the transition to a consumer culture.

II. PLAYING

The whole test of the worth of any sport should be the demand that sport makes upon those qualities of mind and body which in their sum we call manliness.

THEODORE ROOSEVELT

In the late nineteenth century, America went "sports crazy" (Dubbert, 1979: 175). The nation had never been as preoccupied with physical health and exercise; Americans flocked to health spas, consumed quantities of potions and elixirs (like the 63 imported and 42 domestic bottled waters advertised by one firm in 1900), lifted weights, listened to health reformers extoll the tonic virtues of country air and bland high-fiber diets, raced through urban parks on bicycles, and tried their hands at tennis, golf, boxing, cricket and baseball (see Green, 1986). The search for individual physical perfection masked a deeper hopelessness about the possibility of social transformation, and also linked fears of cultural enervation and individual lethargy and failure of nerve.

Sports were heralded as character-building; health reformers promised athletic activity would not only make young men healthier, but instill moral virtues as well. Sports were a central element in the fight against feminization; sports made boys into men. In advice books, which counseled concerned parents about proper methods of child rearing, sports were invariably linked with the acquisition of appropriate gender-role behavior for males. Sports had been recommended as early as the 1840s and 1850s, when the "confusion and ambivalence within the baseball fraternity over the boundary between men and boys resembled the tensions between the culture of respectability and the culture of the street" (Goldstein, 1989: 48). Now they were *necessary,* according to D.A. Sargent, to "counteract the enervating tendency of the times and to improve the health, strength, and vigor of our youth" since they provided the best kind of "general exercise for the body, and develop courage, manliness, and self-control" (cited in Dubbert, 1979: 169). Sports aided youth in "the struggle for manliness," wrote G. Walter Fiske in *Boy Life and Self-Government* (cited in Mrozek, 1983: 207). Sports were especially advised for boys because, as physical education professor Luther Halsey Gulick, Jr. put it, "athletics do not test womanliness as they test manliness" (cited in Rader, 1983: 165).

Manhood required proof, and sports were a "place where manhood was earned," not as "part of any ceremonial rite of passage but through the visible demonstration of achievement" (Adelman, 1986: 286). Such demonstration was particularly important because lurking beneath the fear of feminization was the fear of effeminacy and homosexuality, which had emerged in visible subcultures in urban centers. One English newspaper championed athletics for substituting the "feats of man for the 'freak of the fop,' hardiness for effeminacy, and dexterity for luxurious indolence" (Adelman, 1986: 284).

Some were less sanguine about sports' curative value. Thorstein Veblen's blistering critique of the nascent consumer culture, *The Theory of the Leisure Class,* suggests that organized sports are an illusory panacea. For the individual man, athletics are no sign of virtue, since "the temperament which inclines men to [sports] is essentially a boyish temperament. The addiction to sports therefore in a peculiar degree marks an arrested development of the man's moral nature" (Veblen, 1899: 200). And culturally, sports may be an evolutionary throwback, as they "afford an exercise for dexterity and for the emulative ferocity and astuteness characteristic of predatory life" (*Ibid.,* p. 203).

Most commentators saw sports as the arena for men to achieve physical manhood, but believed that organized sports would instill important moral values as well.[6] Here, especially, the masculinist response to the crisis of masculinity resonated with the antiurban sentiments of those who feared modern industrial society. Sports could rescue American boys from the "haunts of dissipation" that seduced them in the cities—the taverns, gambling parlors, and brothels, according to the *Brooklyn Eagle* (cited in Adelman, 1986: 277). Youth needs recreation, the *New York Herald* claims, and "if they can't get it healthily and morally, they will seek it unhealthily and immorally at night, in drink saloons or at the gambling tables, and from these dissipations to those of a lower depth, the gradation is easy" (cited in *Ibid.,* 277).

And what was true of sports in general was particularly true of baseball. Theodore Roosevelt listed baseball in his list of "the true sports for a manly race" (along with running, rowing, football, boxing, wrestling, shooting, riding and mountain climbing). Just as horse racing had resulted in better horse breeding, Edward Marshall claimed in 1910, so baseball "resulted in improvement in man breeding" (cited in Spalding, 1911: 534). "No boy can grow to a perfectly normal manhood today without the benefits of at least a small amount of baseball experience and practice" wrote William McKeever in his popular advice manual, *Training the Boy* (McKeever, 1913: 91).

The values that baseball called into play were important to the man and central to the nation. The baseball player was "no thug trained to brutality like the prizefighter," noted baseball pioneer A. G. Spalding, nor was he a "half-developed little creature like a jockey" but an exemplar of distinctly "native" American virtues, which Spalding alliteratively enumerated in *America's National Game* (1911):

> American Courage, Confidence, Combativeness; American Dash, Discipline, Determination; American Energy, Eagerness, Enthusiasm; American Pluck, Persistence, Performance; American Spirit, Sagacity, Success; American Vim, Vigor, Virility (Spalding, 1911: 4; see also Levine, 1985).

Essayist Addigton Bruce added:

> Physical fitness, courage, honesty, patience, the spirit of initiative combined with due respect for lawful authority, soundness and quickness of judgement, self-confidence, self-control, cheeriness, fairmindedness, and appreciation of the importance of social solidarity, of 'team play'—these are traits requisite as never before for success in the life of an individual and of a nation (Bruce, 1913: 105).

And Henry Chadwick tossed in "courage, nerve, pluck and endurance" (cited in Adelman, 1986: 173).

Such values were not only American, but Christian, replacing the desiccated values of a dissolute life with the healthy vitality of American manhood. Chadwick saw baseball as a "remedy for the many evils resulting from the immoral associations boys and young men of our cities are apt to become connected with" and therefore deserving "the endorsement of every clergyman in the country" (cited in Adelman, 1986: 173). McKeever added that "baseball may be conducted as a clean and uplifting game such as people of true moral refinement may patronize without doing any violence to conscience" (McKeever, 1913: 101). Baseball was good for the body and the soul of men; it was imperative for the health and moral fiber of the body social. From pulpits and advice manuals, the virtues of baseball were sounded. Baseball "took manliness beyond a mere demonstration of physical prowess and linked it to virtues such as courage, fortitude, discipline . . . [and] concluded that if ball games called these virtues into play—as in fact they were critical to doing well at such sports—then ball playing was obviously one way of demonstrating manhood" (Adelman, 1986: 106).

One central feature of the values that were instilled by playing baseball was that they appeared, on the surface, to stress autonomy and aggressive independence, but they simultaneously reinforced obedience, self-sacrifice, discipline and a rigid hierarchy. This was also the case with the Organized Play movement, and other organizational efforts to counter cultural feminization (see Levine, 1985). The Boy Scouts instilled a "quest for disciplined vitality" (Green, 1986: 261) in which scouts are taught, in the words of founder Lord Baden-Powell, to "give up everything, their personal comforts and desires, in order to get their work done. They do not do all this for their own amusement, but because it is their duty to their king, fellow country-men, or *employers*" (cited in Rosenthal, 1984: 45–46; emphasis added). The results of this and other efforts were noted with glee by Octavia Hill, the celebrated English social reformer in the 1880s:

> There is no organization which I have found influence so powerfully for good the boys in such a neighborhood. The cadets learn the duty and dignity of obedience;

> they get a sense of corporate life and of civic duty; they learn to honour the power of endurance and effort; and they come into contact with manly and devoted officers . . . These ideals are in marked contrast with the listless self-indulgence, the pert self-assertion, the selfishness and want of reverence which are so characteristic of the life in the low district (cited in Hargreaves, 1986: 61).

For the boys learning to play baseball, these values were also underscored. The team always came first, and one always obeyed one's coaches and manager. What Veblen claimed about football is equally true about baseball:

> The culture . . . gives a product of exotic ferocity and cunning. It is a rehabilitation of the early barbarian temperament, together with a suppression of those details of temperament which, as seen from the standpoint of the social and economic exigencies, are the redeeming features of the savage character.
>
> The physical vigour acquired in the training for athletic games—so far as the training may be said to have this effect—is of advantage both to the individual and to the collectivity, in that, other things being equal, *it conduces to economic serviceability* (Veblen, 1899: 204; emphasis added).

Sports reproduced those character traits required by industrial capitalism, and participation in sports by working-class youths was hailed as a mechanism of insuring obedience to authority and acceptance of hierarchy. Baseball's version of masculinity thus cut with a contradictory edge: If the masculinity expressed on the baseball field was exuberant, fiercely competitive, wildly aggressive, it was so only in a controlled and orderly arena, closely supervised by powerful adults. As such, the masculinity reconstituted on the baseball field also facilitated a docility and obedience to authority that would serve the maintenance of the emerging industrial capitalist order.[7]

III. WATCHING

Just as on the field, so in the stands—baseball as a spectator sport was double edged, both facilitating accommodation to industrial capitalism as a leisure time diversion for the urban lower-middle and working classes, and, at the same time, being reshaped by them. Ballparks were located in the city and admission fees were low, so that "attendance at baseball games was more broadly based than at other spectator sports" (Adelman, 1986: 149).

Baseball did not spring to such popularity overnight, as restorer of both individual virility and national vitality; its emergence as the "national pastime" was deliberately crafted. In fact, in the early half of the nineteenth century, cricket was hailed for its capacity to instill manly virtues in its players. "Whoever started these boys to practice the game deserves great credit—it is manly, healthy, invigorating exercise and ought to be attended more or less at all schools," waxed the *New York Herald* (cited in Adelman, 1986: 105–106). In 1868, the *Brooklyn Eagle* informed potential spectators of a cricket match that they were about to see a "manly game" (cited *Ibid.*, 169). Baseball, in fact, was regarded as less than fully manly; one letter to the editor of a newspaper contended that:

> You know very well that a man who makes a business of playing ball is not a man to

be relied upon in a match where great interests are centered, or on which large amounts of money is pending (cited in Adelman, 1986: 167).

By the late nineteenth century, this relationship between baseball and cricket had been reversed. The man who played cricket, Albert Spalding warned, thought that his match was a chance "to drink afternoon tea, flirt, gossip, smoke [and] take a whiskey and soda at the customary hour" (Spalding, 1911: 7). How can we explain such a change? In part, the shift from cricket to baseball can be understood by looking at the changing class and regional composition of its players and its observers. Whereas earlier in the century baseball had been the domain of upper-middle-class men, by the end of the century it was played almost exclusively by lower-middle-class men. Similarly, the rise of mass spectator sports—the erection of the urban stadium, the professionalization of teams and leagues, the salaries of players—changed dramatically the class composition of the baseball fan (see Reiss, 1980, and Barth, 1980). The values that were thought to be instilled by *playing* baseball had made the imaginative leap to an ability to be instilled by *watching* baseball. And values of discipline, self-control, sacrifice for the team, and an acceptance of hierarchy were central to the accommodation of a rapidly developing working class to the new industrial order.

It was during this period of dramatic economic expansion in the late nineteenth century that baseball "conquered" America. In the first few decades following the Civil War, the baseball diamond was standardized, teams and leagues organized, rules refined, game schedules instituted, and grand tours undertaken by professional baseball teams (see Barth, 1980: 159). And though the earliest baseball teams, like the New York Knickerbockers, were made up of wealthy men, baseball was soon being played by small town lower-middle-class men and watched by their urban counterparts (see Mrozek, 1983: 104).

As Gunther Barth (1980) argues, the urban baseball park was one of the new important locations for social life in the burgeoning late nineteenth century city, especially for white, middle- and working-class, native-born men. Like the vaudeville theater, the department store, and the urban park, the stadium provided a world of abundance and fantasy, of excitement and diversion, all carefully circumscribed by the logic of urban capitalism. Here the pain and alienation of urban industrial work life was soothed, and the routine dull grayness of the urban landscape was broken up by these manicured patches of green. The baseball park was a constructed "imitation of a pastoral setting" in the city, in which identification with one's professional team provided a "feeling of community" with anonymous neighbors; the ballpark was "a rural haven of shared sentiments" in the midst of the alienating city (Barth, 1980: 190, 191).[8]

If masculinity had earlier been based on economic autonomy, geographic mobility, and success in a competitive hierarchy, baseball—among the other new social institutions of the turn of the century—allowed the reconstitution of those elements in a controlled and contained location. On the field, baseball promoted values essential to traditional masculinity: courage, initiative, self-control, competitive drive, physical fitness. In the stands, the geographic frontier of the mid-century was replaced by the outfield fences and by the mental frontiers between rival cities. (What we lose in reality, we recreate in fantasy, as a Freudian axiom might have it.)

Baseball was fantasy, and it was diversion. "Men anxious to be distracted from their arduous daily routines provided a natural market for the product of the new industry" (Barth, 1980: 151). And baseball was viewed by boosters as a safety valve, allowing the release of potential aggression in a healthy, socially acceptable way; it was a "method of gaining momentary relief from the strain of an intolerable burden, and at the same time finding a harmless outlet for pent-up emotions" which otherwise "might discharge themselves in a dangerous way" (Bruce, 1913: 106). For the fan, baseball was, Bruce noted, "catharsis."

To some supporters, the virtue of spectatorship was analogous to the virtues instilled by participation. Supporters of Sunday baseball extolled the healthy, invigorating and uplifting atmosphere of the ballpark. William Kirk, for example, called baseball "one of the greatest agents for clean living and temperate living." As he explained, "it is far better for the young boys and the old boys to be out in the light and the open air, watching a clean and thrilling struggle that is played where all may see, than to sit with legs crossed under some taproom table, dealing out grimy cards or grimier stories" (Kirk, 1908: 48). In 1912, President William Howard Taft proclaimed himself a baseball fan, linking class, gender, and moral virtue:

> Baseball takes people into the open air—it draws out millions of factory hands, of tradesmen and interior laborers of all kinds, who spend their afternoons whenever possible in a healthful, genuinely inspiring contest in the warm sunshine and fresh air, when many other sports, and in fact all natural tendencies conspire to keep them indoors engaged in various kinds of unwholesome and unhealthful pastime (Murphy, 1912: 3–4).

Like the frontier, the baseball park was also celebrated as "democratic." The experience of spectatorship, baseball's boosters claimed, was a great social leveler:

> The spectator at a ball game is no longer a statesman, a lawyer, broker, doctor, merchant, or artisan, but just plain every-day man, with a heart full of fraternity and good will to all his fellow men—except perhaps the umpire. The oftener he sits in grand stand or 'bleachers,' the broader, kindlier, better man and citizen he must tend to become (Bruce, 1913: 107).

"The genius of our institutions is democratic," Albert Spalding gushed, and "Baseball is a democratic game" (Spalding, 1911: 6).

Supporters of Sunday baseball celebrated the "real democracy of spirit" that baseball embodied. "One thing in common absorbs us," wrote the Rev. Roland D. Sawyer in 1908, "we rub shoulder, high and low; we speak without waiting for an introduction; we forget everything clannish, all the petty conventionalities being laid aside" (Sawyer, 1908: 31–32). And novelist and former minor league ballplayer Zane Grey echoed these sentiments when he wrote:

> Here is one place where caste is lost. Ragamuffins and velvet-breeched, white collared boys stand in that equality which augurs well for the future of the stars and

stripes. Dainty clothes are no bar to the game if their owner is not afraid to soil them (Grey, 1909: 12).

Such mythic egalitarianism, however, ignored the power relationships that made American democracy possible. For the experience of incorporation into community was based on exclusion: the exclusion of nonwhite men and the exclusion of women. The ballpark was a "haven in a heartless world" for white lower-middle-class men, and the community and solidarity they found there, however based on exclusion, facilitated their accommodation to their position in class society. Professional spectator sports maintained the "rigid gender division and chauvinist masculine identity," as well as the strict separation between whites and nonwhites that provided some of the main cultural supports of class domination (Hargreaves, 1986: 43). While providing the illusion of equality, and offering organized leisure time distraction, as well as by shaping working-class masculinity as constituted by its superiority over women, baseball helped white working-class men accommodate themselves to the emergent order. Embedded in a constellation of institutional and organizational solutions to the crisis of masculinity at the turn of the century, baseball was an expression of men's powerlessness—working-class accommodation to class hierarchy and workplace obedience—on the one hand, and simultaneously an expression of men's power—or at least the power of men over women and of some men (white, native-born) over other men, as well as the power of the working class to reshape the institutions in which they found themselves to better serve their needs. Thus it may have allowed men to experience their incorporation as alienated workers as a series of minor victories, so that their loss in the larger class war was far less painful.

IV. REPRODUCING

Baseball, as participatory sport and as spectator sport, served to reconstitute masculinity whose social foundations had been steadily eroding, and in so doing, served to facilitate the reproduction of a society based upon gender, racial, and class hierarchies. For it was not just "masculinity" that was reconstituted through sports, but a particular kind of masculinity—white and middle-class—that was elaborated. And part of the definition of that masculinity was hierarchy—the power of whites over nonwhites (including all ethnic immigrants to the cities), of the upper classes over the working classes, and of men over women. Baseball as a solution to the crisis of masculinity perpetuated hierarchy even as it seemed to challenge it.

By the end of the second decade of the century, some of the innocence of this illusory solution was lost. In 1919, this world was shaken during the World Series scandal that involved the infamous Chicago "Black Sox," who had apparently "fixed" the series. The scandal captivated American men. Commercialism had "come to dominate the sporting quality of sports" (Filene, 1986: 139); heroes were venal and the pristine pastoral was exposed as corrupt, part of the emergent corporate order, and not the alternative to it that people had imagined. But by then it was too late: the corporate order had triumphed and would face little organized opposition from a mobilized and unified working class. The reconstituted masculinity that was encouraged by baseball had replaced traditional definitions of masculinity, and was fully accommodated to the new capitalist order. The geographic frontier where masculinity was demonstrated was replaced by the outfield fence; men's workplace autonomy and control was replaced, in part, by watching a solitary batter squaring off against an opposing pitcher. What had been lost in real experience could be reconstituted through fantasy. In collective terms, then, baseball was also designed, as A. Bartlett Giamatti quipped, to break our hearts, the hearts that yearned for collective solutions to class, race, and gender inequality.

The baseball diamond, as I have argued in this essay, was more than a verdant patch of pastoral nostalgia; it was a contested terrain. The contestants were invisible to both participant and spectator, and quite separate from the game being played or watched. It was a contest between class cultures in which the hegemony of middle-class culture was reinforced and the emerging industrial urban working class was tamed by consumerism and disciplined by the American values promoted in the game. It was a contest between races, in which the exclusion of nonwhites and non-European immigrants from participation was reflected in the bleachers, as racial discrimination further assuaged the white working class. And it was a contest between women and men, in which newly mobile women were excluded from equal participation (and most often from spectatorship); the gender hierarchy was maintained by assuming those traits that made for athletic excellence were also those traits that made for exemplary citizenship. The masculinity reconstituted on the ball field or in the bleachers was a masculinity that reinforced the unequal distribution of power based on class, race, and gender. In that sense, also, baseball was truly an American game. And if we continue, as I do, to love both playing and watching baseball, it is also a deeply ambivalent love, which, like the love of family or country, to which it is so intimately linked, binds us to a place of both comfort and cruelty.

REFERENCES

Adelman, Melvin L. *A Sporting Time: New York City and the Rise of Modern*
1986 *Athletics, 1820–1870*. Champaign, IL: University of Illinois Press.

Angell, Roger. *Late Innings: A Baseball Companion*. New York: Simon and
1982 Schuster.

Barth, Gunther. *City People: The Rise of Modern City Culture in Nineteenth*
1980 *Century America*. New York: Oxford University Press.

Broun, Heywood. "The Happy Days of Baseball" in *Brown's Nutmeg*, May 6.
1939

Douglass, Ann. *The Feminization of American Culture*. New York: Alfred
1977 Knopf.

Dubbert, Joe. *A Man's Place: Masculinity in Transition*. Englewood Cliffs, NJ:
1979 Prentice-Hall.

Filene, Peter. *Him/Her Self: Sex Roles in America* second edition. Baltimore:
1986 Johns Hopkins University Press.

Goldstein, Warren. *Playing for Keeps: A History of Early Baseball.* Ithaca, NY: 1989 Cornell University Press.

Green, Harvey. *Fit for America: Health, Fitness and Sport in American Society.* 1986 New York: Pantheon.

Grey, Zane. "Inside Baseball" in *Baseball Magazine,* 3(4). 1909

Hall, Donald. *Fathers Playing Catch with Sons.* San Francisco: North Point 1985 Press.

Hantover, Jeffrey P. "The Boy Scouts and the Validation of Masculinity" in *The* 1980 *American Man* (Elizabeth Pleck and Joseph Pleck, eds.). Englewood Cliffs, NJ: Prentice-Hall.

Hargreaves, John. *Sport, Power and Culture.* New York: St. Martin's Press. 1986

Hartman, Mary. "Sexual Crack-Up: The Role of Gender in Western History," 1984 unpublished paper, Rutgers University.

Jackson, Kenneth. *Crabgrass Frontier: The Suburbs in American History.* New 1985 York: Oxford University Press.

Kimmel, Michael. "Men's Responses to Feminism at the Turn of the Century" 1987 in *Gender & Society,* 1(3).

Kimmel, Michael and Tom Mosmiller. *Against the Tide: Pro-Feminist Men in* 1991 *America, 1775–1990 (A Documentary History).* Boston: Beacon Press, in press.

Kirk, William. "Shall We Have Sunday Baseball" in *Baseball Magazine,* 1(3). 1908

"Know Baseball, Know the American" in *American Magazine,* 76, September. 1913

Lears, T. Jackson. *No Place of Grace: Anti-Modernism and the Transformation* 1982 *of American Culture, 1800–1920.* New York: Pantheon.

Levine, Peter. *A.G. Spalding and the Rise of Baseball: The Promise of American* 1985 *Sport.* New York: Oxford University Press.

Macleod, David. *Building Character in the American Boy: The Boy Scouts,* 1983 *YMCA, and their Forerunners, 1870–1920.* Madison, WI: University of Wisconsin Press.

McKeever, William. *Training the Boy.* New York: Macmillan. 1973

McLoughlin, William G. *Billy Sunday Was His Real Name.* Chicago: University 1955 of Chicago Press.

Montgomery, David. *Workers' Control in America: Studies in the History of* 1979 *Work, Technology, and Labor Struggles.* New York: Cambridge University Press.

Mrozek, Donald J. *Sport and American Mentality.* Knoxville, TN: University of 1983 Tennessee Press.

Murphy, Charles. "Taft, the Fan" in *Baseball Magazine,* 9(3). 1912

Reiss, Steven. *Touching Base: Professional Baseball and American Culture in* 1980 *the Progressive Era.* Westport, CT: Greenwood Press.

Rogin, Michael. *Fathers and Children*. New York: Pantheon.
1975

Roszak, Theodore and Betty Roszak. *Masculine/Feminine*. New York: Harper
1975 and Row.

Sabo, Donald and Ross Runfola, eds. *Jock: Sports and Male Identity*. En-
1980 glewood Cliffs, NJ: Prentice-Hall.

Sawyer, Rev. Roland D. "The Larger Side of Baseball" in *Baseball Magazine*,
1908 1(6).

Spalding, Albert. *America's National Game*. New York: American Sports Pub-
1911 lishing Company.

Thompson, Maurice. "Vigorous Men, A Vigorous Nation" in *Independent*, 1
1988 September.

Veblen, Thorstein. *The Theory of the Leisure Class*. New York: Funk and
1899 Wagnalls.

Wright, Frank Lloyd. *The Future of Architecture*. New York: Dover.
1970

NOTES

1. Earlier versions of this essay were published in M. Messner and D. Sabo, eds., *Critical Perspectives on Sport, Men, and the Gender Order* (Human Kinetics Press, 1990) and A. Hall, ed. *Baseball and the American Culture* (Meckler, forthcoming). For critical and supportive readings of this work I am grateful to Judith Barker, Ron Berger, Peter Levine, Mike Messner, George Robinson, Michael Schwartz, and an anonymous reviewer for *Baseball History*. This essay is dedicated to George Robinson who can acknowledge baseball's sexism, racism and venality, and still remain a devoted fan and a loyal friend.

2. The material in this section is adapted from my "Men's Responses to Feminism at the Turn of the Century" in *Gender & Society* 1(3), 1987.

3. This dispossession and historical de-skilling does not mean, however, that industrial work was stripped of its gendered quality. It remained resolutely masculine, which is why the meanings of masculinity were suddenly contested terrain (see Montgomery, 1984).

4. Of course many masculinists were vigorously antifeminist. But the thrust of masculinism was indifferent to the institutional gains for women, and sought only the preservation of "islands" of masculinity.

5. An editorial advertisement in *Baseball Magazine*, 2(3), 1909.

6. The key term here is, of course, "organized" and I will return to that aspect in the next section.

7. I realize that this analysis gives a rather one-sided perspective, stressing the accommodationist qualities of organized sport, and the use of baseball particularly as a vehicle to pacify a potentially threatening working class by stressing both aggression and its structural boundaries for expression. Social historians of working-class life have also made clear the ways in which those against whom such leisure-time activities were deployed, or, more benignly, those for whom the spectacles were produced, also transformed those events, shaping them to fit their needs and maintain cultures of resistance, as much as they were rendered docile and obedient workers by them (see, for example, Rosensweig, and Peiss, 1986). I will elaborate this theme in the next section as well.

8. Such experiences of community are reproduced by baseball across generations, so that community with neighbors is linked with a relationship between father and son as fans. I recall vividly, for example, my first ride on the subway to Ebbets Field, when I knew everyone in the train was as adoring of the Dodgers as my father. And, of course, me. I remember reaching up to hold his hand as we walked to that sagging building, and gasping as we entered the stands when I

saw how bright and green the field itself was. One needn't be a psychoanalyst to understand how feeling so close to 32,000 neighbors was intimately linked to feeling so close to that most special person. The memory of community is linked to the memory of family love for generations of American men. And the sinews of that community are the shared idols of boyhood—his Rube Walker and my Sandy Koufax. Such links may help explain my continued passion for the game, both as a player and as a spectator. And, perhaps, why I still root for the Dodgers, who, from my perspective, are simply on a very long road trip.

On December 31, 1972, Pittsburgh's all-star outfielder Roberto Clemente took off on a mercy flight full of clothing and medical supplies for Nicaraguan earthquake victims. Sometime that night his plane went down in the ocean. His body was never recovered.

Searching for January

W. P. KINSELLA

The sand was white as salt but more finely textured, powdery as icing sugar, cool on my bare feet, though if I pushed my toes down a few inches yesterday's heat lurked, waiting to surface with the sun.

It was 6:00 A.M. and I was alone on a tropical bay a mile down the beach from our hotel. This close to shore the calm ocean was a clear, heartbreaking blue, the color that when viewed in a travel brochure sends pale northerners flocking to travel agents begging for a few winter weeks in one flower-scented paradise or another.

Fifty yards out a few tendrils of sweet gray fog lazed above the water. Further out, the mist, water and pale morning sky merged. On the walk down I had stopped to touch a few dew-covered hibiscus, soft as a lover, cool as the other side of a pillow.

The raft appeared slowly out of the mist, like something from an Arthurian legend. It was a large, inflatable life raft, colored the depressing khaki and olive drab of military camouflage.

It contained one man, kneeling in the front, directing the raft with a paddle. He waved when he saw me, stood up and called something in an urgent voice but I couldn't make it out. As the raft drifted closer I could see the lone occupant was tall and athletic-looking, dark-skinned with a long, lantern jaw and flashing eyes.

"Clemente!" was the first word I heard clearly. "I am Clemente! The baseball player. My plane went down. Days ago! Everyone must think I am dead."

The implication of what he said was slow to register with me. Clemente! It had been fifteen years. Was this some local fisherman playing a cruel joke on a tourist?

"Yes," I called back, after pausing too long, scanning his features again. There was no question in my mind that it was Roberto Clemente. "I believe everyone does think you're dead."

"We crashed on New Year's Eve," he said. "I'm afraid I'm the only one who survived."

He stepped lithely into the water, pulled the raft up onto the beach, tossed the single paddle back into the raft.

"Five days I've been out there," he said. "Give or take a day. I sliced up the other paddle with my pocket knife, made a spear. Caught three fish. Never thought I'd enjoy eating raw fish. But I was so hungry they tasted like they were cooked. By the way, where am I?"

I told him his location.

He took a minute to think.

"It's possible. We crashed at night on the way to Managua. The plane was carrying three times the weight it should have, but the need was so great it was worth the risk. Supplies for the earthquake victims.

"You look so surprised," he said after a pause. "Have they called off the air search already, given us up for dead?" When I remained silent he continued. "Which way is your hotel? I must call my wife first, she'll be so worried."

"I'm very surprised. More than surprised. You are Roberto Clemente, the baseball player?" I asked.

"Of course."

"You were lost at sea?"

"Until now."

"There's something not quite right," I said.

"Like what?" said Clemente.

"Like what year do you think this is?"

"When we took off it was 1972, but New Year's Eve. We crashed in the ocean. It must be January 5th or 6th, maybe even the 7th, 1973. I haven't been gone so long that I'd lose track of the year."

"What if I told you it was March, 1987?"

"I'd laugh. Ha! Look at me! I'd be an old man in 1987. I'd be . . ."

"Fifty-two, 53 in August."

"How do you know that?"

"I know a little about baseball. I was a fan of yours."

He smiled in spite of himself. Everyone likes to be recognized, made to feel special.

"Thank you. But 1987? Ha!" He flexed his large hands, touched his spread fingers to his chest. "These are the clothes I wore the night we crashed. Do I look like I've been wearing these clothes for fifteen years? Is this a fifteen-year growth of beard?" he asked, rubbing a hand across his stubby chin. "A six-day beard would be my guess," he added.

His eyes studied me, thoroughly, as if I were an umpire who just called an outside pitch strike three: my pale, tourist's skin, the way I stoop slightly as if the weight of paradise is too much for me.

"Say, what are you doing out here alone at dawn? Are you escaped from somewhere?"

"No. But I think you may be. Believe me, it is 1987."

"Can't be. No way it can be. I'm me. I can tell. I'm 38 years old. I play baseball. I'm me. Roberto (Bob) Clemente. See my World Series ring." He thrust his hand toward me; the gold and diamond ring glittered as the sun blushed above the horizon.

While he was talking I was digging frantically in my wallet.

"Look here!" I cried. "I'm from Seattle. Here's the 1987 Seattle Mariners schedule." I held the pocket sized schedule out for him to look at.

"Seattle! Seattle doesn't have a team anymore."

"They have a new franchise, since 1977. Toronto came in the same year. Read the schedule, all the other teams are there."

He studied it for a moment.

"Well, it does say 1987. Still, it's crazy, man. I've only been gone a few days."

We sat down on the sand and I showed him everything in my wallet that might confirm the time frame: the issuance and expiration dates of my credit cards, an uncashed check, my driver's license, coins and bills.

"Try to remember when, and after, your plane went down. Maybe there's a clue there."

We walked slowly along the beach in the direction of the hotel and resort, but at the edge of the bay, at the point where we would turn inland, Clemente stopped. We slowly retraced our steps.

"It was late in the night, the plane was old; it groaned and creaked like a haunted house. I was sitting back with the cargo: bales of clothes, medical supplies, when the pilot started yelling that we were losing altitude. We must have practically been in the water before he noticed, for we hit the ocean a few seconds later, and I was buried under boxes and bales as the cargo shifted. A wooden box bounced off my head and I was out for a few seconds, or a few minutes.

"When I woke up I was in front of the emergency door, the cargo had rolled right over me and I was snug against the exit. The plane must have been more than half submerged. There was this frightening slurping, gurgling sound, as water seeped in. It was then I realized my clothes were wet. The raft was on the wall right next to the door. I pulled the door open and the ocean flooded in. I set out the raft, inflated it, reached back and took the paddles, and the big water canteen off the wall. I yelled for the others but I don't know if they were alive or if they even heard me. There was a mountain of cargo between me and the front of the plane.

"I climbed into the raft, paddled away a few yards, and when I looked back the plane was gone. I've been drifting for five or six days, and here I am."

"I don't know where you've been, but you went missing New Year's Eve 1972. They elected you to the Baseball Hall of Fame in 1973, waived the five-year waiting period because you'd died a hero."

"If what you say is true, what if I go back with you and call in?"

"You'll create one of the greatest sensations of all time. A veritable second coming."

"But my wife, my family. Will they all be 15 years older?"

"I'm afraid so."

"My kids grown up?"

"Yes."

"Maybe my wife has remarried?"

"I don't know, but it's certainly a possibility."

"But I'm 38 years old, strong as a bull. The Pirates need me in the outfield."

The 3,000th hit of Robert Clemente, September 30, 1972. (Photo by Les Banos; courtesy of the National Baseball Library, Cooperstown, N.Y.)

"I know."

"My teammates?"

"All retired."

"No."

"If I remember right, Bruce Kison was the last to go, retired in 1986."

"Willie Stargell?"

"Retired in 1982. He's still in baseball but not playing. He's 47 or 48 years old."

"Hard to believe. Then I suppose everyone in the Bigs that played at the same time, they're gone too? Marichal? Seaver? Bench? McCovey? Brock? McCarver? Carlton?"

"Carlton's won over 300 games, but he doesn't know when to quit. He's a marginal player in the American League. So is Don Sutton, though he's also won 300. Jerry Reuss is still hanging on, maybe one or two others from when you last played. Hank Aaron broke Babe Ruth's home run record, then a guy from Japan named Sadaharu Oh, broke Hank Aaron's record."

"And my Pirates?"

"Gone to hell in a handbasket, so to speak. They won the World Series in '78, Willie Stargell's last hurrah. They've been doormats for several seasons, will be again this year. Attendance is down to nothing; there's talk of moving the franchise out of Pittsburgh."

"They need a Roberto Clemente."

"Indeed they do."

He looked longingly up the inviting path that eventually led to the resort and the town. We sat for a long time in sand white as a bridal gown. He studied again the artifacts of my life. Finally he spoke.

"If I walk up that path, and if the world is as you say—and I believe you—I will become a curiosity. The media will swarm over me in a manner unlike anything I've ever known. Religious fanatics will picnic on my blood. If I see one more person, I'm certain I'll have no choice but to stay here."

"What are your alternatives?"

"I could try to fit in, to pass as an ordinary citizen who just happens to look like Roberto Clemente did 15 years ago. But if I see that other person, if I become real to the world, I may suddenly find myself white-haired and in rags, 53 years old."

"What about baseball?"

"I could never play the game again; I would give myself away. No one plays the game like Clemente."

"I remember watching you play. When you ran for a fly ball it was like you traveled three feet above the grass, your feet never touching. 'He doesn't touch the earth,' my wife said one night, 'he has invisible pillows of angel hair attached to his feet, that's what makes him appear to glide across the outfield.'

"Perhaps you could go to the Mexican Leagues," I suggested. "Remember George Brunet, the pitcher? He's still pitching in the badlands in Mexico and he's nearly 50."

"I also suffer from greed, my friend, from wanting to claim what is mine: my family, my home, my wealth. I'm afraid my choice is all or nothing."

"The nothing being?"

"To continue the search."

"But how?"

"I've searched a few days and already I've found 1987. Time has tricked me some way. Perhaps if I continue searching for January, 1973, I'll find it."

"And if you don't?"

"Something closer then, a time I could accept, that would accept me."

"But what if this is all there is? What if you go back out there," and I pointed to the hazy intersection where sky and water met, "what if you drift forever? What if you drift until you die?"

"I can't leap ahead in time. It's unnatural."

"If you came back to baseball Three Rivers Stadium would be full every night. You could make Pittsburgh a baseball city again. It would take great sacrifice on your part; you'd have to put up with the media, the curious, the fanatics. But perhaps it's worth what you're destined to do."

"I am destined to be found, maybe even on this same beach, but 15 years in the past, your past. I intend to do just that. I'll keep searching for January."

He walked a few steps in the direction of the raft.

"Wait for a few moments. I'll go and bring you supplies. I can be back in 20 minutes."

"No. I've managed well so far. I have five gallons of water, a bale of blankets to warm me at night, the ingenuity to catch food. I don't want to carry anything away from this time. Perhaps my footprints in the sand are already too much, who knows?"

"Well, good luck. I hope you find January."

He was wading in the clear water, already pushing the raft back into the ocean.

"If you find January, if the history I know is suddenly altered, I hope I went to see you play a few times. With you in the lineup the Pirates probably made it to the World Series in '74 and '75. They won their division those years, you know . . . you would have been the difference. . . . If it happens I'll be the only one to know . . ."

But Clemente had drifted beyond hearing. I watched as he paddled, his back broad and strong. Just as the mist was about to engulf him, as ocean, fog, and sky merged, without looking back he waved his oar once, holding it like a baseball bat, thrusting it at the soft, white sky.

A Dodger Boyhood

JACK KAVANAGH

The longest journey of my life began with a single, tentative step out of my Brooklyn neighborhood in 1930. Another 10-year-old boy and I, restless on a sunny Saturday morning, began walking toward Grand Army Plaza. We lived on 12th Street, just off Prospect Park. We had invaded the park many times but had never tried to cross the three miles to the other side. Small boys test the limits of parental tolerance by pushing toward increasingly distant goals. I am sure we followed the outer perimeter of Prospect Park because it seemed safer than venturing into the depths, which were still unexplored. I don't believe we had a particular destination that day, just a sort of "I dare you" challenge to range beyond the familiar nearby streets. So, we began a journey which, for me, still goes on although it has doubled back on itself and is traveled only in memory. It is the trail worn by Brooklyn Dodger fans who, since 1958, have no direction to move except backward in time. The traces of my own footsteps grow fainter as more recent travelers scuff away signs of my passage. Mine was a time when "Wait till next year" meant another try for first division, not a repeat meeting with the Yankees in the World Series.

* * *

Two small, knicker-clad boys walked along the Park Slope side of Prospect Park and, a mile later, circled Grand Army Plaza with its huge memorial arch. We were asked by a young man if we would pass out handbills to people entering the plaza from Eastern Parkway. He would give us each 50 cents. In advance. Being paid first offered an early temptation to cheat and challenged our budding integrity. We could have pocketed our half dollars and dumped the handbills down a sewer or into a trash basket. We didn't. We disposed of them all the way we had agreed to do. Then, instead of turning back, we pushed on along Eastern Parkway going past the Brooklyn Museum looking for a candy store where we could spend some of the money we had just earned. When we reached Bedford

Avenue I saw Ebbets Field for the first time. I probably had heard about it. Boys assimilate such knowledge. Still, in memory it looms as Camelot.

If an event was needed to fix the moment in my mind, it happened as we walked behind the cement right field wall. Suddenly the street swarmed with other boys running toward us. A baseball, having cleared the screen atop the wall, came bounding toward me. I like to think I fielded it with the grace of Glenn Wright, the Dodgers' star shortstop. I clutched it with suddenly sweaty palms. But it was my mine! In a few days the ball disappeared into pickup games played with other small boys on diamonds we improvised on the meadows of Prospect Park. It probably ended its usefulness wrapped in black friction tape. Small boys don't become collectors of baseball artifacts until they grow up and can buy back the talismans of their youth.

With each year my identification with Ebbets Field grew, as did my personal confidence. I would now cross Prospect Park on a time-saving diagonal just to hang around outside Ebbets Field. I began collecting autographs, cutting pictures from newspapers and pasting them in copy books whose unused pages should have been covered with school work. We lived in a 32-family apartment house and the superintendent stacked newspapers in the basement. He sold them, I'm sure, to a junk man but first he let me cut out the photos.

I went to Alexander Hamilton High School. This pleased my parents because it had a good reputation as a college preparatory school and I was happy because the school was only several miles beyond Ebbets Field from where I lived. If I walked home from school, I would reach the ballpark, where games then began at 3:15, by the second or third inning. There was a place where a game-starved fan could obtain a limited view. A commercial garage provided an accessible rooftop behind the left field grandstand. It could be reached by climbing a ladder inside the garage.

From the edge of the roof you could look into Ebbets Field. You couldn't see the whole diamond but, between the upper and lower tiers of the stands, there was a view of the core area of the game. Home plate, with the batter, catcher and umpire could be seen; the pitcher was visible, as was the first baseman. No other players were in sight. Fly balls disappeared from view but the crowd's reaction would tell whether they had been caught or had fallen safely. On a single, the batter became a visible runner on first base. On the occasional home run, we would see a hitter run toward first base then slow down as he rounded the bag and left our view. Moments later the player would reappear as he trotted back into sight and crossed home plate. We could keep track of the game from the right field scoreboard. It informed us of the score, the batter's number and the outs. There were no radio accounts of the games. The broadcast era would arrive in Brooklyn, with Red Barber, in 1939.

When night baseball came to Brooklyn on June 15, 1938, I was up on the garage roof. Now a high school senior, I had gone home first and then walked back across Prospect Park to Ebbets Field. I was intent on seeing as much as I could of the event. Even though the Cincinnati pitcher, Johnny Vander Meer, had pitched a no-hitter in his previous start, it had been in Boston against the Braves. We had a higher opinion of the hitting ability of our Dodgers. Larry MacPhail, the new general manager, had been providing us with new heroes.

Dolph Camilli, Leo Durocher and Freddie Fitzsimmons had come from other teams to join such sturdy standbys as Babe Phelps and Buddy Hassett. However, Van Mungo had lapsed from being a pitcher we could insist was the equal of Dizzy Dean and Carl Hubbell. We had read that inept front office work had let Vander Meer himself get away after the New Jersey youth had tried out with the Dodgers.

As the game went on, the right field score board registered only zeros for Brooklyn inning after inning. Not only were the Dodgers scoreless, they were also without a hit. Dodger players appeared on first base, but only after we saw them first drop the bat and trot there. Vander Meer was characteristically wild. Our Dodgers fell behind, trailing 6–0 with only one more inning left to win the game. They say that inside the ballpark the fans were rooting for Vander Meer to complete a no-hit game. I doubt it. Most of them probably didn't know the Reds pitcher was on the verge of making history with a second consecutive no-hitter. There were no ubiquitous transistor radios, a future plague of ballparks, to tell a dimly comprehending spectator, and people for rows around, what was happening. Even if the game had been broadcast, the superstition that it was a jinx to acknowledge a no-hitter in progress would have stifled any comment that an attempt to pitch a second no-hitter in a row was under way.

To the dozen or so of us on the garage roof, the game was not yet lost. We would have traded our roles as witnesses to baseball history for a winning Dodger rally in the ninth. When Vander Meer loaded the bases with walks, after two were out, we hoped the pesky shortstop, Leo Durocher, would keep the inning alive. When he sent a fly ball into the night, on a flight invisible from where we watched, a dozen breaths were held. We exhaled in common despair and, strangers again, but forever bonded by the inevitability of Dodger defeats, climbed down the ladder from the roof of the garage and passed into the dark night. The tiers of lights which had illuminated Ebbets Field for the first time were turned off and only the regular street lamps lit the outside of the ballpark. A block away I walked down Franklin Avenue, passing those coming from Ebbets Field. The shared attitude was not one of universal approval for Vander Meer's feat but of disappointment that the Dodgers had lost another game.

It was the last game I ever watched from the limited view on top of the garage behind left field. When the next season arrived I had graduated from high school and was a college freshman in need of a summer job.

* * *

Maybe it wasn't what my mother had wanted me to be when I grew up, but becoming an usher at Ebbets Field was the perfect summer job, one I held for 3 years between 1939 and 1941. After a boyhood spent outside the ballpark, the opportunity to be inside was a golden one. Word came from an older cousin that I should show up at Ebbets Field a week before the season began and apply for an usher's job. My name would be on a list. Jack Collins, the business manager of the Brooklyn Dodgers, had cleared me at the request of his nephew. The nephew was my cousin's best buddy.

Larry MacPhail was about to begin his second year as general manager of the

Ebbets Field. (Photo courtesy of the National Baseball Library, Cooperstown, N.Y.)

Dodgers. He had spent 1938 sizing up the team's needs. Now he was ready to act. Leo Durocher became the new manager; the team was in the market for better players and better ushers. This last news was hardly earthshaking, but MacPhail had been appalled by the ushers who had menaced patrons in the past. Bully boys from the political clubhouses, they had bulged in ill-fitting, sweat-stained red uniforms left over from years of second division squalor.

Larry MacPhail had admired the ushering crews in the Chicago ballparks. At Wrigley Field and Comiskey Park, they were trained and directed by Andy Frain. His ushers were college types: young, lean, clean-cut. Of course they could be corrupted easily with a couple of bucks from a fan in need of a seat on an S.R.O. day, but they were impressive in their uniforms. MacPhail had hired a Frain assistant, a peppery man named Jack Haines, to recruit and train a new corps of Ebbets Field ushers.

A long line of applicants stretched through the rotunda entrance to Ebbets Field. When you reached a certain gate you gave your name. The fellows just ahead of me were turned away. My name got me inside. I joined a growing group sitting in the lower grandstand behind first base. When about 100 of us were in place Jack Haines addressed us. We were hired, he told us, to be ushers. Not everybody would work every game; it would depend on the size of the crowd. For next week's opening day, we would all be used. Come back wearing a white shirt with a detachable collar. A green tie was required and black shoes. New kelly green uniforms would be provided.

The detachable collar was already passé, but maybe not in Chicago. The idea was to save on laundry bills. A man's collar got dirty faster than the rest of his shirt. Cuffs, too, could be detachable, but the changeable soft collar for shirts was basic. The scorned ex-President Herbert Hoover had favored stiff collars, but only he and altar boys wore them. I still had front and back collar buttons from my own recent years as an altar boy. So, with three detachable collars and two collarless white shirts, and a Chinese laundry around the corner from where we lived, I was set. The green necktie was easily come by in an Irish family. It was standard neckwear for St. Patrick's Day.

I needed one more item. There was a new federal requirement. I had to have a Social Security card. Then, newly identified as 067-12-5890, wearing a white shirt, attached collar and green necktie, and (at my mother's insistence) a raincoat and rubbers over my black shoes, I reported at Ebbets Field at 10 A.M. on a rainy Tuesday, April 18. It was to be Opening Day and the New York Giants would be the opponents. If it stopped raining.

I was not one of the ushers issued a uniform. I was given a green visored cap and a badge to pin to my coat. Mr. Haines gathered us behind home plate and read off our assignments. Mine was somewhere upstairs, far out along the left field foul line. We were to be in place when the gates opened and the crowds flooded in. At the moment, the only floods we anticipated were from the rain which pelted down on the infield tarp.

But the rain slowed to a drizzle. The ballpark opened as we ushers scurried to our posts. The players filed into the dugouts and one of them, a new pitcher, Red Evans, began to warm up. The game was played, the Dodgers lost and Evans began a slow exit to anonymity. It was the first of his eight losses, measured against only one victory, before he went back to the minors. It seemed a dismal way to start a season. We had a new manager and 100 newly minted ushers. Maybe it was the overcast day, but it looked as though we would eventually utter the inevitable Brooklyn sigh "Wait'll next year."

However, the team improved. And people heard about it because broadcasting the games on radio was part of the new era. MacPhail had imported Red Barber, with an improbable Southern accent, to report the games. A year before, I would have been happy to even hear the Dodgers games. Now I could simply walk in with the other ushers and see them. I cut as many classes as I could in April and May to be at Ebbets Field when the team was at home. Sometimes I worked, most times I didn't. The ranks of ushers multiplied. Every day new candidates would present letters of introduction from politicians. Borough President Robert Cashman must have sent several dozen nephews himself. Finally, one day, after the number required to work the game had entered Ebbets Field, the rest of us were stopped at the gate.

My first concern was just to get inside and see the game. I hadn't objected to democratically rotating the assignments. Until summer arrived, I had the alternate choice of going to my classes. Actually, I wasn't as upset about possibly losing my usher's job as I was about being denied entry to Ebbets Field on days

Ebbets Field scoreboard. (Photo courtesy of the National Baseball Library, Cooperstown, N.Y.)

when it wouldn't be my turn to work. I went to a nearby drugstore and called Jack Collins, the general manager. I reminded him whose cousin of his nephew's best friend I was and he instructed me to meet him at the rotunda gate. He said, "follow me" and led me at a brisk pace to Jack Haines' office. "The kid works. Every game." A man of few words and decisive action, Collins pointed at me, Haines blanched, and after that I found myself outfitted with a full uniform, no longer being issued only the cap of an extra, and working every game. It was my first experience in the use of influence for advancement.

There really wasn't all that much to know about ushering. The work was crowded into a busy half-hour just before game time. Ushers stationed themselves where ramps led ticket holders into the reserved and box seat sections. You had to find those with tickets in your section quickly and size them up for tip possibilities. The experienced usher ignored customers wearing loud sports shirts, particularly if they were with a date and paired with other couples. They would try to maneuver someone else into tipping the usher. At best, one would slip you a dime after you had led the way to a row of seats, lowered them, removed imaginary dust with a cloth carried in the hip pocket and returned the tickets with the hand held palm up.

The patron you were happy to spot was middle-aged, wearing a hard straw hat and a dark suit. Usually alone, he would put a quarter in your hand. The worst was the out-of-towner. We were never sure whether his effusive thanks, instead of a tip, was an act or naivete. Apart from tips, we were paid $3.00 a game and $5.00 for doubleheaders. On a good day tips would average about $6.00. Standing room crowds gave us an opportunity to make extra money. Working with the special cops, you could get a buck to allow someone to sit on one side of the aisle steps. A small trade could also be conducted by letting people take still empty seats after the game began. A full-time usher made about $80 a week when the team was home.

About half of us were saving most of what we made for college costs. Before a game, until the gates to Ebbets Field opened, the ushers would sit in two groups. On one side, the college students would have opened their books. They were offset by those just as diligently studying the *Daily Racing Form*.

As the season went along and the Dodgers rose in the standings, interest in the team grew. The crowds reached such numbers that, when the final day of the season arrived on October 1, Brooklyn's attendance had neared one million. The Yankees, winning a fourth straight pennant, and the Giants, playing in the bigger Polo Grounds, didn't reach that mark.

The season which had begun in a drizzle ended in one. On Sunday, October 1, the tail-end Phillies came to play a closing doubleheader. The Dodgers, who hadn't finished in first division since 1932, were in third place, a half game ahead of the Chicago Cubs. A rain out would insure they would end there, but Larry MacPhail wanted to play the game and bring the attendance over a million. A brand new car would be given to the one millionth customer. How they figured out who, among the 17,152 who splashed into Ebbets FIeld, was Mr. Million, I don't know. The final total was 1,007,762 and after the game, some happy fan climbed into the car that was driven, with its windshield wipers going, through the center field gate.

* * *

The 1940 season started with the Dodgers winning eight straight, climaxed by Tex Carleton's no-hitter in Cincinnati. There were new faces, one young enough to pass into the park with the college-type ushers. Twenty-year-old Pee Wee Reese became the new shortstop and was joined during the season by another boy wonder, Pete Reiser. Joe Medwick, a surly slugger from the St. Louis Cardinals "Gas House Gang," was added after the season began. He was beaned six days after joining the Dodgers by a former teammate, Bob Bowman. Larry MacPhail, who had been upstairs in the pressroom, raced down ramps and dashed out on the field. He raged in front of the Cardinal dugout, challenging their players to come out and fight. A later version has him vaulting over the railing of his field box. Wrong. I was ushering the section behind the Dodger dugout that day. When you drew that assignment you were particularly aware of where MacPhail was and who his guests might be. The Dodger G.M. rarely sat in his box, to the home plate side of the Dodgers bench. He preferred the pressroom and its bar. But, he was always likely to turn up during the game, and it would cost the usher his job if someone not invited by MacPhail was sitting in his box.

The ushering staff was generally the same as had been assembled the year before. We wore the same green uniforms. Jack Haines had gone back to Chicago, we understood. A younger man, blond and handsome as a matinee idol, Jack Jordan, had replaced him. The theatrical good looks were a family trait: he was the brother of the stage and screen actress, Helen Twelvetrees. Unlike Haines, who rarely donned the gold-braided white jacket of the chief usher, Jordan preened in his. Four others wore white jackets to indicate they had the rank of captain. Oddly, there was little envy among the green-uniformed ushers. A white jacket denied its wearer the opportunity to pick up tips by dusting off seats, and the position was too important to risk by hustling standees for a buck.

There was one other who wore an usher's white coat. As good looking as Jordan in a darker way, Johnny Freund's voice earned him the role of announcing the lineup over the P.A. system MacPhail had installed. Other than irritating umpire Larry Goetz one day by identifying him as "Goats," Freund did his job effectively. One day we ushers were asked to audition to replace him for the summer months, as Johnny would be acting in summer stock somewhere. During that theatrical engagement he changed his name. He left as Johnny Freund but came back in September as John Forsythe.

The Dodgers had been feisty in 1939. In 1940, Leo Durocher turned them nasty. His constant braying, "stick it in his ear," made Brooklyn everyone's enemy. It was "us against the world." Apart from the new young shortstop, Pee Wee Reese, and the player the Dodgers had to call up during the season, Pete Reiser, the team's character changed by acquiring older, hard-nosed players. Joe Medwick was foremost among these. One story that circulated among the ushers involved Reese and Medwick.

There was nothing in the press about the incident and it might have been quietly ignored by the writers covering the Dodgers. More likely, it was hushed up among the players. Forty years after the alleged event, I wrote to Pee Wee Reese asking for confirmation. He didn't deny it outright, only asked that it be left unexplained. I had reminded him of a fight that was supposed to have taken place in the clubhouse.

We had noticed something unusual during a game and Danny Comerford, Jr., an assistant to his father as a clubhouse attendant, explained it to us. We had seen Reese dash out to the left field and do something that required Medwick to bring his glove back to the bench. In those days gloves were left behind when players changed sides each inning. The story we heard was that Medwick, a notorious hazer of rookies, had first spit tobacco juice into Pee Wee's glove when going to his own left field position. Some of the older players urged Reese to retaliate, insisting that he take his own first chew of tobacco and work up an appropriate amount of spit. The next inning, the egged-on Reese raced to left field and unloaded into Medwick's glove.

After the game Medwick charged Reese, an angry bully who wanted to settle things with the slender youngster. At this point the team captain, Dolph Camilli, intervened. He had boxed professionally until his older brother, fighting as Frankie Campbell, had died after a bout with Max Baer in California. Baer became the heavyweight champion and Dolph Camilli an MVP for the Dodgers. The way we heard it, Camilli dropped Medwick with one punch.

Being an usher provided an insider's view of events that sometimes were inadvertently misrepresented in newspaper accounts. Often an usher literally had another point of view than the reporters in the press box behind home plate. For example, Brooklyn's nemesis in 1940 was the Cincinnati Reds. They had won the 1939 pennant with a team largely put together by Larry MacPhail when he had been their general manager. In 1940 they would repeat, mostly because of quirky games they won at Ebbets Field. The one which seemed to settle the pennant race early came in the opening game of a doubleheader on Sunday, June 16. The Dodgers were in first place and had beaten the Reds on Friday and Saturday. The team's emerging ace, Whit Wyatt, and Paul Derringer, one of the best right-handers in the league, pitched the first game. They matched zeros until two were out in the top of the ninth inning. Then Lonnie Frey, a former Dodger, lined a drive to right field. It hit the foot of the screen above the scoreboard and caromed high into the air. It came straight down, but not where right-fielder Joe Vosmik waited expectantly. Frey zoomed around the bases. It was a sure double, but when Frey saw Vosmik still pounding his glove in frustration he kept going. The third base coach waved him on and Frey scored standing up. He could have circled the bases all afternoon. The ball never came down.

The newspaper writers decided the ball had remained on a shelf formed by a wing of the scoreboard. The press box consensus was that the ball became stuck at the foot of the screen. Not so. My view was from Section 1 of the upper grandstand, next to the right field wall. I was looking down at the small, triangular platform toward which the ball had dropped. The ball didn't become stuck, it disappeared.

Before the game a workman had climbed up to replace some rotted boards. As the game was about to begin, he was nailing new 2 by 4s into place on the shelf when the umpires spotted him. Beans Reardon trotted out and ordered him down off the scoreboard. Apparently intending to go back and finish after the game, the carpenter left his toolbox behind. He also left the space for one board uncovered. That's where Frey's ball went, plummeting cleanly through the narrow opening. The next day the carpenter went back and rebuilt the platform so that it sloped, but it had been the missing board that gave Frey his home run and the Reds a 1–0 win.

Both at home and away the Dodgers were embattled. At Ebbets Field they were viewed as playing aggressive baseball. On the road they were vilified as dirty players with head-hunting pitchers and a manager without a conscience. Like hockey players whose brawls contagiously spread to the stands, the Durocher style of play drew people who not only wanted to be where the action was, they also wanted to be part of it.

Fighting among the spectators grew in direct ratio to the battles which broke out on the diamond. Somehow, Larry MacPhail expected his ushers to pacify the beer-swilling hooligans. He again turned to Andy Frain in Chicago, and the Ziegfeld of ushers rushed to Ebbets Field, accompanied by four assistants. We were to get a crash course in mob control. Better we should have been taught karate. After a lecture explaining how to identify the leaders who were stirring up trouble and how to talk them out of their intended mayhem, it occurred to the

Dodger management they already had special policemen to deal with roughneck patrons. Our problem as ushers was that, like in other situations in life, you couldn't find a cop when you needed one. By common consent we adopted the safest rule possible. When trouble loomed, we ran.

The ultimate in inciting the rougher elements in the stands came on September 16 when the Cincinnati Reds were visiting Ebbets Field. The game went into extra innings before the Reds scored a tie-breaking run on an umpire's questionable decision. If anything was arguable, Durocher would storm after the umpires. On a force play at second, Pete Coscarart had juggled the throw. Larry Goetz hesitated, then called the runner out. No, overruled George Magerkurth from third base. He had a clearer view and told Goetz the Reds runner was safe. The run which scored on the play counted, and won the game.

When the game ended several fans stalked the 6′3″ Magerkurth, a hefty giant at over 200 pounds, and one tripped him. The umpire was flat on his back and his assailant, a stubby slugger, was astride him and viciously pummeled him. All this went on behind my back and was unseen for the same reason by those ushers ringing the diamond. The fight took place behind them while they faced the stands. It was another technique imported from Chicago. It didn't make much sense to prohibit people in street shoes from crossing the diamond on the way to the center field exit gate after the players had been ripping it up with their spikes all afternoon. But it looked nice.

My own assignment when the game ended was to open a gate in the low fence that separated the downstairs reserved seat section from the rows of general admission seats farther back from the field. While I was doing this I heard noises that usually meant the blood lust of the crowd had been aroused. Whenever a fight breaks out in the stands at a ball game, people who have paid good money to see professionals compete climb on seats to watch a couple of amateurs maul each other. When I looked around I could see two men wrestling on the ground. One was an umpire. While I was sizing up this unlikely scene, I heard a deep-throated growl. A Neanderthal type was lumbering over rows of seats in my direction, grunting and shaking a ham-sized fist at me. I sensed that my green uniform identified me as "authority" and by some twist of a primitive intellect, this correlated with umpires and Magerkurth's decision. The beady eyes of the approaching beast glowed with hate. I did what any red-blooded usher would have done. I hurdled the rows of seats between me and the playing field.

Later I pretended I had been rushing to the rescue of umpire Magerkurth. Not so. He just happened to be where I was headed. My idea was to join the other ushers. They already formed two sides of a defensive square, although most of them were still blithely unaware that behind them an umpire was in a losing battle. A full-page picture of the huge Magerkurth being pummeled by a stumpy assailant sitting astride his stomach ran on the front page of the *New York Daily News* the next day. Behind them, an ushering colleague of mine, George Phillips, appeared to be gazing bemusedly at the fight scene.

Larry MacPhail was outraged. It was bad enough that his ushers hadn't intervened, the one whose picture was in the paper actually seemed to be enjoying the fight. When he arrived at the ballpark, Phillips was told not to bother putting on his uniform. Instead he was to report directly to Larry

MacPhail so that the general manager could fire him personally. If we'd worn epaulets, MacPhail would have snipped them off Phillips' uniform and handed him a white feather for cowardice.

Soon Phillips was back and putting on his uniform. We crowded around as he buttoned the coat and straightened his hat. Then we saw his swollen and blackened eye. No, MacPhail hadn't done it. In fact, it saved Phillips' job. MacPhail, having been told the picture had been snapped just as the usher had turned to investigate what was happening behind him, assumed Phillips had been slugged in the following melee. Actually, Phillips had gotten the shiner hours after the game was over. He had been the second choice of a young lady he had offered to escort home from a bar. In stepping outside to settle the issue with his rival, Phillips had caught a roundhouse thrown by a different antagonist for a different purpose. However, he accepted MacPhail's interpretation and the assurance of future assignments of choice ushering locations that went with it.

Magerkurth's assailant was a parolee, upset about a lost wager on the game and not a vindictive Dodger fan at all. Still, the hoodlum was portrayed sympathetically in the press. The era of "The Bums" had begun.

* * *

There was little concern expressed among the ushers for what was happening in Europe or Asia in 1941. We had our own wars. The Dodgers fought their way through another season. Strengthened by Kirby Higbe on the mound and catcher Mickey Owen, with Pete Reiser available from opening day and Billy Herman coming from the Cubs early in the season, Brooklyn seemed certain to make 1941 the "next year" we had been waiting for. The last time Brooklyn had won a pennant was the year I was born, 1920. Then, it seemed a longer time than looking back across the past fifty years does now.

There were frequent changes in the ushering ranks during the season. A peacetime military draft was under way. A few ball players went into the army: Hank Greenberg from the American League and Hugh Mulcahy, of the Phillies, from ours. Ebbets Field ushers seemed to be very attractive to draft boards. Every home series ended with a collection being taken up for some one of us who was being inducted. I had been classified 1A and told not to bother to return to college in the fall. The draft board predicted I would be called in October. I was as concerned that I would miss seeing the Dodgers in the World Series as I was about going into the service.

Everyone has a favorite year of his life. Mine is 1941. There was no point in saving money for another college year. Even clothes were a waste of money as I would be trading in my green Brooklyn usher's uniform for a khaki one. One of the summer's activities when the Dodgers were away on a road trip was to use the vacant Ebbets Field to play ball games in a four-team league. The ushers had two teams, one from the ranks of the regular staff and the other from the part-timers who worked when the crowds were large. The field maintenance people made up another team, and the league was rounded off by a team from the vendors. Thanks to a fat peanut seller who played right field for the vendors, I hit a ball off the Abe Stark sign at the bottom of the scoreboard. The sign,

The author at bat, with his father behind the plate, 1930. (Photo courtesy of Jack Kavanagh)

unmarked by a baseball since Woody English was reported to have done it during the 1930s, promised a suit of clothes if a batted ball hit it. Because of the angle, and with a major league outfielder always playing immediately in front of his sign, Mr. Stark got great publicity without having to give away so much as a vest. It's just as well that Uncle Sam was already pledged to give me my next suit as Abe Stark did not return my phone calls.

I was still available for ushering duties when the Dodgers cinched the pennant in Boston and bunting was hung at Ebbets Field in anticipation of a World Series victory over the New York Yankees. As a Dodger fan I was ecstatic. As an usher I was sanguine. The regular crowds would mostly be replaced by the kind of people who get the tickets that are denied to the fans who have supported the team all season. The World Series crowd would be "out-of-towners" who never seemed to know they were expected to tip the usher who showed them to their seats. Worse, there would be no standing room crowds to squeeze into places on the steps. Although we did get to work the three games scheduled for Brooklyn, they were emotional disasters as well as meager paydays.

The first game played at Ebbets Field, after the two games at Yankee Stadium had been split, was on October 4. Freddie Fitzsimmons was knuckleballing the Yankees to impotency until his rival pitcher, Marius Russo, also pitching shutout ball, lined a drive off Fitz's knee. The ball bounced as high as the light towers, finally came down like a pop fly, and was caught by Pee Wee Reese to end the seventh inning. Fitz was on the ground, his knee broken. Hugh Casey couldn't keep New York from scoring twice in the eighth and we lost 2–1.

October 5 is another of those dates forever bitterly fixed in tribal Brooklyn memory. Yet it gave me one of my most unique experiences as an Ebbets Field usher. My assignment was the field boxes between the Dodger dugout and the home plate screen. It was fine for collecting autographs, but not tips. Randolph Scott and Groucho Marx led large parties, effusively greeting everyone but ignoring the usher trying to get one last tip with his soon to be retired seat-dusting rag.

Then Casey Stengel arrived. He was the manager of Boston that season. I remembered him as the Dodgers manager when I had been a kid getting autographs. His was the hardest to get. Then one day, while the others were chasing someone coming down McKeever Place, I saw Casey walking alone along Sullivan St. I waited with my back to him, then wheeled around and held out my book. "Sign for me, Casey, before the others see you." He did.

Now I was too mature to ask another grown man to write his name for me. But I was happy with the opportunity the seating arrangements gave me. Apparently his wife, Edna, had found something to do other than come to Ebbets Field. There was an empty seat beside Casey. At a regular season game I might have hustled a fan without a box seat ticket for a couple of bucks to sit there. This time I took it myself.

Casey accepted me and, with no one else to talk to, the loquacious Stengel carried on a nonstop analysis of the game. He managed for both teams. Like all Brooklyn fans, I had thought I knew everything there was to know about baseball strategy. Casey dazzled me with his anticipation of coming circumstances. He didn't second-guess Leo Durocher or Joe McCarthy, he was two and three innings ahead of the action as he outlined all pending strategy moves.

It looked good for the Dodgers. They overcame a 3-run Yankee lead and went into the ninth inning leading 4 to 3. Hugh Casey retired the first two batters and, as every mournful Dodger fan knows, struck out Tommy Henrich and that should have ended the game. Instead, the ball spun into the dirt and bounced away from catcher Mickey Owen. Henrich ran for first base and the ball rolled all the way to where Casey and I were sitting. It stopped in front of us.

What followed was a nightmare. The savvy Leo Durocher and his brainy assistants, Chuck Dressen and Red Corridon, let a red-faced Hugh Casey go on uninterruptedly trying to overpower the Yankee batters. As base hits rained all over the park, the Dodgers choked. Owen the catcher, in shock himself for the passed ball, didn't go to the mound to confer with Casey. No one called time. The carnage went on.

Casey Stengel was nearly out of his mind with frustration as Durocher remained, out of sight, on the bench. At one point, Casey had his leg over the low railing. I thought he was going to go out and stop the action himself. Actually, he was trying to get the attention of the Dodger bench. The side of the dugout blocked him from the view of the players like blinders on a horse. When the Yankees finally were retired, they had a 7 to 4 lead. The Dodgers batted listlessly in the bottom of the ninth. I guess I said goodbye to Casey Stengel as I went off to my postgame assignment. The loss had left me numb. I don't recall leaving Ebbets Field.

I walked back across Prospect Park to my home neighborhood and instinctively headed for McCauley's Bar & Grill. The bar was lined with silent men. Steins of beer and shot glasses of whiskey were in front of each mourner. I found a vacant stool and Tom McCauley, grief on his face, set up my boilermaker. There were no postmortems, just quiet despair. When a man emptied his glass, a raised finger brought a refill.

Hours later I was shaken from my morbid stupor by the arrival of Jim McDonald, another Ebbets Field usher. He angrily reminded me we had arranged a double date for that evening. He was to pick up the girls and we would meet in the lobby of the Empire Theatre on Broadway. "Life With Father" was enjoying a popular run. We had been lucky to get tickets—the very ones which I still had in my wallet. Jim and our dates had waited for me in vain. In the aftermath of the game, stunned by the misfortune which always seemed to plague the Dodgers, I had blanked out all social responsibility.

The World Series ended the next day and so did my career as an Ebbets Field usher. Actually, my draft board didn't send me off to the military until January. Between the disastrous World Series loss to the Yankees and the start of my military service, the country had gone to war. A real one, not the skirmishes of the Dodgers on baseball diamonds. We were assured we would always "Remember Pearl Harbor" and the sneak Japanese attack of December 7, 1941. Today's peace-oriented society chooses to focus sympathy on the holocaust of Hiroshima that ended it. I remember both. I remember being in the Phillipine Islands and expecting to be part of the blood bath that would accompany an invasion of Japan. The night we heard about the atomic bomb it meant, to some of us, that we would be able to return home and see Ebbets Field and the Dodgers.

I never went back to ushering at Ebbets FIeld. I had married, was working, and going to school at night. The G.I. Bill would cover the expenses of my remaining college semesters better than hustling tips at the ballpark.

I rarely go to major league games anymore. I lost much of my interest when the Dodgers moved to Los Angeles. When I do go to a game, I tip the usher. At times he seems surprised. I understand they belong to a union now and work steady. I had three wonderful seasons as an usher at Ebbets Field. Everything considered, and don't tell the lady I married in 1943 this, it was the best job I ever had.

BOOK REVIEWS

INTRODUCTION TO REVIEWS

Everything Baseball is one of the works discussed in this year's Book Review Section, and I am tempted to borrow the title of Jame Mote's excellent book to describe this portion of the *Annual*. Although we can cover only a small fraction of the vast baseball literature published each year, even this sample is convincing evidence that virtually everything can be found in baseball. In addition to the traditional baseball genres (e.g., autobiographies and histories), the books reviewed this year include sophisticated analyses of how the national pastime can be related to everything from the modern American economy to the mind/body problem in Western civilization and the "power of myth."

Given that everything can be found in baseball, it is appropriate that the *Annual*'s reviewers this year come from practically everywhere in academia. They include scholars in history, cultural anthropology, economics, religious studies, linguistics, and literature.

While these authors and reviewers can find practically everything in baseball, I get the feeling that baseball is not or cannot be everything to most of them. Although research and writing on sports has become more and more academically respectable, it is still all too common to find colleagues—even ones who spend much of their time watching and talking about athletics—who can't believe that baseball should be a serious subject for study.

So, by necessity, scholarly work on baseball is often sandwiched in between more conventional academic pursuits. For those authors and reviewers here who don't have the relative freedom from the clock that the university allows professors, time devoted to baseball often must be taken from even more precious periods of leisure. So, whether you like or dislike, agree or disagree with the books and reviews presented in this section, I hope, at least, that you will appreciate that many are a labor of love, an increasingly rare commodity in our world.

Fred Roberts
Michigan State University

Scully, Gerald W. *The Business of Major League Baseball.* Chicago: The University of Chicago Press, 1989. 212 pp. $24.95.

Winegardner, Mark. *Prophet of the Sandlots: Journeys with a Major League Scout.* New York: Atlantic Monthly Press, 1990. $18.95.

These books are two more examinations of baseball behind the scenes. Gerald Scully is a professor of management at the University of Texas at Dallas, and he has written an economic analysis of baseball that is a valuable and challenging contribution to our understanding of the game.

Among the topics in his book, *The Business of Major League Baseball,* is a systematic review of technical economic data that exposes the effects of the owners' collusion against free agents. Scully concludes that "free agents' salary is a much smaller fraction of their contribution to team revenues than is the case of the non-free agents." In other words, free agents, despite their larger salaries, put disproportionately more money in their owners' pockets than other players do.

In the same vein, Scully concludes that the very best players make a difference of somewhere between ten and fifteen wins per season for their teams. He values those additional wins at between two to three million dollars per club, roughly each of these players' salaries at the time of the study. Prior to free agency, the elite of the game received only ten to twenty percent of the revenues that they added to the franchise coffers.

Scully also considers the old claim from the Ueberroth era that twenty-one of the twenty-six teams were losing money—the canard that was the basis for the owners' collusion. Scully conservatively estimates that fifteen of the clubs were making a profit, and he adds that the year studied, 1982, was an especially difficult one for baseball because it followed the 1981 campaign that lost one-third of its season to a strike.

An economic issue that Scully might have examined in depth is the publicly financed stadium. Since the 1960s, cities and states have been assuming the principal capital investment of the club owners with the effect of bestowing largesse on the owners in the hundreds of millions of dollars. What have been the effects of these enormous subsidies?

Scully uses his economist's eye to look at other topics that might seem to have less to do with dollars and cents. He studies racial discrimination in hiring for managers and front office executives and concludes that the small number of black managers may be related to the small number of black infielders, the position that is most associated with preparation for managing.

In this case, the professor may have overanalyzed things. Bigotry, in this case a failure to see talented leadership, is an irrational impulse that has been prevalent in baseball. Gifted players who happened to have been black were ignored by organized baseball for half a century. Scully generally does well in avoiding the economists' assumption that human behavior is always rational, but he seems to have missed the obvious here: that the owners are again being blind to talent.

The Business of Major League Baseball does not read like a novel. Some may describe the style as "academic," but only if they have not read an academic journal lately. Those who are interested in the business side of baseball will find this book an important study.

Prophet of the Sandlots does read like a novel. Mark Winegardner, who teaches fiction writing at John Carroll University in Cleveland, traveled with Tony Lucadello on his mission to find players for the Philadelphia Phillies. Lucadello signed Mike Schmidt for the Phillies, his greatest discovery among the fifty major league players he found in the fields of amateur baseball.

Lucadello shared with Winegardner his distress at the state of the major league game. His complaint that players are not what they used to be cannot be dismissed as an old man's nostalgia. Lucadello was specific about the problem: the modern player, he maintained, was a better athlete than players of the past, but less skilled in the fundamentals of baseball.

His solution was charmingly low tech. Parents should build walls against which their children would throw and field baseballs. Hitting would be practiced by swinging at two hundred plastic golf balls—a task Winegardner found humbling.

Winegardner does a fine job of contrasting the scouting of old-timers like Lucadello with the modern corporate use of the Scouting Bureau. He also covers the changes in scouting and signing strategies in the modern era of the draft, and he records disagreements between Lucadello and the Phillies front office about which players to select in the draft. As interesting as these issues are, they recede to the background as Winegardner spins his poignant tale of this old man and his travels.

Lucadello is revealed as charmingly eccentric: he looked for lost change beneath the grandstands before the games he saw, and once a year he gave the annual collection of this treasure to the first church he saw. He also took pains to treat people with kindness, never commenting on a player when his friends or family might hear. That practice was also good business, since Lucadello was in constant fear that another scout might discover his favorite players and capitalize on Lucadello's work.

A troubling theme that persists in the book is the loneliness of that kind of life. Lucadello put well over two million miles on his leased cars, representing time away from his family and home. For all of his love for baseball, the time he gave the game seemed to isolate him from other strengths and pleasures that he should have been able to enjoy.

Instead, he found himself less able to influence the scouting policies of the Phillies, and the life to which he was perhaps excessively dedicated gradually narrowed to desperate choices. Winegardner was obviously very fond of Lucadello, but he resists any impulse to become maudlin or to cast the Phillies as scapegoats for Lucadello's fate. The book turns into a powerful emotional tale precisely because Winegardner channeled his own emotions into a tight, disciplined account.

The business aspects of baseball are a scandal to many fans, but Scully and Winegardner have shown that the subject needs to be understood if fans are to truly appreciate what they see on the field. Many qualities of the business of baseball are appalling (let's not forget the pointless lockout of 1990), but ignoring the front office antics is likely to prolong the irresponsible behavior of the game's rulers.

Though their subjects and styles are quite different, both Scully and Winegardner have made significant contributions to the fan who wants to understand baseball beyond the diamond and the clubhouse.

Neil J. Sullivan
Baruch College

MacPhail, Lee. *My Nine Innings: An Autobiography of Fifty Years in Baseball.* Westport, Connecticut: Meckler Publishing, 1989. 253 pp. $35.00.

Every field of human endeavor begins with risks and innovations, settles into routine and predictability, and ends awash in excess and nostalgia for a lost golden age. If America is exempt from the dictates of historical inevitability, and baseball truly is the American game, then baseball may yet escape its date with destiny. Just don't bet on it, Pete Rose. The treble (and related) phenomena of $100,000,000 franchises, $3,000,000 players, and $5,000 baseball cards at least suggest that baseball is lurching toward an uncomfortable rendezvous with history, at which point its own history of risks and routine will appear more innocent, more benign than the truth of the matter at the time. What is nostalgia, after all, if not memory? And what are nostalgic memories if not memories clouded less by the mists of the past than by the darkening ugliness of the present?

Just what has all this Spenglerian speculation to do with the autobiography of a baseball bureaucrat? Lee MacPhail is not Henry Adams, though the parallel is not entirely absurd. Each entertained the idea of making a career of teaching history. Each lived during some portion of their respective eras of excess. (For Adams, it was America during the Gilded Age; for MacPhail, it is baseball since the advent of television and free agency.) And each has written his autobiography. There all similarities end abruptly. *My Nine Innings* is not *The Education of Lee MacPhail.*

By his own account, MacPhail has had too pleasant a life to allow any sense of foreboding to interfere with his next trip to the ballpark or the golf course. Poor Henry Adams. Forced to confront the latest Washington scandal, he couldn't jet to Florida where a condo, a putting green, and spring training awaited him. Unable to erase the memory of federal troops crushing yet another strike, he could never escape to Yankee or Memorial Stadium for the afternoon. For Henry Adams, the only escape was history preferably the twelfth century.

For Lee MacPhail, the game, mostly baseball and now golf, has always been there. Escape has never been more than a box seat away. When the bureaucratic wars threatened to engulf him he could simply watch the players go about their business, which is playing a game, the bureaucratization of which has created his business. Given his endlessly pleasant alternatives, how could he permit any thoughts of doom and gloom to invade the sanctuaries of his mind and his game. And none ever have.

At this juncture in the shared history of baseball and the MacPhail family, Lee MacPhail represents the second of three generations of baseball MacPhails. His father, Larry, was the risk-taking innovator. His son, Andy, is the "executive vice president" (that's bankerese for "general manager") of the Minnesota Twins. As such, he is doing his best to hold off the age of excess by not spending banker-owner Carl Pohlad's oft-counted millions on free agent ballplayers. That leaves son-father Lee as the man in the middle. Which is right where he belongs—and right where he has always wanted to be.

"Like father, like son" does not apply to the first two MacPhails. As a young soldier, Larry MacPhail participated in a harebrained scheme to kidnap the newly exiled Kaiser Wilhelm. As a rising businessman, he lost his fortune in the crash of 1929. As an accidental baseball man, he pioneered night baseball, radio broadcasts, and air travel. The first few "innings" of son Lee's story focus on father Larry, who, one guesses, was at best a disinterested father.

Son Lee, however, is not bitter. Along with Branch Rickey and George Weiss, he includes his father as one of the three "mentors" in his baseball life. Precisely what he learned from them he does not say. At least MacPhail senior and Rickey were innovators. And when it came to dealing with players, all three were accomplished authoritarians. Of Weiss, MacPhail junior will only say that he was "very tough with his players . . . and didn't have a good relationship with them." That is Lee MacPhail at his blandest—and harshest.

This is not an axe-grinding autobiography. Reading between the lines and sifting among the clichés (Casey Stengel was "one of a kind"; Paul Richards had his "plusses and minuses."), MacPhail, the bureaucrat, has had little time for baseball's boat rockers, most particularly Bill Veeck, George Steinbrenner, Charlie Finley, Marvin Miller, and Peter Seitz. As an American League man, he has disdain for the "dinosaurs" in the National League who opposed divisional play and continue to hold out against inter-league play and the designated hitter. By comparison, MacPhail considers himself to be a wild-eyed reformer. It doesn't wash. Lee MacPhail was always a company man, and his reflections are those of a mostly contented company man at that. True, the reserve system was "clearly unfair." Yes, he agrees, more should have been done prior to 1976 to eliminate its abuses. But nothing was done, because it was not in the interest of the MacPhails of baseball to make significant changes in the then-prevailing status quo. Since 1976 the consequences of free agency have been, in MacPhail's view, "disastrous for the game." No, Lee, make that disastrous for those who pretend to rule the game.

From MacPhail's vantage point, only management is "concerned for the game itself." Oh? It would be nice to think that somebody mortal is looking out for the "game itself," but on this issue management has proved itself to be all too mortal.

MacPhail would have us believe that baseball's golden age extended from the 1930s through the 1950s when the Larry MacPhails, Branch Rickeys, and

George Weisses had custody of the "game itself." Then players "devoted their lives to the game." Then the reserve system made life pleasant for baseball's powers that were. Then the players evidenced "little resentment" over its impact on their lives and wallets. Why? Perhaps because of their infuriating lack of concern for the "game itself."

Lee MacPhail would also have us believe that he was a bureaucrat of eminent fairness. In fact, his place in baseball history rests on his occasional implementation of what might be termed the MacPhail Fairness Doctrine. Two incidents come to mind: the pine tar episode of 1983 and the contract negotiations of 1985. As president of the American League, MacPhail overruled his umpires and restored George Brett's Yankee Stadium home run. "Pine tar," he intones, "did not aid in propelling that ball out of the ballpark." The "intent" of the rule was to "curtail the excessive use of pine tar," not to "nullify such a hit once it had occurred." Written like a true bureaucrat—and a fair one at that.

As chief negotiator for the owners in 1985, MacPhail used the approach of pleading poverty on behalf of his bosses. His ploy was to open their books in support of his case—all in the name of fairness. And the Marvin Miller-less players union bought it. The immediate result was a union give back. Eligibility for arbitration was rolled back from two to three years. A longer term result was the protracted 1990 dispute over union's demand to restore its lost year.

Little else in Lee MacPhail's long career will be terribly memorable. If he follows his father into the Hall of Fame, it will either be because of his name or because enough voters will remember enough players who don't belong there either. MacPhail was with the Yankees in their glory days of the 1950s, but any connection between their success and his presence was purely accidental. True, he did help to build the Orioles into a championship team in the 1960s, but by his own account, good fortune had as much to do with the Orioles' success as front office genius.

According to Lee MacPhail, the best job in baseball is that of farm director. Fair enough. One wishes, then, that his memoir had revealed the Lee MacPhail recipe for judging baseball talent. Instead, we are given a few self-effacing stories of Lee MacPhail blunders. In the 1961 expansion draft, the Orioles' brain trust "agonized" over protecting one of two young pitchers. Their names were Arne Thorsland and Dean Chance. Guess which one the Orioles kept.

Trades, we learn, are best made after three or four drinks. It also seems that most of MacPhail's attempts to devise a drug policy for baseball took place after a belt or three. Whether the juxtaposition of elbow-bending and mood-altering was accidental or ironic is unknown. But it is there.

Sometimes, what's not there is equally curious. MacPhail claims that the All-Star game is now played at night because of two games played on horribly hot July afternoons in St. Louis and Minnesota in the mid-1960s. Oh? What about something called television, Lee? For that matter, MacPhail saw nothing wrong with the 1964 CBS purchase of the Yankees. To read this memoir is to pretend that the unholy marriage between television and sport has never been entered into, much less consummated.

To read this memoir is to enter into the pleasant world of a pleasant man whose life just happened to revolve around baseball. Strikes and lockouts have interrupted the rhythm of baseball seasons, but they have not disturbed the placid demeanor of a second generation baseball bureaucrat. Irresponsible owners and wily union leaders, spiraling salaries and indifferent players may have destroyed Lee MacPhail's golden age, but nothing has eaten away at his love for the game.

From the vantage point of the retirement of the next baseball MacPhail, the "nine innings" of Lee MacPhail may take on the appearance of a golden age all its own. In the meantime, the "game itself" remains more or less intact. Barring future strikes and lockouts, even unruffled bureaucrats can still look forward to the rites of spring.

John C. Chalberg
Normandale Community College

Sullivan, Neil J. *The Minors: The Struggle and Triumph of Baseball's Poor Relation from 1876 to the Present*. New York: St. Martin's Press, 1990. 307 pp. $19.95.

If the game was all organized baseball and sandlot in the romantic past, today it is major league baseball. That is where the fans and the money are in the game. Now, the major leagues draw 50 million to the parks, gross over $1.2 billion in revenues, and their superstars make $4 million a year. The other night as I was flipping through the channels of my cable-linked TV, I attempted to watch half a dozen major league games, and an Arizona–USC college game. As fans we have gotten what we wanted—greater access to major league baseball. Somehow, live games in Mudville don't seem important.

Sullivan bemoans this decline in the fate of the minor leagues. The book is a romantic, if superficial, look at the evolution of minor league baseball from times of bust to times of more bust. Today, the minor leagues are in the best financial shape than they have ever been. Triple A clubs now sell for $10 million, a sum that the majors achieved in the early 1970s.

The book consists of a series of chapters on the early years of organized baseball, the great men in the front office and on the playing field, the great teams, the Negro leagues, the rise of the powerful Pacific Coast League, and the events that led to the supremacy of the majors over the minors. As a history of the minor leagues, it suffers from a near total reliance on secondary source material. As such, anyone familiar with the work of Harold Seymour, Robert Obojski, Harvey Frommer, Robert Peterson, or others will not find anything of value in this book. Nor can one get a feel for the romantic past of baseball. There are some anecdotes about players, but they are in the common folklore. There is an attempt to cite the statistics of the great players. But the author seems not aware of the change in the mound from 50′ to 60′6″ in 1893 or the innovation of the lively ball in 1920 and the difficulties that they introduce in making inter-period comparisons of player statistics.

Here is the author's diagnosis of the cause of the decline of the minor leagues: "The short answer is that the collapse of the minors was but one result of major league greed. The prosperity that baseball has enjoyed may seem to confirm the wisdom of policies that were in fact catastrophic. But grasping after short-term gain has cost us most of our minor league teams, historic rivalries at both the major and minor league levels, strong bonds between communities and their teams, and elegant ballparks that enhanced the game. In exchange, we have been treated to domed stadiums, plastic grass, designated hitters, spasmodic expansion and franchise relocation, and other tricks that seem to ensure the privileges of the major league owners but inevitably erode the foundation of the game for everyone. The problem with baseball in recent years is not that a game has become a business, for it was always a business. The problem is that the business is run with so little regard for its heritage."

The fact of the matter is that things change. The America of the 1990s is vastly different from the America of the 1890s. Organized baseball, after all, was not in very good shape until 1903. Rules changed from season to season. Teams came and went. Leagues folded and were reborn. The nineteenth century was a very unstable era for organized baseball. The America of the post-World War II era is the product of a great technological revolution. The automobile accelerated the migration of the middle class to the suburbs, and television brought the world into the living room, if through rose-colored glasses. As baseball fans, we are the better for it. Just as movie theaters, the summer concerts in small towns, and a host of other parts of pre-television society have shrunk, so has minor league baseball shrunk, as well. But the decline of the minors has more to do with these general changes in American society than it does with the greed of the major leagues.

Gerald W. Scully
University of Texas at Dallas

Holway, John. *Black Diamonds: Life in the Negro Leagues from the Men Who Lived It*. Westport, Connecticut: Meckler Publishing, 1989. $32.50.

John Holway is among those who have changed how America remembers its sporting past. Along with Robert Peterson, Donn Rogosin, Craig Davidson, Jules Tygiel and a few other writers, filmmakers, and sports historians, Holway has helped recapture the history of independent black baseball during the epoch of segregation. In a stream of articles and books, Holway has written of the Negro Leagues, their teams, and their stars, during the half century before Jackie Robinson leaped across the color line, when major league baseball was a segregated institution.

In the latest of these works Holway offers the story of twelve Negro League veterans: Paul "Jake" Stephens, Chet Brewer, Ernest "Willie" Powell, George Giles, Gene Benson, John "Buck" O'Neil, Willard "Home Run" Brown, Max Manning, Dave Barnhill, Verdell Mathis, Johnny Davis, and Wilmer Fields. These are men with whom only the aficionados of the Negro Leagues will be familiar. But Holway makes a case for why we should remember them along with Gibson, Bell, Leonard, Paige and the few other Negro Leaguers who have made their way into the nation's collective sporting memory.

Holway lets these men speak for themselves as they recollect the days when black baseball was hidden behind a racial boundary that few whites passed. Their stories are both poignant and upbeat, and collectively introduce the reader to the manifold experiences of this sporting life.

Black Diamonds tells these stories in the players' voices. That is its strength, for it makes the reader feel as if he or she is there with the storyteller, but its weakness, too, for sometimes the memories appear disjointed or in error (as memory is often fallible). Yet the flavor and panache that come through are clear.

Holway offers an important addition to the stories he related in *Blackball Stars: Negro League Pioneers,* winner of *Spitball Magazine*'s Casey Award for the best baseball book of 1988. His editing and intelligent questioning of these men are as important as his finding them and persuading them to relate their sporting lives. In all, it makes for a good read about a fascinating part of our sporting and national history.

Rob Ruck
Pittsburgh, Pennsylvania

Forker, Dom. *The Men of Autumn: An Oral History of the 1949–53 World Champion New York Yankees.* Dallas, Texas: Taylor Publishing Company, 1989. 228 pp. $18.95.

In the tradition of Roger Kahn, who waxed so eloquent about the lovable "Bums" of his youthful haunt—Ebbets Field—baseball writers (like all baseball fans) maintain an endless, unshakable love affair with losers. Kahn's *Boys of Summer* is only the prototype for a flood tide of books on our nostalgic fascination with those childhood diamond heroes who inevitably lost the big game and always evoked the plaintive cry of "wait till next season!" Roger Angell, baseball's other supreme poet-in-residence, echoes the reigning sentiment of the hardened baseball rooter in expressing his preference for "historic teams of defeat" like the Red Sox of Boston and the Tigers of Detroit, teams whose long sagas of frustration are only further ennobled by the fine coincidence that they play in baseball's oldest and most revered ballparks. Like so much that surrounds baseball, this is all something of a myth. The Dodgers of the 1950s seemed always to be there for the World Series—it was only the hated Yankees they could never truly vanquish. The Red Sox and Tigers boast numerous glory years and pennant seasons when compared with baseball's legitimate losers like the St. Louis Browns, the Seattle Mariners, or those perennial American League doormats, Chicago's hapless White Sox.

Given this baseball truism, veteran sports historian Dom Forker thus sets himself a most difficult literary task, that of arresting our attention with accounts of baseball's most victorious (and consequently its least-loved) among legendary teams. Mr. Forker's new book chronicles the events surrounding the

1949–53 New York Yankees, and is in many ways the antithesis of Kahn's classic portrait of the rival 1950s-era Brooklyn Dodgers. On the surface the format is similar—taped interviews with 23 alumni of that Yankee juggernaut which today remains the only team in the century-long history of the sport to capture five consecutive World Series crowns.

Forker's title echoes Kahn's as well—*The Men of Autumn*—although the very point here is that Kahn's melancholy appeal to disappointing summertime dreams of childhood baseball reflects a more tragic tone missing from Forker's less editorial treatment. These Yankees were, after all, supreme winners who always emerged victorious during the money seasons of late September and early October. For these Yankees, it was always this year's celebrations and never next year's vain hopes. Forker's lively interview transcriptions do much to capture the winning attitude and supreme confidence of players like Rizzuto, Bauer, Woodling, Mize, Irv Noren, Joe Collins, and Billy Martin, roleplayers who formed the heart of Casey Stengel's unstoppable teams of the Mantle–Berra–Ford era. In the end, Forker's book is far different from Kahn's in all the most obvious ways. Attention here is focused narrowly on the baseball events of the 1950s, far less on life's struggles, which cursed Kahn's Dodgers long after their brief playing days. While Mr. Kahn's book eventually dissolves into self-indulgent autobiography, Forker's personal involvement with the Yankees of his childhood is appropriately muted and skillfully concealed. Baseball is the sole venue here, and memories of those marvelous Yankee teams during baseball's greatest decade come to full life in the reminiscences of some of the less-celebrated Yankees of the era—Ed Lopat, Charlie Silvera, Tommy Byrne, Gil McDougald.

For those who grew up with baseball in the 1950s, hating the Yankees with vitriol or loving them with boundless passion, Forker's work is a baseball fantasy matched by few other baseball books of the past several seasons. There are small flaws: the two greatest players on this team—DiMaggio and Mantle—fail to appear and were apparently unwilling to participate. Brief introductions to each carefully edited interview often merely repeat, via summary, more lively players' commentaries to follow. And an enticing "Foreword" by Mr. Yankee, Mel Allen, proves all too brief and hopelessly uninsightful. But Forker and his collaborators do transport us once again back to diamond summer afternoons in the Yankee Stadium of our childhood—and what more could we ask of this or any baseball book?

Peter C. Bjarkman
West Lafayette, Indiana

Rose, Pete and Roger Kahn. *Pete Rose: My Story.* New York: Macmillan Publishing Company, 1989. $18.95.

When Peter Edward Rose, one of the great baseball players of all time, was banned from baseball by A. Bartlett Giamatti, he vowed that day that he would soon tell his version of the story. In *Pete Rose: My Story,* he and Roger Kahn claim they have told that story. If their effort is judged solely as Pete and Roger's attempt to set the record straight, the book is a dismal failure. Early in the book Roger Kahn accepts at face value Pete Rose's assertion, "I'll always tell you the truth." That misplaced loyalty on Kahn's part prevents him from examining in any significant way the complex combination in Rose of egotistical single-mindedness about his baseball records and his financial status, and his occasional warmth and concern for others.

On April 20 Peter Rose pleaded guilty to two counts of submitting false income tax returns, and he now joins his accusers, Paul Janszen and Ron Peters, as convicted felons, accusers whom Kahn and Rose denounce as liars. But it was Rose who concocted elaborate schemes to conceal his cash payments from card shows and from selling memorabilia, and who hid his actions from his lawyers and accountants. I wonder if Kahn still accepts Pete's claims of honesty and if he still supports so fully Pete's hollow-sounding cry that he did not bet on baseball. Kahn accepts without question Pete's version of the Pick Six ticket and his account of why he agreed to the banishment from baseball. Rose argues that not only was there no finding that he had bet on baseball, but the commissioner had allowed him to apply for reinstatement after one year, not seven years. Not having done his homework, Kahn does not raise the important point that all banished players have the right to apply for reinstatement after one year. That Rose has that right is not something that he had negotiated.

Since Roger Kahn has written what is for many the classic baseball book, *The Boys of Summer,* and has approached that level in *A Season in the Sun* and *Good Enough to Dream,* this book will also disappoint those who admire Kahn's work. There are flashes that remind us of Kahn at his best, such as the brief account of the 1869 season of the Cincinnati Red Stockings or his description of Pete, Jr., leaving an interview, "a young ballplayer, in a prime of youth and sinew, jogging through sunlight on spikes, gliding and soundless, cruising fresh-cut grass." But too much of the book is the bold, unchallenged voice of Pete Rose extolling his greatness as a ballplayer or his financial status.

And too often Kahn portrays himself as the defender of Rose. When Rose, who has devoted his entire life to baseball, is suspended for thirty days for bumping an umpire, Kahn questions "how much Giamatti knew about pro ball. Not the beau ideal, but the reality." Kahn, who supposedly knows baseball, asks "Thirty days? Try three." Kahn claims he will be asking hard questions of Rose, but when he turns his attention to Rose's relationship with his first wife, he spends much of the chapter attacking Karolyn's article in *Sporting News.* He writes, "With an author's respect for freedom of expression, I could still support a constitutional amendment making it a felony for one party in a crumbling marriage or divorce to publish anything about the other party until fifty years after the final decree, by which time, probably, nobody would remember or care." Perhaps Mr. Kahn should have waited a few more years before writing this book.

One interesting theme that Roger Kahn explores in this book is the relationship of fathers and sons. Pete claims, and there is ample evidence to support his claim, that his father, who played semiprofessional football until he was forty-two, was the most important influence on his life. While Kahn was writing the book, Kahn's own son died, and the relationship between Rose and Pete, Jr. is important to our understanding of Rose himself. This web of connections is one of the strong points of the book, but it is finally underdeveloped, a series of intriguing questions or anecdotes that are never fully explored. There is an interesting parallel between Pete's father's advice to Pete not to attend summer school to regain his high school eligibility: "You can't go to school in the summer. It would get in the way of your baseball," and Pete's own advice to his son to join the Orioles and not accept a baseball scholarship. But Kahn has become a close personal friend of Rose, and it is that friendship that dominates and clouds this study. The true story of Peter Edward Rose still waits to be told.

Robert Johnson
Miami University

Goldstein, Warren. *Playing for Keeps: A History of Early Baseball.* Ithaca, New York: Cornell University Press, 1989. 182 pp. $21.95.

Sentimentalists and anti-intellectuals, unlikely compatriots, will probably make common cause to actively detest this excellent scholarly book. What I also suspect is that cynics will claim—mistakenly—that it reports little or nothing that is new.

Looking at the good old days of more than a century ago, this volume offers an unromanticized interpretation of the origins of our national pastime. As readers encounter careful research and intelligent analysis, simplistic notions must be forever cast aside as unfounded. To state succinctly the author's thesis: key to baseball's survival is that it is played for both fun and profit. To lay claim to just one side of this equation, he believes, is to misinterpret its success.

Warren Goldstein explicates the circumstances under which professional baseball emerged. Situated in the decades following the Civil War, this study reexamines issues and concerns long familiar. But this author reaches unvarnished conclusions that can only be ignored at one's peril.

Playing for Keeps succeeds because its careful assessment of baseball's origins has been informed by academically-trained historians who write about American society and culture. Rather than being interested in baseball in particular or organized sport in general, they are concerned with a multiplicity of categories such as ethnicity, gender, race, occupation, class, religion, geography, politics, material culture, and institutions. When done effectively, as in this instance, the books that evolve offer an artful, nuanced analysis of some key aspect of human agency within a cultural form.

"Unresolvable tensions," reproducing themselves over and again, stand at the center of baseball's history when Warren Goldstein gains custody over it. Take the case of baseball's first professional champions, the Cincinnati Red Stockings of Harry Wright. While this story has been told often, Goldstein's sensitive rendition is noteworthy because he so effectively delineates the symbiotic relationship between baseball and the cultural context of the times.

For example, the author offers an instructive discussion of the proper design of the team uniform, tailored and modulated in the application of color to evoke a proper sense of urbanity. He writes: "Uniforms served the seekers after respectability quite well as they sought to distinguish themselves from the poor and rough—men, boys, and would-be gentlemen who could not afford uniforms."

He also explains why the players' path from amateur to professional status proved so confounding to them. When members of the Red Stockings sought to resort to amateur play after 1870, they discovered that they could not entirely stem the ascent of professionalism. Readers learn from the author, in this instance, about why it is always impossible to successfully move backward into cultural time.

A successful and provocative book such as this whets the reader's appetite. I am a trifle disappointed that Goldstein devoted scant attention to the putative National Brotherhood of Professional Baseball Players of 1890 and the role of John Montgomery Ward. Nor does he pause, except momentarily, to assay the circumstances of African Americans.

Playing for Keeps also would have benefited from some apt comparisons between national cultures. Two possibilities come to mind. The parallels between the professionalization of baseball in the United States and soccer in England could be readily analyzed by turning to Tony Mason's book about the rise of the Federated Association. Likewise, the rationale for the enthusiastic acceptance of American baseball in Japan, beginning in the early 1890s, is recounted in a wonderful cultural study contributed by Donald Roden to the *American Historical Review*.

But nothing should detract from Warren Goldstein's achievement. This book is required reading for anyone who professes to know the history of baseball.

Michael H. Ebner
Lake Forest College

Riess, Steven A. *City Games: The Evolution of American Urban Society and the Rise of Sports*. Champaign, Illinois: University of Illinois Press, 1989. 332 pp. $29.95.

Community finds its expression in games. This reality is as applicable to the urban village as to the small town or farmstead. As Steven Riess argues in his new book, the changes in city life—from the walking city to the radial city, grounded in public transportation, to the contemporary suburban city, which depends on automobiles for its organization—are reflected in the structure of the sports and games of residents.

The implicit themes of Riess's volume are expressed in a few basic concepts: morality, power, space, ethnicity, and economics. These concepts organize the role of leisure within the structure of urban life. One problem with Riess's analysis, at least for the non-historian, is that the conceptual forest is often downplayed in place of the factual trees. We learn more about events and circumstances, a flow of detail, while some of the broader implications of these points are lost. The connections among the facts are ultimately why we read the book. Still, the arguments are present, if occasionally overshadowed.

Throughout the text one is astonished and impressed that for each place and time claims and counterclaims are presented demonstrating the moral effects of leisure on the population. Sometimes, as in the case of the playground movement and ethnic participatory sports, these activities are said to be important for the development of healthy bodies and healthy minds—found also in the themes of "muscular Christianity." Clean air builds character. On other occasions, the effects of sports and games are undesirable, as in the supposed outcome of wagering on leisure activities. In sum, one finds within the American urban landscape a "Protestant ethic" for leisure activities: sport should make us better citizens of the republic.

Americans find it impossible to treat games as activities unmoored from any "serious" purpose. Social actors are continually jostling with each other to find the moral meaning of baseball. Is the game a means for youths to learn mathematical skills, is it a means by which people can gain the benefits of sun and fresh air, is it an exercise that helps to build community, does it promote sedentary lifestyles, or is it a corrupting influence on youth, which encourages them to mix with the most disreputable elements of the city? Significant disputes arise over the moral placement of sports and recreation. Perhaps most dramatic is Riess's treatment of boxing in the early decades of the century. In New York State, for example, there was a significant political battle between the pro-boxing Tammany Democrats of New York City and the Conservative Upstate Republicans, who claimed to find boxing degrading.

As Riess's data make evident, the definition of sport is connected to the use of power. Boxing again serves as a prototypical example of this process. In the early years of the century, politicians were heavy investors in the sport; in time, these roles were taken over by mobsters as many forms of boxing became tied to organized crime. The "ownership" of sport is an important component of political power within a city, as recent attempts to "blackmail" cities to build or renew sports arenas dramatically reveal. The owner of a sports franchise often has, by virtue of that role, a considerable position of influence in the community.

Riess's vision of the city is, at its heart, a spatial model, ultimately grounded in transportation technologies. He proposes three stages of American cities, defined by the prototypical form of transportation: the foot (the walking city), the streetcar (the radial city), and the car (the suburban city). Geography matters in the provisioning of leisure activity. The ability to find open spaces and get access to them determines the type of sport that is available and who is able to participate. As Riess makes clear in his presentation of the changes in baseball, the spatial constraints of the "parks" (and their eventual change to stadia) helped to determine the organization of the game. Land use is not a peripheral issue in the rise of sports, but its core: in Ebbets Field as well as Chavez Ravine.

Ethnicity adds spice to the sporting stewpot. Riess makes a particularly effective argument for the responses of the first generation immigrants of the nineteenth century to the American urban landscape. Each ethnic group brought to these shores its own sporting culture, each different in some measure from all others, and different from the indigenous Anglo-American culture. The gymnastic turnvereins (the turners), shared by German immigrants, are perhaps the most influential of these movements, although by no means the only one.

Finally, Riess describes how sport is lodged within the economic nexus of society. Social class, business corporations, unemployment, and discretionary income each affects how sport will and must be organized within the confines of the city. Economics provides a grounding for the moral organization of sporting enterprises, from the racetrack to the ballpark.

City Games provides the reader with a rich tapestry, depicting how sport has connected to the American urban environment. While Riess fails to emphasize some of his points because of an overreliance on data at the expense of interpretation, the material is present for analysis by others. One leaves this volume with the sense that the analysis of sport, despite the topic's evident playfulness, can never be separated from morality or from economics. Even if we should dare to try, its many participants would never permit this. They know that sport is good, evil, rich, and poor.

Gary Alan Fine
University of Georgia

Mote, James. *Everything Baseball.* New York: Prentice Hall Press, 1989. 429 pp. $14.95 (pbk.).

In James Mote's Preface to *Everything Baseball* he says his work is "baseball's time capsule." It is that and much more. It is an abundant treasure house of information and a fascinating compendium of information about the American response to the game of baseball. The overall effect of the volume is that of impressing one with the extent to which baseball has permeated the American consciousness and found expression and representation in all mediums of expression and communication. It is more than a matter of being reminded of or celebrating baseball outside the ballpark and the actual structure of the game. The presence of baseball in film, television, radio, theater, art and sculpture, literature, music and the spoken arts (the areas around which Mote organizes the book) indicates how the National Game serves as a touchstone of values and attitudes and as a central mythic ritual. As Annie Savoy says at the conclusion of *Bull Durham* (quoting Walt Whitman), our nation sees "great things" in the sport, and it has served to "repair our losses" and has been a "blessing to us."

Mote's labor of love and intelligence in *Everything Baseball* documents what "great things" Americans have seen in the sport, as well as the ways baseball has served commercial purposes or been co-opted and appropriated for entertainment. The entries range from the sublime expression of baseball as a source of the universal meanings of death or the cosmic meanings of life in such poems as William Heyen's "At Season's End" or Philip Dacey's "The Unseen Tenth Man" (with the texts of both poems provided), to the novelty expressions of such songs as Red River Dave McEnery's "The Pine Tarred Bat (The Ballad of

George Brett)" and C.W. McCall's "Pine Tar Wars," both released in 1983. As one reads through the entries, one is reminded of the experience of seeing a particular film or television presentation or reading a certain novel. I recalled being deeply touched and moved by Max Gail's portrayal of Babe Ruth in the ESPN production "The Babe"; and I remember the absolute delight I took in watching the humor and comedy of "Long Gone," a 1987 HBO film that I consider a classic of its genre. A picture of Henry Wiggen and Bruce Pearson from the film version of *Bang the Drum Slowly* reminds me of the achievement of Mark Harris in writing what I believe is a remarkable screenplay based on his novel.

This book is a rich visual text with high quality black and white reproductions of historical photographs, paintings, illustrations, magazine and comic book covers, sheet music and record album covers, frames from films, and movie posters. The amount of work that went into gathering these visual sources as well as compiling the item listings and descriptions must have been staggering and challenging. Mote's extensive Acknowledgments indicate how many individuals, organizations, and institutions contributed generously and cooperatively to his enterprise. The volume is full of surprises and delights as well as oddities like Elmo and Patsy's song "Will You Be Ready (At The Plate When Jesus Throws the Ball)" or Steve Vaus's "Steve Garvey National Anthem." Mote lists 68 versions of "Take Me Out to the Ball Game" since 1908, and the listing makes for fascinating reading.

The book is punctuated with excellent mini-essays on a variety of topics ranging from a history of "Casey at the Bat" to a discussion of Thomas Eakins' masterpiece of painting titled "Baseball Players Practicing." These nuggets of information and history reflect how much Mote has assimilated the materials he has gathered and catalogued, and the essays serve to highlight particular items. Mote also includes some complete texts such as the full lyrics to "Joltin' Joe DiMaggio," "Let's Keep the Dodgers in Brooklyn," "Slide, Kelly, Slide," and "Take Me Out to the Ball Game" to mention only a few. Reproductions of paintings and sculptures document some of the great works of American art and show why the interest in baseball art is developing into significant exhibitions, books, and collecting. These works are national treasures that deserve to be better known, shared, and appreciated.

It is hard to fault Mote on any count in this rich and remarkable book. While it does not feature "absolutely every baseball song, poem, novel, play, movie, TV and radio show, painting, sculpture, comic strip, cartoon" as its cover claims it does, it comes as close as one could expect. For example, I could find perhaps five baseball novels not listed that one might find in such reference works as Suzanne Wise's *Sports Fiction for Adults: An Annotated Bibliography of Novels, Plays, Short Stories, and Poetry with Sporting Settings* (1986) or Grant Burns' *The Sports Pages: A Critical Bibliography of Twentieth-Century American Novels and Stories Featuring Baseball, Basketball, Football, and Other Athletic Pursuits* (1987), but Mote's listing contains novels not included in the Wise and Burns books. Mote does not list all the novels by writers of baseball series for juveniles, such as those by Gilbert Patten, Ralph Henry Barbour, Edward Stratemeyer, William Heyliger, Jackson V. Scholz, John R. Tunis, or others. However, one can consult Anton Grobani's *Guide to Baseball Literature* for these titles.

This book is effectively cross-referenced between sections and items and is extensively indexed so as to provide maximum usefulness. The Selected Bibliography and Selected Guide to Sources and Dealers are extremely useful.

In its concept, execution, format, and contents this book is a triumph. It is an essential and indispensable reference and resource book, taking its earned place with such volumes as Myron J. Smith, Jr.'s *Baseball: A Comprehensive Bibliography* (1986) and Grobani's work. However, it also deserves to be perused and enjoyed as a rich text with contents that reward and delight. Baseball literature is richer for James Mote's remarkable work, and it will undoubtedly make the work of scholars and historians easier as well as make the general reader more knowledgeable and appreciative of the traditions and heritage of baseball.

Douglas A. Noverr
Michigan State University

Benson, Michael. *Ballparks of North America: A Comprehensive Historical Reference to Ball Grounds, Yards and Stadiums, 1845 to Present.* Jefferson, North Carolina: McFarland & Company, 1989. 475 pp. $35.

Wood, Bob. *Dodger Dogs to Fenway Franks.* New York: McGraw-Hill Publishing Company, 1988. 347 pp. Hardcover $18.95; Paperback $7.95.

Both of these books are about ballparks and both are enjoyable, but otherwise they have little in common. Michael Benson has authored what amounts to an encyclopedia of baseball stadiums (stadia?) that have grown, flourished, and often withered and turned to dust over the last century and a half in Canada, the United States, Mexico, and points farther south. Hundreds of ballparks are included—approximately 800, as a matter of fact—and for many of them Benson provides such vital statistics as street location, dimensions of the playing field, seating capacity, attendance records, the teams that played there, and the years that the park was in active use.

In addition, a number of the parks are described at greater length. Sometimes there's only a paragraph or two, but often there's an essay of several informative (and entertaining) pages. The Elysian Fields in Hoboken, New Jersey, for example, was presumably the first baseball park of all time since on June 19, 1846, it was the site of the first modern baseball game. However, Benson makes the Sherlockian observation that although "history has chosen this game as the sport's official premiere, an illustration of the game drawn at the time shows a diamond with basepaths already worn bare."

Did you know that the clock that was atop the scoreboard at Ebbets Field now adorns the scoreboard at McCormick Field in Asheville, North Carolina (where parts of the movie *Bull Durham* were filmed)? Or that Bill Veeck is the one who, in 1937, personally planted the ivy along the base of Wrigley Field's outfield walls? Or that Fenway Park's men's rooms still don't have urinals; they have trenches. *Ballparks of North America* will tell you all that and much more; it is a scholarly work and a labor of love that is a delight to peruse at leisure.

Leisure is one commodity that is hard to find in *Dodger Dogs to Fenway Franks,* Bob Wood's chronicle of his frantic journey along the Interstates of America in the summer of 1985 when he succeeded in attending a game in each and every major league ballpark during a seven-and-a-half-week period. A junior high school history teacher by profession, he took along his academic gear and "graded" each ballpark with respect to layout and upkeep, bathroom and parking facilities, food and beverage quality, employee courtesy, atmosphere, and so on.

Dodger Stadium (Los Angeles) and Royals Stadium (Kansas City) wound up with the only overall A's. Houston's Astrodome and Toronto's Exhibition Stadium (no longer in use) were at the bottom of the class, with D+'s. Those perennial favorites, Wrigley Field and Fenway Park, received B+'s. Comiskey Park and Tiger Stadium got only B's.

Living on a teacher's salary, Wood chose to *drive* 12,000 miles in 52 days rather than fly between cities. Economically that was probably wise—especially since deregulation has sent air fares soaring. In terms of the validity of his grading system, however, it was a disastrous decision because it meant that he was always in a hurry and thus could hardly ever spend more than a single day at a ballpark. A few hours are simply not enough time to get an accurate fix on employee courtesy, food quality, or any number of other aspects of a ballpark. A grouchy security guard, a one-sided game that day, who knows what else, can give a warped view of normal conditions. Students are always complaining about how teachers grade. In this case, I think they would be justified. Everything considered, shouldn't one see at least three or four games in a ballpark to give it a fair grade?

Naturally, many of Wood's impressions are (necessarily) subjective. For example, a major annoyance for me nowadays is the extraordinarily loud nonstop music that bombards the audience in many ballparks—it starts even before batting practice, continues during the game, and only lets up momentarily when the pitcher stares at the catcher, looking for his sign, and then goes into his windup. Apparently many general managers believe that *something*—be it loud music or cartoon highjinks on the scoreboard or a raffle for some sort of prize—has to be going on every single instant or baseball fans will get bored. Normal relaxed conversation with one's neighbor during or between innings is about as feasible as at a heavy-metal rock concert or a birthday party for hyperactive five-year-olds. Wood, however, loves this multimedia circus atmosphere. A pulsating beat and crazy cartoon scoreboards are his cup of tea, as sure to be rewarded with an A+ as an honor roll student who stays after class to help erase the blackboard.

In my own grade book, I've given Bob Wood an A for effort, a B for writing style, and a C for content. As just about anyone at NYU will tell you, though, I'm a notoriously easy grader.

Lawrence S. Ritter
New York University

Lansche, Jerry. *The Forgotten Championships: Postseason Baseball, 1882–1981*. Jefferson, North Carolina: McFarland & Company, 1989. $35.

Jerry Lansche has packed into this useful reference work more than four hundred brief game accounts and box scores for four kinds of "forgotten championships": (1) the nineteenth-century World Series, ignored by most compilers, even those that bill themselves "official"; (2) the postseason city and state series, which flourished in the 1880s and the early years of this century, but which disappeared entirely after 1942; (3) the six major league tiebreaker series and single games played between 1946 and 1978 which, except for the famous home runs by Bobby Thomson in 1951 and Bucky Dent in 1978, leave few traces in the literature of the game; and (4) the series that many fans (Lansche included) wish they *could* forget, the 1981 divisional play-offs that excluded from postseason play two clubs with the best overall records in their divisions. Lansche's compilation saves the researcher many eye-watering days—weeks, even—at the microfilm reader; box scores and descriptions of most of the games he records have not been readily available since the original newspaper accounts were published.

The first postseason meeting between major league champions is here—a pair of 1882 exhibition games split by Chicago (NL) and Cincinnati (AA)—as are twelve of the thirteen nineteenth-century series touted at the time as national or world championships. (Lansche omits without explanation the 1900 Chronicle-Telegraph Cup "World Series" in which National League pennant winner Brooklyn defeated second-place Pittsburgh three games to one.) Nearly three-fourths of the book, though, is given over to the seventy-plus major league postseason city and state championships contested between 1882 and 1942. Lansche omits the "Maryland" series of 1886 and 1887 between Baltimore (AA) and Washington (NL), but he has tracked down nearly every game of every series in St. Louis (fourteen series between 1885 and 1917), Philadelphia (ten between 1883 and 1912), Ohio (eight between 1882 and 1917), New York and Brooklyn (seven between 1883 and 1914), Boston (1905 and 1907), Missouri (1889), and the longest lived, Chicago (twenty-five series between 1903 and 1942, of which eighteen were won by the usually underdog White Sox). In his search Lansche missed only a couple of games: the final game of the first St. Louis series in which the Browns (AA) extended their sweep of the NL Maroons to 4–0, and the fourth game of New York's 1886 Mets–Giants series, the only Mets win. (Lansche seems to have found Game 6 of the 1889 Philadelphia series only at the last minute, too late to include its box score or to revise his description of Game 5 as the series "finale.") Some of these city and state series were as loosely contested as meaningless exhibition games, but a surprising number (especially in the twentieth century when they were often played under the aegis of the major leagues' National Commission) were battled as seriously as any World Series, and received press coverage well beyond the cities in which they were played. Unfortunately, Lansche gives us little of the context in which these forgotten series were played. While he surfeits us with details of individual games, he provides little interpretation to help us digest them. The analysis he does provide tends to be flip and superficial.

The final section of *Forgotten Championships* somewhat confusingly lumps together the league tiebreaker play-offs with the 1981 divisional series, failing to explain that the former are, strictly speaking, extensions of the regular season rather than postseason games. Also, while nearly every game in the book is covered in some detail, Lansche limits discussion of the 1951 Dodger–Giant tiebreaker series almost entirely to the series' final half-inning, surely the one half-inning of baseball history least in need of resurrection from the tomb of forgetfulness.

There are other annoyances. Sometimes the box scores omit such crucial information as the times-at-bat or runs-scored columns. Sometimes, too, Lansche contradicts his box scores in his game descriptions. And once in a while he loses his way in the mass of information (erroneously reporting the 1886 season records and standings of the Athletics and Phillies, for example, or commenting that the Dodgers' "1959 season was about to end" when in fact a Dodger loss in the game under discussion would simply have evened their series with Milwaukee at one win apiece). But for the most part Lansche has control of his facts. And there are pleasures to balance the annoyances: a freedom from grammatical and typographical errors noteworthy in this era of careless writing and editing, and a full index that is particularly useful for tracking down individual ballplayers.

Forgive the flaws. In his diligent unearthing of a century of neglected championships, Lansche has given us a work unique in its coverage, and more enduring in its usefulness than a whole shelf of Steinbrenner biographies or fantasy baseball previews.

Frederick Ivor-Campbell
Warren, Rhode Island

Dorfman, H. A. and Karl Kuehl. *The Mental Game of Baseball: A Guide to Peak Performance*. South Bend, IN: Diamond Communications, 1989. 337 pp. $14.95.

It's a pleasure to give this volume a positive review, since the authors of the book have clearly steeped themselves in the positive approach to performance that they recommend to baseball players. The book is balanced, orderly, interesting, and instructive. Its message about affecting performance with mental attitude and discipline has applicability beyond baseball (in fact, it helped me with a particularly thorny problem in college politics I was grappling with while I was reading it). The authors' sensibilities invite us to recognize the general implications of the lessons they outline for baseball, as they draw on the likes of Socrates and Suzuki, Goethe and Yoda, to make their points clear. Their dedication is, appropriately, "to all who love this game of baseball—and the vigorous pursuit of excellence."

The focus on the mental may take a bit of adaptation for natives of Western culture, baseball players and others, who tend to separate the mind conceptually from the body, and associate sports activity more with the latter than the former.

Dorfman and Kuehl, however, quickly remind us that the most excellent sports performers have discipline, control, and achievement in both areas, as well as good communication between the two. As they remind us that working on both the mental and the physical simultaneously is beneficial, or that getting out of a slump has both a physical and a mental component, we begin to sense that separating mind and body in the first place has provoked artificiality in our thinking. The authors step in the direction of eliminating the mind/body schism in the final chapters, where they present very specific examples of the interrelations of physical and mental states (i.e., breathing and emotional tensions, poor judgment and restricted blood flow). They also work well to document and interrelate the cognitive and the emotional; their reference on the first page of the introduction to "thinking and feeling" is carried out consequently in material in the body of the book.

The chapters in the first section of the book deal with specific mental activities or states in turn, i.e., dedication, responsibility, attitude, confidence, learning, preparation, visualization, etc. The four chapters in the second section of the book focus on mental conditioning for hitting, pitching, fielding, and base running, and the appendix provides task-specific goals for each activity (as well as for bunting and catching). The book is well organized for those who will use it as a manual for mental conditioning (although an index might also have been helpful). The authors make suggestions for dealing with the mental environment within which one functions, focusing first on oneself as a mental force affecting performance, but also accounting for the effects of media, friends, fans, etc.

Throughout the volume, examples of points illustrated are copious and interesting. One is never left with the concepts alone to wonder "How would this work in practice?" There's an example of how it works in practice, and most often an historically memorable one at that, making the volume a contribution to baseball lore as well as a "how-to" book.

The heart of the matter, which this book approaches with a performance emphasis, is that baseball functions as a (if not *the*) central American ritual. We define being American by playing baseball, and by the way we play baseball. A recent public television special about baseball was littered with words like icon, ritual, mythic, initiation rite, drama, miracle, etc. In rituals in general, people recreate their sense of who they are socially by making symbolic statements on the subject.

In some cultures, ritual participants go into trances (an altered state of consciousness in which high frequency brain waves are subordinated in favor of lower frequency waves). When we play sports effectively, we create a similar frame of mind ourselves, leaving behind ego, consciousness of the immediate environment, and so on. This state is referred to by Dorfman and Kuehl and their informants as a "flow experience" or "having it together." This getting together of mind and body is doubtless more difficult for those who have conceptually separated them to begin with. In this frame of thinking though, the body becomes as much an instrument as the bat, and the elaborations of hours worth of mental and physical preparation for a game, performed sequentially the same way every time, promote an atmosphere in which baseball is as much a religion as it is a sport.

Those players who attain this ritualistic consciousness (if not full trance, something closer to it than normal high frequency wave-dominated consciousness) are often also the most successful players physically speaking (not "tightening up" or overthinking). Dorfman and Kuehl are definitely barking up the right tree. Baseball is indeed mind games, games we play with ourselves and with others. Furthermore, since baseball players are sometimes symbols as much as they are people, and since baseball acts as a strainer through which we filter our perceptions of ourselves, the player whose biofeedback capabilities produce "statistical" success is the one we most readily recognize as a hero or shaman, a manifestation of the very ideal we celebrate by having the game. The ritualistic aspect of baseball may, in fact, be the reason Americans so readily accept films which associate baseball with creative magic, and with personal identity, e.g., *The Natural, Bull Durham, Field of Dreams.* A key element of success, metaphorically in the films, and practically in baseball games, is self-visualization.

Whether one comes to Dorfman and Kuehl's volume with the willingness to entertain matters of the relationship between symbolism, physical performance, and identity, or from a more circumscribed traditional Western viewpoint, which distinguishes mind and body for working purposes, but results nevertheless in a kind of squeaky-clean mental approach to baseball (à la Hershiser), this volume is well worth investing in.

Karen Larson
Gustavus Adolphus College

Krich, John. *El Beisbol: Travels through the Pan-American Pastime*. New York: Atlantic Monthly Press, 1989. $18.95.

Say, are you interested in looking at the summer vacation photographs of a complete stranger? Anyone who enjoys the hulking presence of an unknown human being standing in front of historic scenes and blocking the view of foreign sites qualifies as the major market for this book, beyond, of course, the author's immediate relatives.

This book is not about baseball, nor is it about Latin America, and most assuredly it is not about Latin American baseball. The evidence suggests that *el beisbol* is a noun in some bizarre Esperanto that means "pointless chatter about oneself," because there is nothing in this volume except continuous yammering about the author.

A few examples from the book, written by someone who claims to love baseball: Our intrepid author crosses the border into Mexico, south of San Diego, and attends a game on Christmas Day with a neighbor named Kim. A play-off berth hangs on the outcome of the contest, but our author tells "that's hardly something I can get whipped up over" so we never learn the result, nor do we learn much about Kim except that she is a baseball virgin. Next, the author, without Kim, heads for Puerto Rico, where he wanders around, comments on the state of hotels, goes to the beach to watch a hotel fire, does a couple of interviews with old players and Roberto Clemente's wife, but never tells the reader much about the substance of their remarks. The author does learn that attendance is down in the Puerto Rican league, but an analysis of the causes goes beyond this book. Arriving in the Dominican Republic, the author visits San Pedro de Marcoris, the village that has produced more major leaguers than anyplace else in the world. The author never even speculates on the reason.

After recovering from his journey to the islands, the author joins a Berkeley, California group called Baseball for Peace that takes baseball equipment to Nicaragua to aid the Sandinistas, and uses the occasion to play a few games against Nicaraguan ball teams. Want to know something about Baseball for Peace? Try another book. Want to know something about baseball in Nicaragua? Try another book. Want to know something about the author's companions on the trip, beyond the fact that one was politically conservative and that the best ballplayer was this Republican's son? Try another book.

On to Venezuela to find the southern boundary of baseball. The author hires a guide and translator and drives to Ciudad Bolivar, where he finds the muddy Orinoco River, a baseball field, and his ultimate conclusion: "Though the old ballgame has driven me thousands of miles on this curious odyssey, it just doesn't seem worth getting this worked up over." No reader will get worked up.

Don't buy this book, it won't even serve to keep a door open. Unless, of course, you are curious about the rather tedious remarks the author makes about himself. Go watch a game, go watch *Field of Dreams*, go read a good book about baseball. Skip this one.

William H. Beezley
Texas Christian University

Higgins, George V. *The Progress of the Seasons.* New York: Henry Holt & Co., 1989. 228 pp. $18.95.

Lelchuk, Alan. *Brooklyn Boy.* New York: McGraw Hill, 1990. 298 pp. $19.95.

While it would be dangerous to make a sociological generalization from these two books alone, their juxtaposition is evocative. For the Irish-American George Higgins, author of the baseball memoir *The Progress of the Seasons,* growing up in Boston in the 1940s, commitment to the Red Sox supplied a close male bonding between the boy and both his father and grandfather. But for the pseudonymous Aaron, youthful version of the Jewish-American Alan Lelchuk in his novel *Brooklyn Boy,* the boy's beloved Dodgers, also of the Forties, force wedges of miscommunication and anger between the intransigent Russian immigrant father and the eagerly American assimilated son. In both books baseball history provides not only a controlling metaphor but actually the sole organizing element for works that are sometimes moving, sometimes banal, but always willfully rambling.

George Higgins, lawyer and chronicler of Boston's Irish politicians and other varieties of shady characters, has sustained—like many New England intellectuals—a lifelong affair with the Red Sox. He loved them as a boy, critically put up with their ultimate collapses as a man, and writes about them with the special baseball language of nostalgia and analysis that the game evokes. What he knows best about baseball are its emotions, which are tightly bound to his love for the two male authorities of his childhood: Charlie, the grandfather, and John, the father. Although women exist in this text as wives, mothers, girlfriends, they are peripheral; *The Progress of the Seasons* is a gendered text about a ceremony, very much in Faulknerian terms. Here, the ball game at Fenway Park parallels hunting in the Big Woods. Baseball, like the hunt, commences as "the ceremonial beginning of more than forty years, so far, of following the Boston Red Sox, and trying to understand other complicated things as well." The book opens with the boy's first introductions to baseball, passes through the games that the three males attend and discuss, and finishes after the deaths of the older generation. Of course, as with the best baseball writing, the ultimate tone is sentimental: "If God is good—and I have been pretty good, at least—when I die, St. Peter at the Pearly Gate will direct me down the ramp, then up the ramp, to Section 17, and John and Charlie will be sitting there, wondering why I'm late." Echoing Donald Hall, Higgins muses on loss, joining the 1966 Red Sox record (72–90) with his father's death. "How much we depend on our sons, and how much we depend on our fathers."

The book stretches from Higgins' first game in 1946 to the end of the 1966 season, with later interpolations. For Higgins, however, that first announced batting order will always be *his* Red Sox: Dom DiMaggio CF, Pesky SS, Williams LF, York 1B, Doerr 2B . . . the others (Metkovich, Wagner, Russell, and a pitcher, perhaps Ferris) are not important to his memory so are glossed over. Not baseball history, then, but memoir, lyrically selective, is Higgins' method, for "all the ball games, hundreds of them, merge with a few exceptions into a long brilliant skein of incalculable value."

The book oddly mixes novelistic excess—"All novitiates first require the mastery of rituals," referring only to his father's act of entering Doerr's name on the scorecard—with factual reportage: Higgins observing Ted Williams in his late sixties trying to adjust Rich Gedman's swing. Part interviews with the veterans Williams, Radatz, DiMaggio, Doerr, Pesky, and Lonborg, part analysis (there are some fine comparisons between baseball and writing), part baseball reminiscence, and, largely, autobiography, the book sustains some fine moments. But in a league dominated by winners like Roger Angell and Bill James, George Higgins' baseball text, like Bill Buckner's (and Pesky's, and Yaz's) Red Sox team loses at the end.

Alan Lelchuk's *Brooklyn Boy* also fails to achieve distinction in comparison to some of the classic evocations of baseball's effect on a young man growing up absurd in a Jewish acculturation dilemma—such as Irwin Shaw's *Voices of a Summer's Day* or Gerald Green's *To Brooklyn with Love*—but the novel is of genuine interest for two reasons. First, the book treats baseball as part of a political framework. The protagonist's alienated (from wife and child) father is a left-winger, investigated by FBI men who, Aaron the teenage son discovers, do not know baseball history. The father may be a fellow traveler, yearning for

Russia, but the son feels securely patriotic because he knows, plays, and adores baseball: "What saved the boy perhaps was the deeper loyalty, baseball and the Dodgers. For on the field it didn't matter much whether you were an imagined leftie or actual fellow traveler; if you could hit the curve, scoop the short hop, throw the high hard one, run the bases, that's what really counted" (similar motifs run through Howard Senzel's odd *Baseball and the Cold War* and Carl Bernstein's recent *Loyalties*). Second, *Brooklyn Boy* is a traditional Jewish novel, about generation differences—the awful father detests baseball—about politics, urban traumas, school, sex, jobs, growth of a mind, development of a writer . . . but the book *needs* baseball established as a cultural metaphor even when, or perhaps particularly when, halfway through, the narrator's interest in the game fades. Thus, whether talking about gang rumbles, pool hall exploits, gambling, sexual initiations, or merchant seamanship in the latter parts of the book, the author employs baseball phrases as referents to assist the reader's judgment and to provide continuity.

Mostly, the early parts of this novel treat the typical 1940s Jewish, second-generation boy's cultural love affair with the national game. Aaron plays well, learns (cf. Philip Roth, "My Baseball Years") the geography of baseball—" 'But where's Ebbets Field?' Of course Papa didn't know *that*"—contrasts baseball (America) to religion (Russia): "Better to be a Dodger sinner, he knew now for sure, than a pious believer," and identifies Dodger passion and pain with his own love and fear in the Brooklyn streets. One-third of the way into the book, the entire form alters from the sentimental education of Aaron Schlossberg, as Roth or Bellow might have presented it, to a long evocation in the manner of Roger Kahn's *The Boys of Summer*—poetic, mock-religious, portentous. Short chapters appear on The Shrine (Ebbets Field: "a little bit of heaven purchased cheaply," "Could anyone ever understand an American if he didn't understand what baseball meant to a young boy or girl?"); The Voice (Red Barber); The Stranger (Jackie Robinson); The Arm (Carl Furillo); The Glove (Billy Cox); Four Goodly Creatures (Reese, Campanella, Snider, Hodges). From these flowing, descriptive passages springs the moment of truth in the novel, the political/psychological struggle for Aaron between an assimilated man who takes the boy to Dodgers games and his violently opposed Yiddish-oriented father who believes only in schooling.

Like George Higgins, Alan Lelchuk writes an uneven book in a familiar genre. In both cases, the history of baseball helps to string together heterogeneous scenes and characters. But the point both books make is clear: baseball represents in many ways the best aspects of the American scene. The game also helps to explain why one of the great observers of that scene, Henry James, found it a complex fate to be an American.

Eric Solomon
San Francisco State

Brock, Darryl. *If I Never Get Back.* New York: Crown Publishers, Inc., 1990. 424 pp. $18.95.

When Bernard Malamud published *The Natural* in 1952 he created a new genre of baseball fiction. Since then, Robert Coover, Mark Harris, Philip Roth, W. P. Kinsella and others have followed Malamud in mixing fact and fantasy about the national pastime. Darryl Brock's new novel is a worthy addition to this special class of baseball stories. In this entertaining yarn, Sam Fowler, an alcoholic reporter for the *San Francisco Chronicle,* collapses on a train station outside of Cleveland after attending his father's funeral. He wakes up in 1869 and soon joins the Cincinnati Red Stockings as they are beginning their legendary undefeated season. From June to November he travels with the team to the East Coast, then back to their home city, and finally on to California. Along the way he encounters Mark Twain, several murderous gamblers and thugs, and Fenian Irish revolutionaries. He also falls in love with Caitlin, the beautiful widowed sister of one of his teammates. Sam chooses to remain in San Francisco and to wait for his destiny to unfold as the Red Stockings return to the midwest. The book's climax is not quite as clever or satisfying as the rest of the narrative, but overall this is an entertaining tale.

Readers who enjoy American social history in general and baseball history in particular will find much to admire in *If I Never Get Back.* Brock has done meticulous research on post-Civil War urban America and the early years of the national pastime. He describes in detail everyday life in the cities and towns of the early Gilded Age and the Wild West of the era of cowboys and Indians. As a newspaper reporter, Fowler records the rather primitive pre-modern state of the streets, hotels, saloons, and trains. He is fascinated by an early experiment with a flying machine, and he is foolish enough to speculate in gold just before a giant crash on Wall Street.

Brock's presentation of early baseball is excellent on both the technical aspects of the sport and its social and cultural ambience. He takes his readers back to a time when skilled players ("ballists") competed on rough fields with rudimentary equipment that did not include gloves. Pitchers hurled underhand, often mixed fast and slow twisting balls. Batters ("strikers") could call for a low or high pitch. Games were generally high scoring but usually included a number of spectacular plays. The novel brings the stars of the Red Stockings to life; its play-by-play accounts of their matches against the Troy Haymakers, New York Mutuals, Brooklyn Atlantics, and lesser nines are quite exciting. The author also depicts the boosters, hustlers, and other colorful characters who transformed early baseball from an amateur game into a highly commercial and professional sport. The novel features club managers, reporters, gamblers, ruffians, and the ladies who decorated the stands but who did not curb the rowdies who attended the games. Just for fun Brock has Fowler invent the bunt, the intentional walk, hot dogs, hamburgers, and Cracker Jacks.

While Brock presents an accurate and wonderful recreation of early baseball, he does commit three minor errors. He implies that Jim Creighton, star pitcher of Brooklyn's Excelsiors and probably the sport's first paid player, died of an injury he sustained playing baseball. Actually, he was hurt in a cricket contest.

Secondly, baseball was not introduced into the South after the Civil War by returning soldiers and prisoners. New Englanders and New Yorkers brought early versions of the modern game into New Orleans, St. Louis, and other southern cities prior to 1861. Finally, contemporary newspaper accounts credit the 1869 Red Stockings with fifty-seven wins and one disputed tie with the Haymakers, not sixty games without a defeat. But these are mere quibbles. *If I Never Get Back* may never join *The Natural* in baseball's literary hall of fame, but it certainly makes it into the major leagues of baseball fiction.

George B. Kirsch
Manhattan College

Deford Frank. *Casey on the Loose*. New York: Viking, 1989. $15.95.

With fanciful imagination akin to W. P. Kinsella's *Shoeless Joe* and with a beguiling conflict reminiscent of Malamud's *The Natural*, Frank Deford expands the excitement of Ernest Thayer's poem "Casey at the Bat" as he muses on "what really might have happened" following Casey's famous fanning in the ninth inning on that Saturday in Mudville long ago. But Deford's story, an elaboration of a shorter version that appeared in *Sports Illustrated*, is more than paraphrase of the poem or hyperbole of baseball lore.

Printed in sepia tones and illustrated with sepia photographs of and about the era, the book serves well as a fanciful, sympathetic introduction to popular American culture in the latter portion of the nineteenth century. With delightful detail about cures and clairvoyants, about fashions and fears, about work patterns and recent inventions, and about popular literature and common entertainment, Deford exemplifies the spirit of popular culture in late nineteenth-century America. In this context, then, he casts baseball as a form of plebeian play—an entertainment popular among the working class—that was on the verge of gaining thorough cultural acceptance and respect. "For baseball," Deford both writes and displays, "was developing a kind of adhesive that held together the evolving modern city and all its diverse types."

Like much of baseball history, the significance of Deford's story is in its telling, not the tale itself. If revisionist history interprets and tells the past in terms of present concerns, Deford here presents us with revisionist myth, doing what all good sports writers do: "They always only tell it their way." For the story schemes to relate legendary figures—such as basketball inventor James Naismith, champion boxer John L. Sullivan, and journalist Richard Fox of *The National Police Gazette*, besides Timothy F. X. Casey himself—to fictional characters like Casey's faithful fiancée and an almost predictable corrupting gambler. So although the convergence of the cast of characters seems contrived, the telling of their encounters creates a nostalgic baseball magic that lends playfulness and hope to the sense of sadness that has lingered past Casey's swing and a miss a century ago.

Unlike Casey's fateful futile swing, however, Deford scores a hit with baseball fans who enjoy its legendary heroes. For with a final swing and a twist in the spirit of Thayer's striking account of Casey's turn at bat, Deford's story evades the predictable outcome of Mudville's game and Casey's career while staying within the rules of the game itself.

Joseph L. Price
Whittier College

CONTRIBUTORS

Gary Gildner is a poet, short story writer, novelist, and professor of English at Drake University. His books include *Blue Like the Heavens, The Second Bridge,* and *A Week in South Dakota.* He has received the Robert Frost Fellowship, the National Magazine Award for Fiction, and other prizes. At age sixteen he threw an American Legion no-hitter.

Louis Jacobson is a sophomore at Princeton University who, since 1985, has been researching the subject of Jews in major league baseball. A member of the biographical research committee and the oral history committee of the Society for American Baseball Research, he has also published an article on Mose Solomon, "the rabbi of Swat," in its *Baseball Research Journal.*

After careers in advertising, publishing, broadcasting, and working with the mentally retarded, Jack Kavanagh is enjoying retirement by writing about baseball. Currently he is writing a juvenile novel that will be published by Gallaudet University Press. He has also completed juvenile biographies of Grover Cleveland Alexander and Dizzy Dean for the Chelsea House series on Legends in Baseball.

Michael Kimmel is an assistant professor of Sociology at the State University of New York at Stony Brook. His books include *Changing Men: New Directions in Research on Men and Masculinity* and *Men Confronting Pornography.* He is the shortstop on the National Writers Union softball team and has been chosen as the all-star shortstop for the past four seasons.

W. P. Kinsella needs no introduction to baseball enthusiasts. He is an award-winning author, best known for his novel *Shoeless Joe* and its film version, *Field of Dreams.* His present contribution to *Baseball History* is the title story for his next collection of baseball stories.

Bruce Kuklick is Mellon Professor of the Humanities in the History Department of the University of Pennsylvania. His examination of the departure of the A's from Philadelphia is adapted from a history of Shibe Park that he is now completing. *To Every Thing a Season: Shibe Park and Urban Philadelphia, 1890–1990* will be published by Princeton University Press on opening day, 1991.

Rob Ruck is author of *Sandlot Seasons: Sport in Black Pittsburgh* and co-author of *Steven Nelson, American Radical.* He is a Fellow of the Pittsburgh Center for Social History and an associate of the Center for Latin American Studies at the University of Pittsburgh.

Jim Sumner is staff historian for the North Carolina State Historic Preservation office. His essay on baseball at Salisbury Prison during the Civil War appeared in *Baseball History*'s first annual.